THE WORKS OF SRI CHINMOY

PRAYERS

VOLUME II

THE WORKS OF SRI CHINMOY

PRAYERS

VOLUME II

★

MY CHRISTMAS-NEW YEAR-VACATION-
ASPIRATION-PRAYERS

MY EARLY MORNING
PRAYER-JOURNEYS

MY EARLY MORNING
HEART-CLIMBING PRAYERS

LYON · OXFORD

GANAPATI PRESS

© 2021 THE SRI CHINMOY CENTRE

ISBN 978-1-911319-36-8

See appendix for notice regarding this edition.

FIRST EDITION WENT TO PRESS ON 31 MARCH 2021

PRAYERS

VOLUME II

MY CHRISTMAS-NEW YEAR-VACATION-ASPIRATION-PRAYERS

MY CHRISTMAS-NEW YEAR-VACATION-ASPIRATION-PRAYERS

1

Today
My Lord Beloved Supreme
Is examining the full record
Of my gratitude-heart.

2

May my Master always find me
At the shrine
Of my heart-temple.

3

My Lord Supreme
Wants me to do
Something very special
For the love, joy, peace
And bliss-starved mankind.

4

A true seeker's heart-tree
Always and always offers
The sweetest gratitude-fruits.

5

At every moment
I must be fully awake
And not half-awake
In my aspiration-life.

6

My Lord Supreme
Is asking my heart-tears
To accompany Him
Along His own Eternity's Road.

7

My Lord Beloved Supreme
Wants me to deeply enjoy
The full harvest
Of His Satisfaction-Smiles.

8

Every day
My God-obedience-heart
Offers its devotion-gratitude
To God's Will.

9

My heart
Is an ever-increasing
God-Affection-experience-
    happiness.

10

God tells me
To take my mind's impurity,
My heart's insecurity
And my life's futility
Very, very, very seriously.

11

Alas,
It is always too late
When our disobedience
Takes God seriously.

12

In my inner life,
God is God the Compassion-Eye
Far beyond the flights
Of my imagination.
In my outer life,
God is God the
    Forgiveness-Heart
Far beyond the flights
Of my imagination.

13

The Hour of God
Accepts
No excuses.

14

Who is my Lord Supreme?
My Lord Supreme is He
Whose Concern for me
Echoes and re-echoes
From sky to sky.

15

Nobody could stand against me
When God's God-blossoming
    Moment
Began inside my heart.

16

My Lord, I know, I know,
Your Tolerance
Of my disobedience-life
Has cost You dearly.

17

My God-gratitude
Is my divinity's
Only source.

18

My heart
Is a God-aspiration-choice.
My life
Is a God-manifestation-voice.

19

May my Master's eye
Proudly occupy
Every space in my heart.

MY CHRISTMAS-NEW YEAR-VACATION-ASPIRATION-PRAYERS

20

I was my mind-dryness,
But now I am
My Lord's Compassion-Rain.

21

I was born to smile
At God the Creator
And God the creation,
But alas,
My life's sadness-clouds
Are hanging in my heart-sky.

22

My Lord,
All I have
Is ignorance-frown.
All I need
Is Your Compassion-Smile.

23

Today my soul
Is smiling and dancing
Inside my heart-tears.

24

Today God wants my heart
To be only one thing:
A roaring strength of
   cheerfulness.

25

Today God wants my mind
To be only one thing:
An ever-climbing
   consciousness-altitude.

26

I must not allow my days and
   nights
To sleep any more
Inside my idle eyes.

27

I have come to learn
That there is no real God
For those who do not
Bend their knees
And extend their arms.

28

God loves and values
My heart's God-needs
More than anything else.

29

Unlike our faith in God,
God's Faith in His children
Remains unwavering.

30

My heart, my vital and my body,
Stay away—
As far as possible—
From my mind's negativity.

31

As today
Is in God's Hands,
Even so, tomorrow
Will be in God's Hands.
Therefore, we must not worry.

32

My Lord tells me
That my sincerity-mind,
My purity-heart
And
My simplicity-life
Are bound to please God
In God's own Way.

33

At every moment
I must blend into the dust
Of my Beloved Lord's Will.

34

God's Grace
Is ever-present
And not an accident.

35

May my life on earth
Be a multi-dimensional
God-service.

36

What am I doing?
I am planting gratitude-plants
In my heart-garden.

37

Alas,
How is it that I have not seen
That my life's ignorance-time
Has expired?

38

My Lord Beloved Supreme,
I shall no more permit
Your Heart to bleed
For my abominable misconduct.

MY CHRISTMAS-NEW YEAR-VACATION-ASPIRATION-PRAYERS

39

I shall not live
Between "can" and "shall".
I shall live only
Between "must" and "done".

40

Do not recline,
Do not recline!
If you recline too much,
You are bound to decline
Too soon.

41

God does not hesitate
To welcome my heart.
Alas, I hesitate
To welcome God's Eye.

42

My mind, be careful!
There is every possibility
That soon you will be
    excommunicated
From God's inner circle.

43

Although it may not be a
    best-seller,
My heart is an open book
To both God and humanity.

44

God needs me
As an unconditional lover
And not
As an unsolicited adviser.

45

A devotion-life
Is a divine
Miracle-performer.

46

May my mind see all
    human beings
As jewels
And my heart feel all
    human beings
As angels.

47

God does not want me
To improve my past.
He wants me only
To build a perfect future.

48

My God-surrender-heart
Is
My God-Paradise-life.

49

My sweet Beloved Supreme,
Do give my heart the capacity
To love and adore
The golden dust of Your Feet
With every breath.

50

My Supreme,
Only You, only You, only You
I can and I want to claim
As my own, very own.

51

My Supreme,
Please, please bring
My dead aspiration-heart
Back to life.

52

Not God-speakers
But God-lovers
Are found in God's
Remembrance-Heart-List.

53

My Lord has repeatedly told me
That there is no such thing
As a negligible mistake.
Each mistake can be fatal
In the spiritual life.

54

My Lord,
I must not fail You in any way,
Even for a single day.

55

There comes a time
When God remains absolutely
    silent
If He has to repeat to us
Certain soulful things
Again and again.

56

Our volcano-mind
And our tornado-vital
Can be silenced
Only by our Lord's
Compassion-flooded Eye.

MY CHRISTMAS-NEW YEAR-VACATION-ASPIRATION-PRAYERS

57

Every day God is dying
To introduce our minds
To His Infinity's Peace.
But alas, He sadly fails.

58

A true God-lover
Is
God's universal burden-carrier.

59

Each seeker
And his gratitude-heart-tears
Must live together.

60

O seeker, do not shelter
The heart of unreadiness
And
The breath of unwillingness.

61

Love God the man,
Serve man the God.
Behold!
God the Real,
God the Universal
And
God the Transcendental
Is come.

62

If the God-surrender-
  summit-height
Frightens you,
Then God-realisation shall
  remain
A far cry.

63

I must bind my life to God's Feet
If I want my mind to escape
From the piercing
Anxiety-worry-arrows.

64

The desiring mind opens its door
To the earthly amazements.
The aspiring heart opens its door
To the Heavenly enlightenments.

65

My heart sleeplessly cries
For God's Face.
God's Heart endlessly weeps
For my embrace.

66

God tells me that
My beauty is exquisite
When I kneel
In the temple of my heart
And worship Him.

67

Only a sleeplessly and
 breathlessly
God-hungry heart
Is God's fondest child.

68

My happiness-heart
 fully blossoms
Only inside
My God-gratitude-
 heartbeat-tears.

69

An unconditional God-lover
Lives in the sleepless ages
Of God's Satisfaction-Delight.

70

A spiritual Master is
An all-illumining torch-gift
From the Father Heaven
To the Mother Earth.

71

The mind is chained
To a huge ignorance-bondage-
 rock.
Alas, the mind does not mind!

72

The day I do not love
My Lord Beloved Supreme only,
I live in my God-disobedience-
 inferno.

73

In every walk of life,
Enthusiasm is of supreme
 importance
To take a progress-step.

MY CHRISTMAS-NEW YEAR-VACATION-ASPIRATION-PRAYERS

74

My Lord,
Please, please awaken my mind
From its darkest midnight sleep.

75

A God-surrender-life
Has to be always on time
For the fulfilment
Of God's express Will.

76

God's choice warriors
Shake hands with impossibility
With a roaring laughter.

77

Every desire-man
Is eventually forced to dance
With frustration-tragedies.

78

My Master is my
    life-transforming
Dreamer, lover and doer
Inside my aspiration-heart.

79

Like blind beggars
We are discarding
God's Compassion-flooded
Blessing-Love-Concern-Peace-
    Bliss-Gifts.

80

Each obedience-thought
Adds joy
To our inner will-power.

81

Alas,
In man's unwillingness-mind
The entire world is fast asleep.

82

I cannot believe
That my tiny heart-cave
Is my Lord's real
    Satisfaction-Home.

83

Stop, my mind, stop!
Do not cast any more
Your dark
Doubt-suspicion-frustration-
    shadows
Upon my God-loving
    aspiration-heart.

84

Every day
As my gratitude-heart
Collects most devotedly
My Lord's Smiles,
Even so, my Lord's Pride-Heart
Collects most affectionately
My tears.

85

May my aspiration-heart-
    pilgrimage
Know no halt
Along Eternity's Road.

86

Mine is the heart
That constantly needs
Intense eagerness
To realise
My Absolute Lord Beloved
    Supreme.

87

My life's perfection-
    manifestation
Is not more of God
And less of me.
My life's perfection-
    manifestation
Is all in God, all with God
And all for God.

88

I am, as usual,
My life's poor God-service.
God is, as usual,
His Heart's rich Reward.

89

At long last
My heart is successful
In compelling my mind to
    surrender—
At long last!

90

God's Eye
Is unimaginably beautiful:
This is what I learn
From the tears of my heart.
The tears of my heart
Are extremely powerful:
This is what I learn
From God's Eye.

MY CHRISTMAS-NEW YEAR-VACATION-ASPIRATION-PRAYERS

91

Those who serve God
Must never swerve
From spontaneity and intensity.

92

The inquisitive mind's powerful
    altar
Is science.
The pure heart's sure
    God-discovery
Is spirituality.

93

The love divine says to me:
"My Lord is always in.
My Lord is always in.
He never goes out.
He never goes out."

94

My prayer is as deep
As my belief.
My meditation is as certain
As my Inner Captain:
God.

95

I call it my gratitude-heart.
God calls the same thing
His own Beatitude-Face.

96

My Lord Beloved Supreme
Answers only
His Heart-Home telephone calls.

97

I do not fight against
My doubting mind.
I beg my Beloved Lord Supreme
To deal with it.
He immediately does the needful.

98

My mind secretly measures
My heart-tears.
My Beloved Lord Supreme
Proudly treasures
My heart-tears.

99

My Lord most compassionately
Blesses the human in me.
My Lord most affectionately
Cradles the divine in me.

100

With everything that I have
And I am,
I devotedly stay in the shade
Of God's Concern-Tree.

101

God smiles and smiles and smiles
When I most powerfully bind
   Him
With my heart's devotion-cord.

102

I keep not even an iota
Of God-disobedience-thought
In my aspiration-heart.

103

A seeker without
The God-fulfilment-eagerness-
   Heart-hunger
Is not a real seeker.

104

I love dire challenges
In my inner life,
I love.
I love great triumphs
In my outer life,
I love.

105

My Lord,
You have been living
All the time
Inside my tiny heart.
Can You not live
Before my two big eyes as well?

106

With my heart's intensity
And immensity-devotion-hunger,
I avidly devour
My Lord's Sweetness-Smiles.

107

Whenever I get an opportunity,
I look at my Lord's Feet
To awaken my mind
And enlighten my heart.

108

God's Heart blesses me and
   embraces me
In expected ways.
God's Eye blesses me and
   embraces me
In unexpected ways.

MY CHRISTMAS-NEW YEAR-VACATION-ASPIRATION-PRAYERS

109

There can be no excess
Of my heart's devotion
To my Lord's Will.

110

Only a sleeplessly
God-loving heart
Is indomitable and invincible.

111

The abysmal abyss we have
  visited.
Now we must climb up
God's Pinnacle-Height
And have there our permanent
  abode.

112

Only the tears of my heart
Practise rush service
To God.

113

God fulfils my dreams
With the Beauty
Of His Eye
And the Fragrance
Of His Heart.

114

I fulfil God's Visions
With the light
Of my self-mastery
And the delight
Of my God-discovery.

115

Centuries ago
I started my pilgrimage
To God's Paradise-Feet.
I am sure at God's choice Hour
I shall succeed.

116

My happiness-heart
Never, never
Doubts God.

117

Run, speedily run!
Covet, greedily covet
God-service-opportunities.

118

My Lord,
Out of His infinite Bounty,
Pilots my life-boat
To His own Golden Shore.

119

God begs us every day to study
The life-transformation-course
Given by Him.

120

Devotion is not
An emotional exuberance.
Devotion is
Our God-love-perfection
And our God-service-satisfaction.

121

I must never allow
My aspiration-heart
To be blighted
By God-doubts and self-doubts—
Even for a fleeting second.

122

May my present God-love,
God-devotion and God-surrender
Be dwarfed by my future giant
God-love, God-devotion
And God-surrender.

123

When my mind fails,
   my heart cries.
When my heart fails,
   my soul cries.
When my soul fails,
   my God cries.
When my God fails,
He tries again and again
   and again
Until He ultimately
And unmistakably succeeds.

124

As God's Forgiveness
Is not far away,
Even so, my life's absolutely new
   start
Must not take a long time.

125

Day in and day out
God has made Himself available
So that He will not be assailable.

MY CHRISTMAS-NEW YEAR-VACATION-ASPIRATION-PRAYERS

126

God loves and treasures
My sleepless selflessness
Infinitely more than
My uniqueness.

127

A self-offering prayer
To God's Will
Is a most sacred sunrise
Upon my heart's horizon.

128

God-seekers, God-lovers
And God-servers
Are definitely on the right track.

129

While asking ignorance-night
To get lost,
Alas, I find myself
Totally lost instead.

130

Unlike our minds,
Our hearts are always
Deeply in love
With God's Sweetness-Will.

131

I cried and cried
Pitifully and helplessly
When I saw God's Tolerance-Eye
Was narrowing.

132

God's Eye receives
All the questions from me.
God's Heart immediately
Answers them.

133

A sea of self-giving tears
Is needed
To open the floodgates
Of my inspiration-mind,
Aspiration-heart and
    dedication-life.

134

If I worship God's Feet,
Love God's Heart
And serve God's Eye,
Only then
My God-realisation-impossibility
Surrenders to me.

135

My God-surrendered life
Is heading towards Heaven
To receive from God
His Infinity's Bliss.

136

My deep ignorance-friendship
Is truly a great shock
For my Beloved Supreme.

137

I call it
My devotion-heart.
God calls it
His own living Body.

138

Man's home in God's Heart
Is transient.
God's Home in man's heart
Is permanent.

139

Without a devotion-ticket,
God does not allow any seeker
To participate
In His Cosmic Game.

140

God loves everything of me,
Save and except
My indifference.

141

What I desperately need
Is a lion-roaring
Devotional life.

142

Alas,
I am a desire-boat
Without a boatman.

143

My meditation has taught me
How to escape
From the desire-mind-prison.

144

As it is true
That I am not God,
Even so, it is quite true
That I love God only.

MY CHRISTMAS-NEW YEAR-VACATION-ASPIRATION-PRAYERS

145

My unconditional
God-surrender-life
Is a high jump
Into Infinity's Immortality.

146

A self-loving man
Is a half man and a half animal.
A God-loving man
Is not only a full man
But also a half God.

147

The greatness-mind
Of the Father Heaven
I wish to see.
The goodness-heart
Of the Mother Earth
I wish to become.

148

O God-seeker, be careful!
Your sacred compassion-heart
May be nothing other than
Your secret attachment-life.

149

My Lord Beloved Supreme
Tells me
That everything I need
Is within the limitless orbit
Of my love divine.

150

No oneness-heart-love
Can ever be found
Inside the mind's abysmal abyss.

151

My mind's sincere
   God-acceptance
And God-surrender
Are, indeed, two great surprises
For my God-loving
And God-surrendering heart.

152

No tremendous zeal
Of a seeker's heart,
No true God-satisfaction—
Never!

153

Alas, alas!
My mind's surrender
To God's Will
Is unthinkably overdue.

154

I am absolutely sure
That my God-faith
Shall stand the test of time.

155

May all God-seekers,
God-dreamers and God-lovers
Be peace and bliss-melodies
To the aspiring world.

156

O my desire-beggar-mind,
Step back from the public eye,
Step back from the spotlight.
Lo and behold,
God's boundless Pride-Heart
Is beckoning you.

157

I have made my sleepless
And breathless commitment
Only to my
   Lord Beloved Supreme.

158

My crying and smiling heart
Is a very important member
Of God's immediate Family.

159

My hopes are no match
For God's continuously
Torrential Blessings
Upon my devoted head
And surrendered life.

160

God's Pride in me is unlimited
When He sees even a partial
   death
Of my ego-life.

161

At long last
My heart has come to learn
How to implore and invoke
My Lord's express Presence.

MY CHRISTMAS-NEW YEAR-VACATION-ASPIRATION-PRAYERS

162

My inspiration-mind breathes
The breath of the earth.
My aspiration-heart breathes
The breath of Heaven.
I breathe the Breath
Of my Absolute Lord Supreme.

163

My life of constant
    God-obedience
Entirely depends on the
    intensity-heart
Of my love for God.

164

I am
My mind's proud achievement.
My surrender-heart is
A most sublime achievement
    of God.

165

What I desperately need
Is a God-sanctified heart
And not a computerised mind.

166

Alas, my disobedience-mind
Has completely muddled and
    polluted
The most charming
And the most peaceful pond
Of my heart.

167

My oneness-heart
Is God's infinite Breath.
God's Sadness-Eye
Is my immediate death.

168

My Lord,
Out of Your infinite Bounty,
You have allowed me
To be a frequent visitor
To Your Forgiveness-Heart.

169

My Lord,
The human in me
Wants to need countless things.
The divine in me
Wants to need You only.

170

My Lord,
When I obey You cheerfully,
I immediately become
The full Bloom of Heaven.

171

O my mind,
You are such a fool!
You are forcing
Our Lord Beloved Supreme
To please you in your own way.

172

Alas, every day
We are squandering our Lord's
Blessing-flooded opportunities.

173

We must smile
With our God-ordained
   commitments
Long before we can shine
With our enlightenments.

174

What is my self-doubt,
If not a formidable rival
Of my Lord's faith in me?

175

The aspiring heart knows
That there is a way out
Of every dark mind-corner.

176

God tells me that
My God-service-happiness
Can easily equal
God's Heaven-Happiness.

177

My Lord,
You can do anything You want to
Except one thing:
You cannot escape my
   surrender-life.

178

God wants me to climb
Every day without fail
My life's spiritual
   progress-staircase.

179

My Lord,
May my inspiration-eyes
And my aspiration-heart
Every day long for a
   newness-dawn.

MY CHRISTMAS-NEW YEAR-VACATION-ASPIRATION-PRAYERS

180

My Supreme is telling me
That one disobedience-moment
Can give birth
To lifelong misery.

181

God is extremely happy with me
And extremely proud of me
Even when I offer Him
My belated gratitude-heart.

182

I want my heart
To be God's sleepless
Victory-drummer.

183

All the disciplines of the mind
Have to be tightened
If we truly want to expedite
Our Godward journey.

184

My heart-home belongs
To God alone.
I shall not allow anybody
To trespass.

185

Every day my heart and I
Write a book of devotion
With my devotional songs.
My God the Pride
Every day publishes it.

186

I must never, never
Spin out of
My God-Compassion-
   obedience-orbit.

187

My Lord Supreme,
Here and now
Do give me the capacity
To love You and need You only.

188

I am so ashamed of my mind.
It specialises in doubting
My Lord Beloved Supreme.

189

My Lord Beloved Supreme,
Long before I prayerfully
And soulfully
Touched the dust of Your Feet,
You had firmly caught my heart.

190

My Lord,
With Your Love
I become a fulness-heart.
Without Your Love
I become Eternity's
   nothingness itself.

191

My aspiring heart
Accepts everything divine
Infinitely faster than
My unaspiring mind can reject.

192

At long last
I have come to learn
That my loneliness-life
Is, indeed,
My heart-destruction-blow.

193

My Lord tells me that
My heart's soulful smile
Is my love divine in action.

194

We must never allow
Our God-manifestation-dreams
To gather dust.

195

Every day God wants
My God-searching mind
And my God-crying heart
To communicate.

196

My happiness-heart paves
The clearest and brightest road
To my God-Destination.

197

Today God has given me
A new name:
An ever-blazing enthusiasm-sun.

198

The desiring mind
Does not need God.
The aspiring heart needs God,
But it is too impatient to wait
For God's blessingful Arrival.

MY CHRISTMAS-NEW YEAR-VACATION-ASPIRATION-PRAYERS

199

May my God-fulfilment-
    promise-boat
Sleeplessly sail
In my heart-river.

200

Paradise is where
God asks my heart to cry,
And I ask God's Eye to smile.

201

May my heart be
An ever-blossoming
Purity-temple-flower.

202

O my mind, can you not see
That your prayerful and soulful
    attention
To our Lord Supreme
Is overdue?

203

A minute out of
My Beloved Lord's Boat
Is a well-deserved, lifelong
    punishment.

204

I call it
My God-obedience-heart.
God calls it
His Sweetness-Fondness-Nest.

205

God wanted me, God wants me
And God will forever want me
To be His lion-roaring
    Power-Life.

206

My divinity's heart
Lives far beyond
The sea of time.

207

My life loves the beauty
Of the finite.
My heart enjoys the fragrance
Of the Infinite.

208

When life knocked
At my door,
Joy accompanied my life.
When death shall knock
At my door,
Peace shall accompany my death.

209

God's Forgiveness-Heart
Perhaps has time to waste,
But not God's Justice-Eye—
Never!

210

God Himself cradles
My devotion-heart
In His Power-Blessing-Arms.

211

Mine is the life
Of sleepless and breathless
   surrender.
God's is the Heart
Of priceless and tireless
   Satisfaction.

212

May my mind always remain
   empty
Of freedom.
May my heart be always full
Of God-surrender
And God-oneness-freedom.

213

A universe of book knowledge
Cannot quench even an iota
Of the heart's thirst for God.

214

I must trumpet
My soul—
The ignorance-challenger
And ignorance-conqueror.

215

My mind,
The impossibility-sower,
Must finally surrender
To my heart,
The God-manifestation-
   fulfilment-grower.

216

My aspiring heart prays
   and prays,
But it does not expect
Prayer-results
The way my desiring mind
Always does.

217

No enthusiasm-light,
No progress-delight.
No progress-delight,
No God-satisfaction.
No God-satisfaction,
Life is death itself
For a God-seeker.

218

God appears before me
And nears me
And finally enters into my heart
To see if my heart's streaming
 tears
Are fed.

219

My God-gratitude
And my God-surrender
Are two divine seeds
That God Himself has sown
Inside my aspiring heart-garden.

220

Prayer is a drop
That flows into the
 meditation-ocean.
Meditation is a drop
That flows into the
 contemplation-ocean.
Contemplation is a drop
That flows into the
 God-realisation-ocean.

221

God does not want
His Justice-Light
Forever to sleep
Because He does not want
His beautiful world
To meet with destruction.

222

Only a fully awakened heart
Can make a God-climbing
Progress-delight-journey.

223

My Lord Supreme wants me to
 take
My morning beauty-walk
Not only in my heart-garden
But also in every heart-garden.

224

My sleepless and breathless
God-devotion-heart
Is a fountain-ecstasy
In my Lord's Heart.

225

Only a heart that is blessed
By God's Compassion-Eye
Can wipe away
The mind's frustration-tears.

226

My Supreme, my Supreme,
You are killing Yourself
To please me.
The least I can do
Is give You a sweet smile
From my heart.

227

My Lord, I beg of You,
Do not delay any more.
May Your Heart-Sun break
　　through
My thick mind-clouds.

228

My Lord Beloved,
Day in and day out
You try so hard to make me
　　happy.
Can I not try
To do the same for You,
At least once in a while?

229

I need a sincerity-mind
And an intensity-heart
Desperately
To be worthy of my Lord's
Infinite Affection.

230

My only desire
Is to desire You,
My Beloved Lord Supreme,
And nothing else and nobody else
In this incarnation.

231

My Lord, from now on
And for the rest of my life,
I shall need only
The Compassion-Beauty
Of Your Eye
And the Satisfaction-Fragrance
Of Your Heart.

232

Alas,
Why is it so difficult
Either for us to conquer
Our doubting minds
Or to allow God to conquer
Our doubting minds
Once and for all?

233

God loves to enjoy
My simplicity-mind
And not my stupidity-mind.

234

A purity-heart
God treasures infinitely more
Than we can ever imagine.

235

God runs infinitely faster
Than the speed of light
To reach me
When He sees that my heart
Has a burning need for Him.

236

I know, I know,
Definitely I know the way
To my Lord Beloved Supreme,
Even in the stark darkness
Of my ignorance-night.

237

No more towering promises,
But flowering
God-manifestation-fulfilments—
More, ever more.

238

Every day
My Lord Beloved Supreme
Devours the golden tears
Of my silver heart.

239

To my great astonishment,
Today delight is dancing
From my lotus-heart
To my rose-eyes.

240

Every day without fail
I ply my life-boat
Between my resolute mind-river
And my aspiring heart-river.

241

God's Hand, God's Eye
And God's Heart
Are unconditionally showing me
    the way
To Eternity's Peace and
    Infinity's Bliss.

242

My Lord, today I have
Two very special presents for
    You,
And I am placing them
Cheerfully and unconditionally
At Your Feet:
My tearful heart and
    my grateful life.

243

God does not like at all
My fearful and doubtful mind.
God immensely loves
My tearful and blissful heart.

244

My heart's aspiration-cries
And
My life's dedication-smiles
Thrive only
In my God-surrender-life.

245

I keep my ever-blossoming
Gratitude-heart
Safe in the homeland
Of my soul.

246

My heart's devotion-train
Knows
No full stop.

247

What is expectation
In my spiritual life,
If not an ever-empty cup?

248

My Lord Beloved Supreme
Allows me to feed Him
    sumptuously
Only when my aspiration-heart
Flies at top speed.

249

God has been telling me all along
That self-pity
Is the worst possible crime
In a seeker's life.

MY CHRISTMAS-NEW YEAR-VACATION-ASPIRATION-PRAYERS

250

My mind has been studying for
 years
To receive a doubt-diploma.
My heart has been studying
For years and years
To receive God-love,
 God-devotion
And God-surrender-diplomas
From God Himself.

251

May the smiles of my inner sun
Illumine the dense clouds
Of my outer mind-sky.

252

We cry and cry
For the Compassion-Moon
Of God's Eye.
God cries and cries
For the satisfaction-sun
Of our heart.

253

When our aspiration is on the
 rise,
Paradise lovingly, cheerfully and
 proudly
Beckons us.

254

God tells me
That my expectations and
 frustrations
Do not have the last word.
He also tells me
That my love of God
Has ever the last word.

255

Today I have made
A solemn promise to myself
That I shall not compel my
 Lord Supreme
To go hungry for my smile.

256

My heart and I always whisper
Sorrows and joys
In our God-manifestation-
 activities.

257

Nobody is exempt
From God's ultimate
Justice-Light-Examination.

258

I shall not waste my life any more
By begging the mind
To be good.
I shall from now on
Love my heart more and more,
Infinitely more.

259

The life of a seeker
Is meant to be ever-transcending
In his God-search
And God-discovery.

260

I must realise by this time
That to try to perfect others
Is, indeed, a blind
And hopeless quest.

261

May my life be
A long-forgotten
World-attachment-story.

262

All good seekers are commanded
By God Himself
To answer His Heart-Calls
On the very first ring.

263

To run away
With the mind's freedom
Is to lose one's own
Heart-wisdom.

264

My heart, keep climbing,
Keep climbing,
Even if on rare occasions
You slide down.

265

Only a heart
Of sleepless God-surrender
Knows the way
To God's blissful Eye,
God's peaceful Heart
And God's powerful Feet.

266

My Lord,
In my outer life
You are Your Compassion-Eye.
In my inner life
You are Your Protection-Feet.

MY CHRISTMAS-NEW YEAR-VACATION-ASPIRATION-PRAYERS

267

I do not want to unearth
My past ancestry.
I want to prepare myself
For my future God-discovery.

268

My Lord's Fulfilment-Ocean
Is eagerly waiting for the arrival
Of my life's enthusiasm-river.

269

With our soul's indomitable
    heroism
We must silence
Our ignorance-terrorism.

270

The man-discussion-minds
I like.
The God-conversation-hearts
I adore and love.

271

The human life is torn between
The division-mind-night
And the oneness-heart-delight.

272

O seeker, do not be afraid
Of temptation-obstacles.
You can definitely conquer them.
God is more than willing to help
    you.

273

O seeker, do not bury
Your God-gratitude-heart
In the night of your mind-forest.

274

We cannot climb
The liberation-mountain
Unless we have a heart
Of God-surrender-fountain.

275

My Lord, do give me the capacity
To stop once and for all
My life's imperfection-downpour.

276

My Lord,
Although my spiritual progress
Is most deplorable,
I beg of You a million times:
Please, please do not allow me
To go back to my old,
Desire-bound, ordinary life.

277

My Lord, please, please devour
Everything that I have
And everything that I am.
Be pleased to start with
My abominable pride.

278

My body-fitness-trainer
Is my resolute mind.
My heart-fitness-adviser
Is my luminous soul.
My soul-fitness-leader
Is my Absolute Supreme.

279

My mind's
Insincerity and impurity-flights
Frighten me.
My heart's
Sincerity and purity-flights
Enlighten me,
My very existence.

280

My unconditional God-surrender
Has paved the shortest
And brightest road
To Paradise.

281

The unfortunate many
Cry and cry and cry ceaselessly.
The fortunate few
Fly and fly and fly sleeplessly.

282

My mind and my vital
Are terribly afraid of God's
Forgiveness-flight-cancellation.

283

My Lord Supreme wants
Every moment of my life
To be my aspiration-thrill-ride.

MY CHRISTMAS-NEW YEAR-VACATION-ASPIRATION-PRAYERS

284

Man's promise to God:
A very quick start.
God asks:
"Are you sure?"
God's Promise to man:
A very quick start.
Man says:
"Sorry, I am not interested."

285

God immediately stops
Inspiring me and encouraging me
The moment He sees my mind's
Deliberate indifference-walls.

286

To my greatest joy and
    satisfaction,
Mine is a God-enthusiastic heart
And mine is a God-energetic life.

287

My mind, you are such a fool!
You are never ready to receive
Our Lord Beloved Supreme.

288

I do not know why,
But it is absolutely true
That God loves my
    God-claiming heart
Infinitely more than He loves
My God-loving and
    God-serving life.

289

Only my happiness-heart
Embodies and reveals
Abundant God Smiles.

290

O my God-obedience-heart,
Shake, shake powerfully
    and ceaselessly
My shameless
    God-disobedience-mind!

291

A world-indifference-mind
Is
A God-forsaken life.

292

God's ever-blossoming
Compassion-Eye
Is my heart's rock-solid choice.

293

Doubt, enough!
Get out, get out!
Faith, enough!
Get up, get up!

294

An attention-begging mind
And an expectation-begging heart
Have turned my spiritual life
Into a complete failure.

295

Each time you see God,
Think and feel
That you are meeting with Him
For the first time.
Only then your love, devotion
And surrender
Are bound to increase.

296

My Lord,
My heart is all gratitude to You,
For You are shaping my life
To Your own liking.

297

Tomorrow's golden dawn-smiles
Are beckoning
My today's silver heart-tears.

298

God the Eye asks me
Many difficult questions.
God the Heart answers them
Very easily for me.

299

If we soon do not change
The mind-channel,
Then we shall be forced
To enter into
The darkest and endless
Vital-tunnel.

300

My curious mind is always eager
To collect world-news.
My spiritual heart sleeplessly
   desires
Only God-views in everything.

MY CHRISTMAS-NEW YEAR-VACATION-ASPIRATION-PRAYERS

301

Alas, when shall I realise
That my whimsical seeking
Is hurting very badly
The Heart
Of my Lord Beloved Supreme?

302

God is extremely eager
To share with His
Unconditionally surrendered
    seekers
All His Heart-Secrets.

303

My Lord loves to hear
Only my heart-history,
And He vehemently discards
My mind-mystery.

304

This morning
I was so surprised and excited
To see my heart-river speedily,
Charmingly and self-givingly
Entering into my
    soul-beauty's sea.

305

My Lord Beloved Supreme,
Do make my aspiring heart
An eternal prisoner
Of Your Love infinite.

306

My aspiration-heart-harp
Plays only God's
Infinite Ecstasy-Melodies.

307

Between my sleepless prayer-life
And the Satisfaction-Answer
Is God the Compassion-Eye.

308

Repeated defeats can make
A genuine seeker's life
Eventually invincible.

309

When we expect rush service
    from God,
God complies.
When God expects rush service
    from us,
In the twinkling of an eye
We disappear, we hide
And we continue our
    ignorance-ride.

310

God wants each and every
    human being
To cherish God's uniqueness
In each individual.

311

God sleeplessly loves me
And breathlessly treasures my all.
This much is unmistakably true.

312

The silence-sky of my
    Lord's Heart
Immediately embraces
The thunder-sighs of my heart.

313

Every morning
God teaches my heart
How to become
An ever-climbing cry.

314

God tells me
That my gratitude-heart-songs
Are extremely pure and sacred.
They must never be
Published or publicised.

315

My Lord, You are at once
The Breaker
Of my ignorance-frown-life
And the Maker
Of my heart's golden hopes
And my soul's diamond promises.

316

My Lord, I really want to stop
Playing desire-games.
Please, please, please help me.

MY CHRISTMAS-NEW YEAR-VACATION-ASPIRATION-PRAYERS

317

My Lord, I really do not want
To live any more in the
   desire-arena.
Please, please, please help me.

318

Alas, the mind-made compromise
In the spiritual life
Is a very, very serious
   heart-ailment.

319

Today my Lord Supreme
Has commanded my soul
To proclaim
Worldwide ignorance-
   illumination.

320

May my mind be liberated
From the loudest clamour
Of brooding frustrations.

321

May I spend the rest of my life
With my life's pure prayers
And my heart's sure meditations
For the speedy progress
Of my fellow seekers.

322

Alas, an endless battle is going on
Between my heart's silence-light
And my mind's sound-night.

323

May my outer life and
   my inner life
Be suffused with the Sunshine
Of my Lord's Compassion-Eye.

324

Once we open the floodgates
Of our heart's aspiration
And our life's dedication,
Then God-realisation
Can never remain a far cry.

325

I must go forward.
I have no time to enjoy
My past stabs of remorse.

326

My heart's blossoming
Rainbow-dawn
In my tomorrow's sky
Is predestined.

327

In the spiritual life,
Each forward step
In the march of time
Is extremely and extremely
Significant.

328

My strong, very strong
And extremely strong
　heart-muscles
I have developed
From my constant
　soul-obedience.

329

I want everything that is divine
　in me
To grow and glow
And anything that is undivine
　in me
To shrink and fade.

330

The mind's ego-assertion
Is the life's unavoidable
And inevitable destruction.

331

I shall devote my life to
　spirituality
Throughout Eternity
And never, never return
To worldliness and ordinariness.

332

Anything divine, either in our
　inner life
Or in our outer life,
Can never be exhausted.
It can only be astronomically
　increased.

333

The mind guesses quickly
But incorrectly.
The heart blesses slowly
But unreservedly.

334

I shall no more read
My yesterday's failure-stories.
From now on, I shall sing
　and sing
Only my tomorrow's destined
Victory-songs.

MY CHRISTMAS-NEW YEAR-VACATION-ASPIRATION-PRAYERS

335

Humanity's faith-heart
Is a most admirable service
To Divinity's Life.

336

God proudly smiles
At the seeker's
Mind-vital-jungles' conquest.

337

God tells me not to forget
That the sadness, sorrows
    and tears
Of this world
Are overwhelming.

338

My Lord, even yesterday
I tried hard, very hard,
To convert You to my side.
But today I am begging You
In all sincerity
To convert me to Your side.

339

It takes many, many years
Of very hard work
To convict the clever mind,
But today I have done it!

340

At long last I have come to realise
That compromise in any sphere
    of life
Is, indeed, the stupidity-flooded
    wisdom
Of two weak parties.

341

I want my aspiration-life to end
At the Feet of my
    Lord Beloved Supreme
And not in the arms of my
    desire-life.

342

God keeps His Heart-Room
    wide open
And most beautifully decorated
To welcome a seeker
Of sleepless obedience.

343

Heaven selects
Both ignorance-fighters
And world-peace-dreamers.

344

My aspiration-heart
And
My dedication-life
Thrive
Only on my
 Lord's Nectar-Smiles.

345

It is only when
My unconditional surrender-life
Is complete and perfect
That my Lord's infinite Joy
And infinite Satisfaction
Befriend my soul, my heart,
My mind, my vital, my body—
Everything that I have
And everything that I am.

346

My gratitude-heart-prayers
Hasten my God's God-Hour
To transform my entire life.

347

Each time I want to perform
Something divine,
I am immediately helped
By the firm hand of my
 God-faith.

348

Alas, ceaseless, worthless and
 useless
Anxieties and worries
Are devouring the peace of my
 heart.

349

Only the unparalleled power
Of my silence-mind
Can put an end to my
 topsy-turvy life.

350

Run away, run away,
My mind, my vital and my body,
From the temptation-hounds!

351

Alas, my unlit vital
Is obstinately continuing
In its own inimitable way.

MY CHRISTMAS-NEW YEAR-VACATION-ASPIRATION-PRAYERS

352

If you want to live
All the time in the heart
To satisfy your Inner Pilot,
Then take proper care
Of your heart-vessel
And never allow it to spring
   a leak.

353

If I constantly enjoy
My bondage-chain-life,
Then God is bound to withdraw
His Compassion-Fountain-Heart
From me.

354

I am cultivating
My heart-blossoms.
No more do I see
My mind-weeds.

355

May my life every day
Place a most beautiful flower
At the Feet
Of my Lord Beloved Supreme.

356

Life is short.
Hope is long.
Promise is vast.
Promise-fulfilment is
   perfect perfection.

357

Life is a journey.
Death is the continuation of
   the journey.
Heaven is a temporary rest
For the commencement and
   fulfilment
Of a new life, a new hope
And a new promise.

358

My Lord,
Do bless my breath, my heart,
My mind and my life
With implicit faith
In my Master's will.

359

Today I see
My ignorance-world
In total destruction-fire.

360

My Master
Proudly cradles
My life's
Progress-heart-plants.

361

My aspiration-heart
And my dedication-life
Today have taken a decisive turn
Towards my
    God-manifestation-eagerness.

362

My Lord,
I beg of You to grant me
Conscious and continuous
    progress
In my spiritual life
And to make despair
A thing totally foreign.

363

May my God-manifestation-
    readiness,
Willingness and eagerness
Know no wink
Of ignorance-sleep.

364

My aspiration-climbing heart,
No more fear-clouds,
No more!
No more doubt-storms,
No more!

365

I was born
To realise God, reveal God
And manifest God,
And for nothing less
And nothing else.

366

My unconditional surrender
To God's Will
Has brought me
A most precious gold medal
In every field of my
    aspiration-life.

367

Out of His infinite Bounty,
My Lord Supreme has dropped
Many, many hints
As to how I can realise Him
In the near future.

MY CHRISTMAS-NEW YEAR-VACATION-ASPIRATION-PRAYERS

368

The human in me says,
"Better to die than to descend!"
The divine in me says,
"Ascend and ascend,
Sleeplessly and breathlessly—
Ascend and ascend!"

369

My Master-Lord,
May my mind thrive
And my heart feast
On your divine scoldings
Every day
So that I can have the
    fastest speed
To realise
My Lord Absolute Beloved
    Supreme.

370

Every day God wants
Only my gratitude-heart
To read
His secret Life-Stories.

371

Sweeter than the sweetest
When my Lord Beloved Supreme
    and I
Meet in my heart-garden.

372

When self-indulgence-boat
Sails,
Ignorance-night
Assails.

373

There shall come a time
When humanity's heart
Shall win
Divinity's God-President-
    election.

374

O seeker,
Be careful, be careful!
Your all-desiring mind
Can at any moment be attacked
By the most ruthless nightmare.

375

Expectation-rejections
Are immediately invited
And proudly blessed
By the Light of the
    Absolute Beyond.

376

O seeker,
You must spend all your time
On your aspiration-heart-friend
And spend no time
On your desire-mind-foe.

377

My Lord Supreme,
May I ply my life-boat
Between Your
    Compassion-Eye-Shore
And Your
    Forgiveness-Heart-Shore
Every day.

378

God is telling me
That soon, very soon,
He will broadcast
The celestial fragrance
Of my aspiration-heart.

379

God is extremely eager
To liberate me
From the pain of my
    uncomely thinking.
But, alas, I prevent Him
Each and every time
From fulfilling
His Compassion-flooded Love.

380

If it is my genuine
    aspiration-heart,
Then it is bound to love
Every little thing about God.

381

My heart is extremely dear
    to God
Precisely because
It never dares to imagine
God's displeasure.

382

At long last
I am enjoying
My Lord's unconditional
Forgiveness-Ecstasy-Breath.

383

Not one,
But two paradises I have:
My God-devotion-heart
And
My God-surrender-life.

MY CHRISTMAS-NEW YEAR-VACATION-ASPIRATION-PRAYERS

384

My Lord Beloved Supreme
   tells me
That I am absolutely perfect
Only when I turn all my
   attention
To His Needs.

385

My God-gratitude-tears
And God's Nectar-
   Delight-Smiles
Are inseparable.

386

God tells me
That He is completely fulfilled
Only when I feed Him
With my heart's aspiration-seeds.

387

Soulfully and self-givingly
Every day, every hour,
   every minute
And every second
I must serve God the creation.

388

Each time I dare to dream,
I get a most beautiful glimpse
Of God's infinite Beauty.

389

Wake up, my body!
Get up, my vital!
Shut up, my mind!
Fly high, my heart,
Far beyond the skies!

390

May each nerve of mine
Serve my Lord Supreme
Soulfully and self-givingly
Every day, every hour,
   every minute
And every second.

391

Meditation and nothing else
Has the rare capacity
To discover, reveal and manifest
The diamond-beauty
Of our God-longing heart.

392

God has no time
To read my mind-stories,
But He has His Eternity
To hear my heart-songs.

393

Only my heart's devotion-stars
Have the capacity to twinkle
In my mind's teeming darkness.

394

My life's progress-promise
Shines only in
My sleepless and breathless tears.

395

God says to me,
"My child, you will be able
To find Me
Only if you dare
To bind Me
In your climbing aspiration."

396

In the spiritual life, O seeker,
Never, never worry
About running too fast.
True spirituality knows
No speed limit.

397

If you are truly in love
With God's Feet,
Then God will secretly give you
What He has and what He is.
What He has
Is Infinity's Delight.
What He is
Is Immortality's Satisfaction.

398

Unlike all human beings,
God has only one hobby:
Unconditional Forgiveness.

399

My Lord's endless Concern
Covers all spheres
Of my earth-existence-life.

400

May my God-hunger-breath
Never stop,
Never!

401

My Lord Supreme wants me
To achieve distinction
In my aspiration-world,
And not in my desire-world.

MY CHRISTMAS-NEW YEAR-VACATION-ASPIRATION-PRAYERS

402

Right from today,
Throughout Eternity,
May God's Will
Lead my way.

403

My aspiration-heart
And
My dedication-life
Exist exclusively
For God's Fulfilment, Joy
And Satisfaction.

404

Why was I born?
I was born to serve,
Lovingly, prayerfully
And soulfully,
The golden dust
Of my Lord's Nectar-Feet.

405

My Lord Supreme,
I shall never, never, never
Allow You to shed tears.
This is my life's
Most solemn oath.

406

My Lord tells me
That I can easily belong
To His inner School,
Only after I have performed
My ego-extinction-miracle.

407

Our Lord Supreme whispers,
"My sweet children,
Have faith, have faith, have faith!
Ignorance-night comes
Only to go."

408

My constant God-obedience-life
Is always
On the right track.

409

Even one tear
From my aspiration-heart
Expedites
My Godward journey.

410

My long-treasured mind-noise
Has finally surrendered
To my heart's
    ever-blossoming poise.

411

The difference between
My desire-mind
And my aspiration-heart
Is very simple:
My desire-mind
Is reward-expectation;
My aspiration-heart
Is God-satisfaction.

412

Beautiful,
Divinely beautiful,
Supremely beautiful,
Beautiful beyond compare,
The tears of my
    God-loving heart.

413

May God constantly
Shape my life
To His liking.

414

During the entire day
I must remember
My God-gratitude-prayer.

415

May my aspiration-heart-sky
Be filled
With my God-fulfilment-
    promise-stars.

416

Each divine thought
Is a God-embodiment,
God-revelation
And God-manifestation-
    fulfilment-delight.

417

Self-giving
Is a bountiful
God-harvest-ecstasy.

418

No more
My earth-attachment-chain!
No more
My bondage-night-pain!
From now on I need only
God-enlightenment-game.

419

Let us all pray
For the universal defeat
Of self-doubts and God-doubts.

MY CHRISTMAS-NEW YEAR-VACATION-ASPIRATION-PRAYERS

420

If you want to be
A supremely divine instrument
    of God,
Then you must be always aware
Of your ingratitude-mind
That is still alive and kicking
And destroying all the
    divine things
That you have within.

421

I must never, never, never
    disappoint
The Compassion-flooded Will
Of my Lord Beloved Absolute
    Supreme.

422

I must sleeplessly
Keep in touch
With my Beloved Lord's Will.

423

My life's God-fulfilment-promise
Must always maintain
An uncompromising firmness
When it deals with the
    desire-world.

424

Like my soul,
My heart, my mind,
My vital and my body
Must walk along Eternity's Road
To please God in His own Way.

425

I must become a real member
Of God's Vision-flooded
Peace-Mission-Manifestation
Here on earth.

426

In my spiritual life
I need only one thing:
A burning God-hunger.

427

When I am absolutely sincere,
I receive the smile of the
    millennium
From Above.

428

I must pray and meditate
    every day
Soulfully and self-givingly.
If not, idle thoughts shall tumble
From all directions.

429

My deep meditations
Are always blessed
By the ever-inspiring
Voice of the Beyond.

430

My God tells me that
My unconditional surrender-life
Is the most haunting melody
To His Ears.

431

When I am
My indomitable faith in God,
God becomes
His immeasurable Love for me.

432

God never reads
My mind's secret letters.
He reads only
My heart's sacred letters.

433

God completely trusts us
Only after we have become
The faithful lovers of humanity.

434

An unseen God-seeker,
God-lover and God-server
Is an unparalleled God-treasure
In God's own Heart.

435

I am succeeding
In my outer life
And I am proceeding
In my inner life
Only because of my Lord's
Outstretched Compassion-Arms.

436

I must cultivate
Sleepless God-love
To liberate me
From my confusing
And confused mind.

437

To be always for God,
And God alone,
Is infinitely more than enough.

438

God Himself rings
Powerfully and proudly
My life's gratitude-heart-bell.

MY CHRISTMAS-NEW YEAR-VACATION-ASPIRATION-PRAYERS

439

My God-eagerness-heart
Shall eventually grow into
My God-satisfaction-smile.

440

I have given God
My last world-attachment-desire.
God has smilingly and proudly
Accepted it.

441

The full Satisfaction
Of my Lord Supreme
Is my life's only victory.

442

I quickly mount
My life's eagerness-chariot
To arrive at
God's Palace.

443

We must raise God's Banner,
Not with our proud hands,
But with our soulful hearts.

444

God wants my life
To live in happiness-smiles,
And not in sadness-tears.

445

Do not open your mind-lock:
You will be in very serious
 trouble.
But keep your heart-lock always
 open:
Yours will be the joy
 unparalleled.

446

God is extremely fond of
My thrilling and thrilled
Aspiration-heart.

447

God's Compassion-Eye
Brightens my mind,
Sweetens my heart
And
Enlightens my life.

448

I offer my gratitude-heart-songs
To my Lord Supreme.
He immediately carries me
Away from the boundaries
Of ignorance-night.

449

No more, no more
Ego-intoxication,
But ego-transformation,
More, ever more.

450

Out of His infinite Bounty,
My Lord has given me the
    capacity
To steer my life-boat
To a far-off God-realisation-
    destination
Today.

451

My heart-tears
Are made of
My God-gratitude-songs.

452

If we want to make
The fastest progress
In our spiritual life,
We must silence the mind first.

453

We must not allow
Our world-attachments
To eclipse the face
Of our inner divinity's sun.

454

When I am in my mind,
My only choice is reward-
    expectation.
When I am in my heart,
My only choice is
    God-Satisfaction.

455

My Lord Beloved Supreme
Proudly crowns
My humility-life.

456

God wants me to believe
That He is simply fascinated
By the beauty of my heart
And the fragrance of my soul.

MY CHRISTMAS-NEW YEAR-VACATION-ASPIRATION-PRAYERS

457

God does not want me
To waste any more
My heart's precious love
On my God-doubting mind
And God-denying vital.

458

I have discovered
The beauty of my heart
Inside a leaf.
I have discovered
The fragrance of my soul
Inside a flower.

459

Easily
My gratitude-heart-tears
Steal
My Lord's Compassion-Eye.

460

No more, no more
My God-denying mind.
More, abundantly more,
Infinitely more
My God-crying heart.

461

My Lord Supreme, do tell me,
When are You going to be
    proud of me?
"My child, I shall be proud of you
The moment you dare to claim
Me
As your own, very own."

462

My Lord Supreme, do tell me,
When are You going to love me?
"My child, since the very
    beginning
Of My creation,
What else have I been doing?"

463

I must stop
Telling the world
My life's desire-stories.

464

God does not want me to
    memorise
His infinite Names.
He wants me to memorise
Only three Names:
Concern, Compassion and
    Forgiveness.

465

Every morning and evening
I worship my Lord Supreme
With my heart's
Devotion-lotus-blossoms.

466

My surrender-steps
Reach my Lord's Heart-Home
Infinitely faster
Than any other steps.

467

God often closes
His Justice-Eye,
But He never closes
His Compassion-Eye.

468

To the disobedience-mind God says:
"Come back, come back!"
To the obedience-heart God says:
"I am all yours.
Do whatever you want to do
With Me."

469

Go forward, O seeker, go forward
Towards your destination!
You must never bind the past
With the chains of memories.

470

God is extremely eager
To look at man's happy face
Indefinitely.

471

If I ever lose my devotion-grip
On my Lord Supreme,
Then that will be the end
Of my true spiritual life.

472

Alas, I am eager to know
When God-love, God-devotion
And God-surrender-festivals
Will take place here on earth.

473

I have given my heart
To God for safekeeping.
To my greatest joy,
He has accepted it
Proudly.

MY CHRISTMAS-NEW YEAR-VACATION-ASPIRATION-PRAYERS

474

I must pray to God
As often as possible,
And not at long intervals.

475

May my heart every day
Practise readiness, willingness,
And eagerness-mantras
Without fail!

476

I quickly devour
And divinely enjoy
The dust of my Lord's Feet.

477

I prayerfully invite God,
And He quickly comes
And blesses me
With divine News.

478

My heart and I every day
Embark on our soulful pilgrimage
To God's Feet.

479

Although God does not tell us,
We must feel that
Our ingratitude-heart
Deeply shocks Him.

480

If I truly love God,
Then I must never fear
My Lord's Justice-Light.

481

In my aspiration-life
Nothing can be as important
As my God-hunger.

482

God is always at home,
Available,
When my heart comes
To visit Him.

483

Mine is the heart
That every day flies to God
With devotion-delight.

484

Today God has warned me
Very seriously:
He does not want to hear
Any more bad news and sad news
From me.

485

Nothing shocks my
   Lord Supreme,
Even my Eternity's
Ingratitude-volcano.

486

This morning I have applied
For God's slave-position.
I shall prayerfully wait
For His kind Decision.

487

Although my aspiration-heart-
   temple
Is not always clean and pure,
My Beloved Supreme every day
   visits
My aspiration-heart-temple
And blesses it,
Out of His infinite Bounty,
Unconditionally.

488

Our aspiration-intensification
Is of absolute necessity
If we want to expedite
Our Godward journey.

489

God is always hungry
For my heart's
Self-giving smiles.

490

This world of ours
Will be illumined,
Sooner than at once,
If it falls in love
With God's Eye-Beauty
And God's Heart-Fragrance.

491

Twice God takes us
   most seriously:
Once when we cry most pitifully
And
Once when we smile
   most heartily.

MY CHRISTMAS-NEW YEAR-VACATION-ASPIRATION-PRAYERS

492

In the outer world,
Life is fighting most ferociously
With life.
In the inner world,
Life is living most peacefully
With life.

493

Unconditional God-surrender
Accomplished,
Nothing else remains
To be accomplished,
Either here on earth
Or there in Heaven.

494

My devotion
Is my Lord's
Fondness-Cradle.

495

My perfection-life
Entirely depends on
The aspiration of my
    heart-shrine.

496

Nobody can make the fastest
    progress
In the spiritual life
Without having a
    deep-rooted longing
For God.

497

If I can have an infant-cry,
Then God will become
My real and immediate Mother.

498

With my prayers and
    meditations,
I must occupy
Every unoccupied moment
To manifest my Lord Supreme,
Here on earth and there in
    Heaven,
In His own Way.

499

My Lord's most powerful
    Command:
"My son, throw away
    immediately
Your ignorance-
    membership card."

500

My sound-life
Ends
When my silence-heart
Begins.

501

To doubt God's Love,
Even for a moment,
Is an unpardonable crime.

502

Never question
God's Decision
Even once.

503

Have implicit faith in God.
His Compassion-Eye
Can solve all our problems.

504

To my greatest joy,
My life has become
A perfect slave
To my heart's eagerness.

505

My gratitude-heart
Pleases God
With astonishing speed.

506

A devotion-heart
Has a natural attraction
For God's Compassion-Feet.

507

We have simply no idea
In how many ways
God tries to please us.

508

God has reserved
A very special place
In His Heart
For those who look closely
At everything God does.

509

God's Forgiveness
Plays the most important role
In our nature's transformation.

MY CHRISTMAS-NEW YEAR-VACATION-ASPIRATION-PRAYERS

510

When God calls you
To return home,
You must immediately
And cheerfully
Obey Him.

511

Alas,
Even a thousand smiles
Cannot create one single smile
In the mind.

512

Whenever God sees purity
In our gratitude,
He immediately devours it.

513

An attachment-heart
And a darkness-mind
Are inseparable.

514

Only a self-giving life
Finds its way
To Heaven.

515

God wants me to keep
My love for Him
Hidden
In my heart's deepest chamber.

516

A prayer-song
Is as significant
As a fragrance-rosary.

517

My aspiration-heart has covered
The faraway land
Of Immortality's Nectar-Dreams.

518

God's Heart hungers
Every day
For my heart's morning prayers.

519

My heart sleeplessly cries,
Not for my mind's immediate
    demise,
But for my mind's full
    illumination.

520

O my mind, I am telling you
That you will not be able to deny
My soul's life-transforming
   delight
Indefinitely.

521

The outer advice
Is utterly useless.
The inner prayer
Is absolutely fruitful.

522

I call it
My heart-expansion.
God calls it
His Satisfaction-Delight.

523

My Beloved Supreme,
Your single Touch
Has brought me back
My inspiration-mind,
My aspiration-heart
And
My dedication-life.

524

Desire comes to torture my heart.
Desire comes to kill my life.
Desire comes to take me away
From my Absolute Lord
   Beloved Supreme.

525

If you really love God,
Then you must never, never
Be pleased with yourself
In your own way.
God's Way is the only Way
For you to be pleased with
   yourself.

526

What now I have
Is an earthly mind,
But I must become
A Heavenly heart.

527

My Beloved Supreme
Throws and throws and throws
Aspiration-seeds
Inside my heart-garden.

MY CHRISTMAS-NEW YEAR-VACATION-ASPIRATION-PRAYERS

528

A desire-life
Strikes the mind
Hard, very hard.

529

The fragrance of a devotion-heart
Is unparalleled
In our spiritual life.

530

In my outer life,
My Supreme wants me to be
His Body.
In my inner life,
My Supreme wants me to be
His Breath.

531

If I do not show my Supreme
My gratitude-face,
He will not help me win
My inner race.

532

My meditation-silence
Reverberates
In the Heart-Sky
Of my Lord Supreme.

533

O my foolish mind,
You do not have to understand
 anything.
Just do one thing:
Love and love
Our Lord Beloved Supreme.

534

Implicit faith expedites
Our God-realisation-journey
Unimaginably.

535

An acute shortage
Of gratitude:
This is what a human heart is.

536

The power of patience
Knows
No equal.

537

The mind is deliberate
Truth-limitation.
The heart is constant
Truth-expansion.

538

As doubt is
The most powerful deceiver,
Even so, faith is
The ultimate saviour.

539

We must be extremely,
Extremely careful:
Ignorance-forces are always
   working,
Sleeplessly and vigilantly,
To lord it over us all the time.

540

He who gives joy to others
Unconditionally
Is God's choicest instrument.

541

God, out of His infinite Bounty,
Asks me to collect
His Compassion-Smiles
Infinitely more
Than I have ever expected.

542

Let us bind and blind
All our desires
To please God
In His own Way.

543

If you want to sing
God's Victory-Songs,
Then never yield any space
To self-doubt.

544

God blesses me
With His infinite Pride
When I offer Him gratitude
From the very depths
Of my surrender-life.

545

Two equally formidable
   discoverers:
Mind the war-discoverer,
Heart the peace-discoverer.

546

When we desperately
Need God's help,
God immediately comes
As a human friend.

MY CHRISTMAS-NEW YEAR-VACATION-ASPIRATION-PRAYERS

547

When I am in my mind,
I become the night of sorrows.
When I am in my heart,
I become the beauty
Of a rainbow-dawn.

548

God's Compassion-Tree blossoms
Only when
The tears of my heart
Are absolutely sincere and pure.

549

Meditation is
Desire-reduction
And aspiration-multiplication.

550

When I pray,
I breathe in God's Light.
When I meditate,
I breathe out God's Power.

551

True, the mind does not respond,
But the heart does respond
To God's morning Call.

552

If we want to make the fastest
   progress
In our spiritual life,
Then we needs must have
A doubt-proof enthusiasm-mind
And
A doubt-proof eagerness-heart.

553

When I pray,
I become a crying heart.
When I meditate,
I become a soaring soul.

554

God has a very special fondness
For my whisper-prayers
And whisper-meditations.

555

God wants me to think
Of only peace and bliss
When I look at others.

556

Not our outer government
But our inner enlightenment
Can give us peace.

557

My unconditional surrender
To God's Will
Is God's Heart-Throb.

558

A desire-companion I was,
But now I am
An aspiration-champion.

559

If our hearts are empty of tears,
Then we shall not be able
To claim God as our own,
Very own.

560

To feel God's Presence
Inside our hearts all the time,
Our faith has no equal.

561

Nothingness-fulness
Is another name
For Nirvana.

562

The mind tries
And fails.
The heart cries
And sails.

563

Like your soul,
Fear not, fear not!
Go forward, go forward,
O heart, mind, vital and body—
Go forward, go forward!

564

Aspiration and temptation
Should be taken
As the North Pole
And the South Pole.

565

Sweeter than the sweetest,
When the tears from man's eyes
And the Tears from God's Heart
Meet together.

MY CHRISTMAS-NEW YEAR-VACATION-ASPIRATION-PRAYERS

566

There is a secret and sacred
God-society
That thinks and feels
That e-mail is synonymous
With evil mail.
Fortunately or unfortunately,
I am a solid member
Of that society.

567

My heart-aspiration
Wants me to be
Expectation-rejection.

568

The mind-dictionary houses
    the word
"Additional".
The heart-dictionary houses
    the word
"Unconditional".

569

The human in us died
And
The divine in us was fortified
When the Saviour was crucified.

570

The human mind can win
    the election
In the world-mind.
The divine heart always wins
    the election
In God's own Heart.

571

O my desire-life,
Be fully prepared
For the fast-approaching
Nightmare-attacks.

572

Two are the greatest
    achievements
Of my Beloved Supreme
Here on earth:
My gratitude-heart
And
My satisfaction-mind.

573

Two are my invaluable treasures
Here on earth:
My Lord's Compassion-Eye
And
My Lord's Forgiveness-Heart.

574

My Lord Supreme,
Do give me the
    eagerness-capacity
To co-operate
With Your sweet Will
In every way.

575

I must surrender my all
To my Lord Supreme
If I want to bask
In God's Nectar-flooded,
Sunlit Attention.

576

God wants me to approach
His Throne
Not only with my tearful heart,
But also with my blissful breath.

577

I value infinitely more
The Compassion-Feet of God
Than the Beauty of God's Eye.

578

Alas,
When will my heart be eager
To agree with everything
That God says?

579

From my gratitude-heart-balcony
I have an excellent view
Of God's Sweetness-Eye.

580

My promise to God
Is my God-fulfilment.
God's Promise to me
Is my life-transformation.

581

I must cheerfully follow
My gratitude-heart-road
To the very end.

582

God says to me
That He will never be satisfied
With what I am
Until I become unconditionally
What He wants me to be:
A God-realised soul.

MY CHRISTMAS-NEW YEAR-VACATION-ASPIRATION-PRAYERS

583

Now is the time for me
To claim
My divinity's immortal blue bird
Inside my aspiration-heart.

584

There is only one way
To have peace on this planet,
And that way
Is through constant remembrance
Of God's Love
For each and every human being.

585

It is so heartbreaking
That my mind is always unwilling
To visit
God's Compassion-Eye.

586

In this new century,
I shall have no room
For frustration and failure.

587

I shall keep always
God's Compassion-Feet
In all challenges of life.

588

Without peace in my mind,
I shall not be able
To see peace-blossoms
In my heart-garden.

589

If I have an iota
Of self-doubt,
Then I shall lose
My God-receptivity-heart.

590

God wants us to have
Only a purity-heart,
And not an austerity-life.

591

Just an inch
When my aspiration ascends,
Immediately
God's Satisfaction-Smile
    descends.

592

The moment God reads
My mind's
God-existence-doubt-letters,
He swims in the sea of tears.

593

God wants me to drive
My God-service-chariot
At top speed
All the time.

594

The desiring mind never gives.
The aspiring heart gives,
Cheerfully and unreservedly,
Everything that it owns.

595

The depression of the vital
Is the sad failure
Of life.

596

Readiness I have.
Willingness I have.
Eagerness I have.
What I need
Is intensity.

597

Secretly
God travels everywhere
Only to find
A gratitude-heart
And a surrender-life.

598

I need faith
To the same extent
As I need breath
In my life.

599

We must realise
That God is always ready
With a helping Hand
To take us
To the Promised Land.

600

Religion is the body.
Spirituality is the heart.
Yoga is the breath.

601

When I pray,
I see the height of greatness.
When I meditate,
I feel and become
The depth of goodness.

602

My Lord Supreme,
In Your Compassion-Eye
I see my heart's
Forgotten beauty.

MY CHRISTMAS-NEW YEAR-VACATION-ASPIRATION-PRAYERS

603

My Lord,
You feel my heart's
Helpless tears
Long before they fall.

604

My Lord tells me every day
The same thing:
"My child,
Intensify, intensify
Your heart's inner cry!"

605

My physical health
Every day I need.
My spiritual health
I sleeplessly and breathlessly
    need.

606

My Lord,
I most sincerely thank You,
For You love my tiny world.
My Lord,
I am sleeplessly grateful to You,
For You love the entire world
In and through my tiny heart.

607

Everything in life
Will drive me into the shadows
Of utter failure
Until I start loving
    God unconditionally
In His own Way.

608

The beauty of my self-giving
Is my God-satisfaction
In God's own Way.

609

God is asking me
To tell Him most sincerely
How far I am willing to go
To please Him in His own Way.

610

Self-interest, self-pity
And self-indulgence:
These words are not to be found
Any more
In my life-dictionary.

611

No more self-justification,
No more!
God-adoration more
And ever more!

612

Nothing is as beautiful
And compelling
As my Lord's
    Compassion-Eye-Smile.

613

We love to play
Many, many games,
But God loves to play
Only one game:
Hide-and-seek.

614

He is the hero supreme
Who longs to fulfil God's
Each and every expectation.

615

My Lord,
I need only
Two devotion-flooded hands
And one sleeplessly
And breathlessly crying heart
From You.

616

May each breath
Of my aspiration-heart
Be a communion with God.

617

My Lord tells me that
My heart's sincere cries and tears
Can never remain unheard.

618

O my doubting mind,
What you right now need
Is severe punishment,
And not enlightenment.

619

God-devotion-fire
Can definitely burn to ashes
All earthly obstacles.

MY CHRISTMAS-NEW YEAR-VACATION-ASPIRATION-PRAYERS

620

Since God is all Protection
For me,
Can I not be all affection
For Him?

621

God does not believe
In my self-doubts.
Therefore He always maintains
His implicit Faith in me.

622

God tells me
That mine does not have to be
A lifetime of blunders.
It can be a lifetime
Of my perfection
And God's Satisfaction.

623

My Lord Supreme,
I shall not take,
Even for a fleeting second,
Your Compassion-Eye
And Your Forgiveness-Heart
For granted.

624

Alas,
I do not know how
God is not miserable
When we, all His children,
Are so unspeakably spoiled!

625

Like my Lord's Heart,
I shall make my heart, too,
Ever-new, ever-inspiring,
Ever-aspiring, ever-illumining
And ever-fulfilling.

626

I must always give utmost
   importance
To my
God-remembrance-sweetness-
   moments.

627

My life thrives
Only on one thing:
My sleepless God-devotion.

628

Without a one-pointed
Heart-intensity,
There can be no
God-realisation-achievement.

629

O seeker,
You must realise
That no God-request
Can ever be trivial
Or insignificant.

630

May my morning
God-enthusiasm-leaps
Never stop
During the entire day.

631

I must silence
My mind-counsellor,
My mind-commentator,
My mind-commander
And
My mind-dictator.

632

My soul and I can easily see
That God is constantly smashing
His own
Compassion and
    Forgiveness-records.

633

My heart cherishes
Everything that my Lord does
And every move that He makes
For the betterment of the world.

634

How I wish I could be
With all the real
    God-representatives
When they walk the earth!

635

God laughs and laughs at me
When I do not want to control
My impatient
God-Arrival-anticipation.

636

The Master's heart
Is the silence-voice
Of the Unknowable.

MY CHRISTMAS-NEW YEAR-VACATION-ASPIRATION-PRAYERS

637

To meditate deeply
Is to soar high, very high,
On the wings
Of God's Compassion-Eye.

638

My Lord,
I do not mind Your zigzag path
At all,
As long as I find You
And Your Lotus-Feet
At every turn.

639

For me to sit
At the aspiration-shrine
Is not enough.
I must become
The aspiration-shrine itself.

640

My Master's joy
Knows no bounds
When he sees
My inner progress reports.

641

My heart, my mind,
My vital and my body
Have to be always full
Of my
God-manifestation-
    determination-fire.

642

God wants me
To breathe in deep
Purity-flower-fragrance
All the time.

643

O my mind,
My unaspiring mind,
Will you ever listen
To the pleadings
Of my bleeding heart?

644

I shall no more spend
Even a fleeting moment
In my mind's desire-market.

645

From now on
I shall always find myself
In my heart's aspiration-garden.

646

It is simply impossible
To love God only
And enjoy ignorance-sleep
At the same time.

647

God's Compassion, God's Love,
God's Affection and
　　God's Concern
Have ever-transcending
　　destinations.

648

Humanity is humanity's
Slowest progress.
Divinity is Divinity's
Deepest Concern.

649

To my greatest joy,
This morning I was able
To wave good-bye
To my desire-life.

650

A real devotee
Takes his Lord's Footsteps
As his own heartbeats.

651

God tells me
That it is His supreme Task
To beat my life's victory-drum
At His own choice Hour.

652

My Lord Supreme,
I have only one desire:
Do bless me
With a never-dying
Gratitude-heartbeat.

653

My Lord keeps
His smiling Eye
Inside my heart
And His blessingful Hands
Upon my head.

654

I shall never allow my mind
To be dressed in a dark robe
Of God-disbelief,
Even for a fleeting second.

MY CHRISTMAS-NEW YEAR-VACATION-ASPIRATION-PRAYERS

655

I came into the world
With Heaven's Plenitude-Smiles.
I shall return
With earth's infinitude-tears.

656

God wants me to know and feel
That every hour has to be
A new God-discovery-journey.

657

My heart cries and dies
Only for one thing:
The next ambrosial
God-Touch.

658

May my life always be
Enraptured
In God-manifestation-dedication.

659

No sincere heart
Will ever believe
That God's Will
Is extremely difficult
To grasp.

660

If we live in the heart,
Only in the aspiring heart,
Then we can definitely discover
Ever-new ways to please God
In His own Way.

661

My aspiration-heart
Began its journey
From God's Heart,
And it will forever continue
To God's Feet
Of ever-transcending
    Compassion.

662

When a genuine seeker
Leaves the path,
God's Compassion-Eye suffers
Infinitely more
Than the seeker can ever
    imagine.

663

God secretly and blessingfully
Gives whispering hints
For our continuous inner
    progress.

664

In the spiritual life,
A doubt-enjoyer
Eventually suffers
Enormous failure.

665

May my gratitude-heart-waves
Constantly rise and rise
And rise.

666

A faith-dislocation-heart
Is extremely difficult
To heal.

667

Each seeker must discover
The secret and sacred passageway
From the aspiring heart
To the illumining soul.

668

My only happiness in life
Is my sleepless faith
In my Absolute Lord Supreme.

669

From my Master's fastest glance
I receive
A million blessings.

670

O seeker,
Do not sigh, do not sigh,
Do not sigh,
For with each sigh
You slightly die.

671

The thrill
Of God-service
Is unparalleled.

672

The mind says to God,
"God, can You not give me
What I truly want?"
The heart says to God,
"God, do give me
What I need
At Your own Time."

673

The tears of my heart
Are my only aspiration-guides
To take me to Heaven.

MY CHRISTMAS-NEW YEAR-VACATION-ASPIRATION-PRAYERS

674

No impurity of the mind
Can dare to enter into
My God-gratitude-heart.

675

Either in the near future
Or in the distant future,
My dedication-life-train
Must reach
The God-Bliss-station.

676

Without God-devotion-tears,
We can never have
God-realisation-smiles.

677

When I bow to God
With my humility-heart-prayers,
He immediately blesses me
With His own Crown and
Throne.

678

Every day
I deeply enjoy the beauty
Of my aspiration-seeds
And the fragrance
Of my surrender-deeds.

679

The desire-mind says,
"God is nowhere."
The aspiration-heart says,
"God is right here."
The realisation-soul says,
"God is here and all-where."

680

In the aspiration-election,
The heart always wins.
God the Supreme Judge
Summarily rejects the mind.

681

The heart unreservedly spends
    time
On the mind
For its transformation.

682

O endless desire-mind,
Be careful!
Your own frustration-night
Will not only frighten you,
But also devour you.

683

Quite often
The desire-mind fails
Because God's Compassion
   prevails.

684

The heart does not
Inspect the mind.
It only tries very hard
To connect the mind
With God.

685

When the God-realisation-hope
Disappears,
Bring it back
With your heart's streaming
   tears.

686

A tiny progress-step
Is, indeed, a giant victory
In the inner world.

687

My God-adoring heart cries,
"Where, where, where?"
God's Compassion-Heart echoes,
"Here, My child, here,
And nowhere else."

688

If necessity demands,
Start with a curious mind.
If so is the Will of God,
He will turn your curious mind
Into your serious and precious
   heart.

689

I must dare to dream
Of God's transcendental Smiles
Every night
So that I can manifest God's
   Light
During the entire day.

690

Alas, God's Grace
Is crying for a tiny place
In my heart-room.

MY CHRISTMAS-NEW YEAR-VACATION-ASPIRATION-PRAYERS

691

God wants me
To strengthen my prayer-life
Every day.

692

God wants me
To lengthen my meditation-hours
Every day.

693

No more shall I cry
For earthly fame.
I shall cry only
For a Heavenly flame
Inside my heart.

694

The earthly mind
Does not believe in apology.
It only believes in eulogy
From God.

695

Hope disappears.
This is, indeed, an
    earthly experience.
Tears appear.
This is, indeed, a
    Heavenly experience.

696

God does not want me to think
Of my life's sunset.
He wants me only to think
Of my heart's all-illumining
    sunrise.

697

My progress
Is in my constant
God-adoration.

698

No more
My mind's pride-commotion,
No more!

699

My heart's silence-sea-invocation
More,
Ever more!

700

O seeker,
Can you not feel even once
That your faith in God
Is infinitely stronger
Than your self-doubt?

701

I was, I am
And I shall forever remain
A God-meditation-heart.

702

Those who sincerely invoke God
In the depths of their heart
Can easily become
Life's frustration-depression-
 challengers.

703

The beauty
Of soulful prayers
My life is.

704

The powerful fragrance
Of meditation
My heart is.

705

A desire-bound life
Is infinitely poorer
Than a street beggar's life.

706

A God-surrendered life
Enjoys God's
Infinite Delight.

707

The mind-wall
I see.
The heart-bridge
I become.

708

My God-love
Has to be one-pointed.
If not,
My God-realisation-hope
Shall sadly fail.

709

There is only one
Perpetual problem in my life:
My self-indulgence.

710

My Master's earthly presence
Is a rare opportunity
For me to conquer
Ignorance-night forever.

MY CHRISTMAS-NEW YEAR-VACATION-ASPIRATION-PRAYERS

711

Unimaginably beautiful
And powerful
Are the tears of my
    gratitude-heart.

712

My Lord tells me that what I call
Insignificant disobedience
Is nothing short of a
    fatal blunder.

713

Alas,
All good hearts are crushed
By humanity's cruelty
And indifference.

714

When I live a moment
Without God's Breath,
Death immediately becomes
My possessor.

715

There is no difference
Between a desire-life
And an everlasting
Ignorance-play.

716

To make striking progress,
The human in me prays to God
For repeated chances;
The divine in me prays to God
For His absolutely last Warning.

717

My Lord Supreme,
I have only one desire-prayer:
Please, please send me back
My long-treasured old hope.

718

This morning I was so happy
To offer even
My life's last
    surrender-prayer-breath
To my Absolute Lord Supreme.

719

God wants me to be myself first.
Only then will He turn me into
Another God.

720

May all God-seekers
Every day pray
For the universal conquest
Of self-doubt.

721

Alas,
Even the outstretched arms
Of God's Compassion
Cannot reach my dry mind.

722

My Supreme cries and cries
Before He reads my confidential
  letters.
After reading my letters,
He heaves a very heavy sigh of
  relief.

723

To me,
Each Smile of my Lord Supreme
Is the Smile of the Millennium.

724

Only adamantine
Determination-hammers
Can destroy the mind-walls.

725

May each thought of mine
Be shaded
By my Lord's Protection-Tree.

726

When we most confidently
And most powerfully select faith,
Doubt rejects us immediately.

727

E-mail is man-connection,
And not God-communication—
No, never!

728

My life can escape
From God's Justice-Light,
But it can never escape
From God's Compassion-Height.

729

God-obedience
Is not God-slavery.
God-obedience
Is life-mastery.

730

Sweet is God's Eye.
Sweeter is God's Heart.
Sweetest is God's Will.

MY CHRISTMAS-NEW YEAR-VACATION-ASPIRATION-PRAYERS

731

Religion talks.
Spirituality acts.
Yoga becomes.

732

May my mind's
God-ignoring ignorance-rocks
Be totally shattered
Once and for all.

733

May the entire world
Accept God's Peace-Message
Every day, every hour,
Every minute and every second
For the radical transformation
Of this world.

734

No cruel intimidation
Can ever succeed.
Only illumination shall succeed,
Here, there and everywhere.

735

The frustration of my vital
Can be conquered only
With my heart's patience-light.

736

What I desperately need
Every day
Is a God-commitment-prone
   heart.

737

Expectation-demolition
Is the secret and sacred way
To run the fastest
In the inner life.

738

If you hide
From your Lord's Presence,
How can He give
His ignorance-conquering Lance
To you?

739

My mind-thought-expulsion
I want.

740

My God-invitation-will
I desperately need.

741

God tells me
That if I want to explain Him,
Then He will not allow me
To claim Him.

742

In the spiritual life,
Do not go
Where simplicity, sincerity
And humility-virtues
Are ridiculed.

743

God tells me
That I must not try to
    understand
Others' tears.
I must only become implicitly
    one
With others' tears.

744

If we do not want
To feed God's hungry Heart,
Then we have to face
Sooner or later
God's angry Eye.

745

Fear strangles us.
Courage liberates us.
Courage gives us
What God wants us to have:
God's Victory-promise-
    manifestation
Here on earth.

746

God will never allow
Our God-hunger-heart
To starve.
God will definitely feed
Our God-hunger-heart
    sumptuously
At His choice Hour.

747

May each life
Be a giant
God-enquiry.

748

There comes a time
When we realise
That it is only our mind
That has the capacity
To defeat us.

MY CHRISTMAS-NEW YEAR-VACATION-ASPIRATION-PRAYERS

749

In my case,
The moment I lost my mind,
I gained my heart.

750

Fault-finders
Can never be
True God-servers.

751

God refuses to accept
Our resignation
Because He wants desperately
Our illumination.

752

There is no seat
For frustration
In my life-home.

753

The mind asks,
"Who is right?"
The heart replies,
"Only God is right,
Always right."

754

My life is made of
Aspiration and dedication.
I wish to utilise them equally.

755

The mind-education
Will never be able to give us
Heart-elevation
And life-illumination.

756

Every morning God sings
A very special song
In my heart-home
To inspire me and show me
    the way
To His Golden Palace.

757

Supreme!
God is God's
Compassion-Light.

758

Supreme!
Man is man's
Rejection-pride.

759

Supreme!
God is God's
Mother-Advice.

760

Supreme!
Children are children's
Disobedience-pleasure.

761

Supreme!
God is God's
Illumination-Boon.

762

Supreme!
Children are children's
Ignorance-choice.

763

Supreme!
God's Eye and God's Heart
Are streaming tears.

764

Supreme!
Humanity is humanity's
Uncaring mind.

765

Supreme!
God is God's
Sweetness-Whisper.

766

Supreme!
The world is the world's
Deafness-ears.

767

Supreme!
God is God's
Forward-marching Will.

768

Supreme!
Mankind is mankind's
Backward-crawling desire.

MY CHRISTMAS-NEW YEAR-VACATION-ASPIRATION-PRAYERS

769

I am convinced
That God is always
Pleased with me.

770

Alas,
I am never pleased
With myself.

771

God takes pride
In having me
As His partner.

772

I take pride
In being
God's servitor.

773

God tells me,
"My child,
I have plenty of time.
Take your own time.
Tell Me what you have to say."

774

I tell God,
"My Lord,
I am in a hurry.
Please forgive me.
My ignorance-friend
Is waiting for me."

775

God tells me,
"My child,
Until you take Me
As your only Friend,
Neither you nor I will have
Even an iota of peace."

776

I tell God,
"My Lord, I surrender.
You have won the race.
I shall fly with You,
I shall dive with You,
I shall run with You,
I shall always be with You,
In You and for You."

777

Supreme!
Man is afraid
Of God's Anger-Eye.

778

Supreme!
God is afraid
Of man's sorrow-heart.

779

Supreme!
God wonders why
Man does not pray to Him
Even once a month.

780

Supreme!
Man wonders why
God hides all the time.

781

Supreme!
Only the world-awakening souls,
The God-aspiring hearts
And the God-serving lives
Are invited to participate
In God's morning Meals
And evening Meals.

782

Supreme!
Finally I have stopped criticising
God
For everything that happens
In my life.

783

Supreme!
God is asking me
Not to blame Him any more
For the world-crisis.
God tells me,
"My child,
I am wide awake,
I am wide awake."

784

Supreme!
In my outer life
I have become a lamb
To charm You.
In my inner life
I have become a lion
To manifest You.

785

Supreme!
God tells me
That if I unreservedly love Him,
Then I must bury my past
In oblivion-cave.

MY CHRISTMAS-NEW YEAR-VACATION-ASPIRATION-PRAYERS

786

Supreme!
Heaven bountifully descends
Only when earth cheerfully offers
Its bleeding tears to God.

787

Hope and faith
From deep within
Can challenge and defeat
The outer cruel fate.

788

Supreme!
He who rejects his Master's advice
Summarily
Loses immediately
His God-identification-life.

789

The inner God-surrender-heart
Has to become
The outer world-prosperity-life.

790

The mind-admirer
And the mind-enjoyer
Cannot be
The heart-sky-climber.

791

My prayer-life
Tells my mind
Where it must go.

792

My meditation-life
Tells my heart
What it must become.

793

Aspire, aspire!
God is extremely eager
To share with you
All His supreme Secrets.

794

My prayer loves
My bended knees
Inside my mind-cave.

795

My meditation loves
My deepening heart
Inside my soul-temple.

796

Wherever I go,
God's Compassion
Walks ahead of me
And His Protection
Walks side by side with me.

797

There is only
One Source:
God-Infinity's Delight.

798

My faith in God
Is my inner freedom.
My faith in God
Is my outer confidence.

799

My God-obedience
Is my God-centred life.

800

God and I always speak
The language of heart-fondness
And life-oneness.

801

The love of power
Dominates the outer world.
The power of love
Liberates the inner world.

802

Alas,
When the mind's tunnel
    invites me,
I immediately accept the
    invitation
And run towards the tunnel.
But when the heart's palace
    invites me,
I get frightened. I hesitate.
Finally, I decline the invitation.

803

My prayer-tears
Quickly take me to God.
My meditation-smiles
Immediately bring God to me.

804

I must keep my aspiration-heart
And my dedication-life
Far beyond
The limitations of my fate.

MY CHRISTMAS-NEW YEAR-VACATION-ASPIRATION-PRAYERS

805

The sweetness of the heart
Unmistakably nullifies
The bitterness of the mind.

806

My heart-tears
Are my thunders
To demolish my mind's
Pride-walls.

807

I am hopeless,
Worthless and useless
Until I sincerely feel
That I am of God
And I am for God.

808

My heart-flower
Is God-Beauty.
My life-hour
Is God-Duty.

809

I am my
Three hundred and sixty-five
Tearful days,
Yet my Lord Supreme
Is far, far away
From me.

810

My Lord Supreme tells me
That my sincere nothingness
Embodies His complete Fulness.

811

To have the mind
As the sole master
Of my life
Is to invite confusion-disaster.

812

With my heart's
Sleepless devotion-tears
I drink deep the Beauty
Of my Beloved Lord's Feet.

813

Supreme!
Each and every citizen
Of this world
Must cry and smile
In love and trust.

814

My Lord,
At every moment
I need Your supreme Guidance
To solve all my inner
And outer problems.

815

My Lord,
I must not allow my self-doubt
To mar my heart's inner peace.

816

My Lord,
I must not allow
Anxieties and worries
To eclipse my heart-sun.

817

Every day the Compassion-Eye
Of my Lord Supreme
Leads me
In so many unexpected ways.

818

Every day my Lord Supreme,
Out of His infinite Bounty,
Commands me
To say things and do things
Challenging, daring,
Surprising, astonishing
And startling.

819

My Lord tells me,
"My child,
Start praying and meditating
For you to reach the
    Summit-Goal.
I shall do the rest."

820

God tells me,
"My child,
He who is obedient
To My Voice
Is My immediate Choice."

821

My love of God
Is my only religion.
I must break through
All my mind-occupied
Religion-curtains.

MY CHRISTMAS-NEW YEAR-VACATION-ASPIRATION-PRAYERS

822

For me
There is only one way
To reach my Goal,
And that way
Is by raising the standard
Of my self-discipline
And my God-dedication.

823

I must keep quiet.
I must keep my mind-road
Absolutely clear.
God is on His way
To come and speak to me.

824

My Lord tells me
That even if I do not see Him,
Even if I do not feel Him,
I must believe in Him
When He says
That His Compassion-Eye
Is upon me all the time
In loving watchfulness.

825

My Lord tells me,
"My child,
Be not overcharged
With worries and fears.
I shall gladly be
Your heavy burden-bearer."

826

I must realise
That God's Heart-Eye
Is always open
To my tears.

827

I must realise
That God's Heart-Ear
Is always open
To my cries.

828

My Lord tells me,
"My child,
Do not think
Of your tomorrow's needs.
Like today,
Tomorrow also I shall be
Your cheerful and sure supplies."

829

My Lord tells me,
"My child,
Have implicit faith in Me.
What am I here on earth for,
If I am not going to deliver you
From all your imaginary and real
Trials and tribulations?"

830

No matter what the world
Does to me,
No matter what the world
Thinks of me,
No matter what the world
Says about me,
I shall always be for the world,
For the betterment of the world,
As long as I am in the world
    of the living.

831

My Lord tells me,
"My child,
Be not afraid of your life's
    dire crisis.
I shall be your life's
All-conquering Strength.
You just carry My
    Victory-Banner
Throughout the length
    and breadth
Of the world."

832

My Lord,
From now on
I shall always abide
By Your supreme Plans.
Whenever I plan anything,
I only create disaster.
Therefore, my planning
Is nothing short of
    my interference.
I know You are the supreme
    Player
And I am Your divine instrument.

833

Why does God have to tell me
What He is going to do
In and through my life?
Why?
Let Him accomplish His Purpose
In my life.
I must always walk along the road
Of ever-increasing faith.

834

My Lord's Correction-Hand
Is upon my life.
I must never
Draw back.

MY CHRISTMAS-NEW YEAR-VACATION-ASPIRATION-PRAYERS

835

My Lord asks me
To give equal value
To His Compassion-Eye
And His Correction-Rod
For my ultimate good.

836

My Lord cradles my heart
Between the newness of
　the morning
And the stillness of dew.

837

My Lord,
Out of Your infinite Compassion,
You are paving the way for me
To arrive at the highest
　destination.
Alas,
Why am I drawing back
In self-doubt?
Why?

838

God can do things
Infinitely more for us
If we can feel
That He is astonishingly
　nearer to us
Than we think.

839

When I hunger
For God's Love,
His Concern-Heart
Comes first.
His Compassion-Eye
Follows.

840

Right from this very moment,
No anxiety will be able to find
A nesting place
Inside my thoughts.

841

If I do not love sleeplessly
My Lord Beloved Supreme
Out of the fulness of my heart,
Then I shall fail,
I shall definitely fail.

842

Every day I must make
My morning meditation
Rich, very rich,
By obeying the Voice within.

843

God tells me,
"My child,
I am eager to make you
An exact prototype of Myself.
Are you ready?"
My Lord,
I am ready.
I am at Your express Command.

844

My Lord,
I am seriously angry with You.
I do not need Your Power.
"What else, My child?"
I do not need Your Love.
"What else, My child?"
I do not need Your Compassion.

"What else, My child?"
I do not need Your Attention.
"What else, My child?"
My Lord,
Truth to tell,
I do not need anything from You.

"My child,
Is your exceptionally powerful
sermon over?" Yes, my Lord.
"My child,
My pithy Sermon begins.
Just because you do not need
    anything
From Me,
That does not mean
That I am not entitled
To have anything from you.
In no way you can prevent Me
From desiring things from you.
I need your affection.
I need your sweetness.
I need your fondness."

My Lord,
As I do not need anything from
    You,
Even so, You have to be
    fully prepared
To live
All by Yourself.

"My child,
You are My Eternity's Heart.
You are My Immortality's Breath.
You want to play the role
Of your volcano-anger.
I want to play the role
Of My Forgiveness-Fountain."

MY CHRISTMAS-NEW YEAR-VACATION-ASPIRATION-PRAYERS

845

"My child,
Why are you so ungrateful?
Can you not see
That I have put My Arm
 around you?
Can you not see
That with My Vision-Eye-Wings
I am sheltering you?

Can you not see and feel
That you are the sole object
Of My very, very special
 Concern?
My Concern for you
Shall remain forever
 unparalleled.

My child,
If you continue to displease Me,
Then I shall compel you
To take human incarnations
Countless times.
Needless to say,
This will be My last resort."

846

My Lord,
I am now so miserable.
I really do not know
What to say and what to do.
"My child,
Keep your confidence in Me.
You will never be disappointed.

Your life-boat shall ply
Between the success-shore
And the progress-shore.
I shall garland you
With My
Immortality's Transcendental
 Pride."

847

Solitude
Prepares me
Multitude
To feed.

848

My philosophy
And God's Philosophy
Are totally different.
God loves me.
Therefore He needs me.
I need God.
Therefore I love Him.

849

In the spiritual life,
The inner awakening
Safeguards again and again
Our outer life.

850

The human in me
Prays for God's Love.
The divine in me
Prays for God's Victory.

851

My Lord,
Please do not allow my desire-life
To draw me away from You
And scorch me
In the wildfire of the world.

852

I must be the absolute master
Of my mind.
I must mould it and shape it
The way my Inner Pilot
   commands me.

853

God asks me only
To keep my mind pure.
He will gladly
Do the rest.

854

By this time I must realise
That my own desire-life
Is the only culprit.
I must not blame anybody else
For my sufferings.

855

The river of time is flowing on.
It does not wait for anyone.
Swimming, we must cross
   the river.
Singing and dancing,
We must spend all the time
At the Destination.

856

When attachment disappears,
Detachment brings God to us
Immediately.

MY CHRISTMAS-NEW YEAR-VACATION-ASPIRATION-PRAYERS

857

My Lord, my Lord!
Do save me
From the snares of self-interest.
Self-interest has caught me taut
In its grip.

858

Living for the mind
Is the spiritual death.
Living for the heart
Is the spiritual life.
Living for the soul
Is the spiritual Immortality.
Living for God
Is becoming a God-representative
Here on earth.

859

By saying that the world
Is a bad place,
We are not making the world
     good.
To make the world good,
We must become good first.
How to become good?
Only by loving God the man
And serving man the God.

860

To please God
In His own Way,
I must become a giant personality
In spirituality.
I must become unique
In God-achievements
And a real asset to humanity.

861

The seeker's inner peace
Is the strongest power
In his outer life.

862

The supreme victory is certain
Only when God's Eye
Touches our hearts.
What is the supreme victory?
God-realisation for God's Sake.

863

An obedience-mind
Receives
God's proudest Smile.

864

A disobedience-mind
Is a seeker's greatest failure
In his spiritual life.

865

When I pray,
The sound-life of the day
Joins me proudly.

866

When I meditate,
The silence-heart of the night
Joins me self-givingly.

867

God's Sadness is measureless
When He sees
My world-aloofness-mind.

868

God sees inside my
    sweetness-heart
The blooms and the blossoms
Of His own countless
    divine Qualities.

869

The unaspiring life lives
In the thickening clouds
Of the mind.

870

The aspiring life lives
In the brightening sun
Of the heart.

871

My happiness
Does not start
Until God's Compassion-Eye
Arrives.

872

My Lord is always
An eager Listener.
Can I not be the same,
At least once in a while?

873

My Lord has His own
Daily challenges:
My mind-illumination
And my life-transformation.

874

At last,
After a very long time,
Today my sincere need of God
Has come back.

MY CHRISTMAS-NEW YEAR-VACATION-ASPIRATION-PRAYERS

875

During the day
I see my Lord Supreme
In the waves of my heart-sea.
At night
I see my Lord Supreme
In the silence of my soul-sky.

876

God Himself
Finds the right path
For my crying and weeping heart.

877

My heart and I are determined
To spend Eternity
With my Lord's
    Compassion-flooded Eye.

878

God's Forgiveness-Heart
Is never
Pressed for time.

879

My mind,
Just for this very moment
Please try to please only God.

880

Sooner or later,
My heart shall hear
God's Whispers.
Sooner or later,
My mind shall hear
God's Commands.

881

My Lord loves
To wait and hope.
From now on
I shall do the same.

882

My Lord wants me to show Him
Only what He wants to see:
My ignorance-pleasure-life.

883

We can serve and worship God
At any time we want to,
But during the day
Is the best time to serve God
And during the night
Is the best time to worship God.

884

Perfection and satisfaction
Shall dawn
Only after we have known God
In all His Aspects.

885

Alas,
We are all satisfaction-seekers
And not aspiration-lovers.

886

If I see myself
The way my Lord sees me,
Then I am on the verge of
God-realisation.
If I see myself
The way others see me,
Then my God-realisation
Shall forever remain
A far cry.

887

Every day
The mind delivers
Destructive blows.
Every day
The heart delivers
God's express Messages.

888

My prayer-life
Loves to live
On bended knees.

889

My body loves to walk
Towards the goal.
My vital loves to march
Towards the goal.
My mind loves to jog
Towards the goal.
My heart loves to sprint
Towards the goal.
My soul loves to fly
Towards the goal.

My Lord tells me
That I do not have to walk,
I do not have to march,
I do not have to jog,
I do not have to sprint
And I do not have to fly
Towards the goal.
The goal will come to me
If I can become
A sea of silence-peace.

890

A perfection-life
Is very slow in blossoming,
But it does blossom
Eventually.

MY CHRISTMAS-NEW YEAR-VACATION-ASPIRATION-PRAYERS

891

Every morning
My Lord teaches me
How to breathe in
His Oneness-Fulness-Breath.

892

I am heartsick
And homesick
For my Lord's
Compassion-flooded Eye.

893

Every morning
God wants me to garland Him
With my devotion-heart-roses.

894

Slowly the body dies.
Quickly the soul flies.
Self-givingly the Lord feeds
Earth's sighs and
    Heaven's promises.

895

The power of silence
Has enriched my life
Far beyond the flights
Of my imagination.

896

Sleeplessly and breathlessly
God wants my
    God-devotion-flame
Burning.

897

God tells me
That I must bring with me
My loving words and my
    smiling heart
When I come to visit Him.

898

Alas,
Why do I get frightened
When my soul wants me to have
A guided tour of Heaven?

899

God most proudly treasures
The devotion-fragrance
Of my aspiration-heart.

900

The less possession
My life has,
The more aspiration
My heart offers to God.

901

God is always eager
To lead us,
But will we ever be ready
To follow Him?

902

O my mind,
For such a long time
I have been with you.
Can you not now allow me
To be alone?

903

God's every Visit
My every breath
Treasures.

904

What each human being has
In common with God:
Tears and smiles.

905

Alas,
By constantly listening
To my desiring and doubting
    mind,
I have now become
My own unfortunate victim.

906

To please our Lord Supreme,
Equality is not enough.
We needs must have oneness.

907

God's Compassion-Smiles
And my gratitude-tears
Are successful in merging.

908

The things that God touches
Every day in my life:
My sincerity-heart
And my simplicity-life.

909

I speak to my shrine:
Where is our Lord Supreme?
My shrine speaks to me:
"Our Lord Supreme
Is right here with me.
But where are you,
And where is your heart?
What are you both doing?"

MY CHRISTMAS-NEW YEAR-VACATION-ASPIRATION-PRAYERS

910

The mind loves
To be the expectation.
The mind loves
To be the exception.

911

The heart loves
To be the aspiration.
The heart loves
To be the perfection.

912

If we look at life
From the divine angle,
We see God blooming
Here, there and allwhere.

913

May I help You, my Lord?
"Correction, My child."
Yes, my Lord.
May I serve You, my Lord?
"Correction, My child."
Yes, my Lord.

May You be my All, my Lord?
"Correction, My child."
Yes, my Lord.
My Lord, You are my All.
"Correction, my child."
Yes, my Lord.
My Lord, I am Your doll.

914

The less I have
In my mind-jungle,
The more I am
In my heart-garden.

915

I have learned
Something absolutely new today.
God has given my mind
An ultimatum:
The mind has to choose
Either God or ignorance.

916

Start is here,
Where my heart cries.
Finish is there,
Where my Lord smiles.

917

The doubting mind
Deserves life-imprisonment.
The aspiring heart
Needs heart-enlightenment.

918

My heart is in between
My life's sorrows
And
My soul's consolations.

919

When we do not aspire,
Life remains an imperfect bloom.
When we aspire,
Life becomes the
    perfection-blossom.

920

My Lord asks me
How I can be so low
That I want to give Him
A solo performance.

921

God the Eye
Feeds my
    God-aspiration-hunger.
God the Heart
Feeds my
    God-manifestation-hunger.

922

Nothing else is our birthright
Save and except
Our inner delight.

923

The more possessions,
The more processions.
The less outer prosperity,
The more inner divinity.

924

God comes down
From His transcendental Height
To measure my heart,
And not
To measure my house.

925

God's visible Love for me
Is my sleepless service-life.

MY CHRISTMAS-NEW YEAR-VACATION-ASPIRATION-PRAYERS

926

I must transform
All my mind-stories
Into my God-pleasing
Heart-songs.

927

The soil of faith
And the seed of love
Receive from God
His transcendental Blessings
And Pride.

928

God cries and cries
When the fulfilment of our
  desires
Gives us endless pleasures.

929

We must not ask God
Why, how, when and where.
We must tell God
That we are sleeplessly ready
With our eagerness-heart
To please Him in His own Way.

930

In our heart-garden,
Each flower reminds us
Of our meditation-hours.

931

Every morning
We shall have to make a choice:
Either to remain in our
  mind-sighs
Or in our heart-skies.

932

Only the
  God-devotion-heart-seekers
Are allowed to drink deep
God's Affection-Ambrosia.

933

Infinitely more concern has
  to bloom
In the heart of Heaven.
Then only
Peace will blossom
On the lap of Mother Earth.

934

May my heart beat sleeplessly
Only for the full manifestation
Of my Lord Beloved Supreme
Here on earth.

935

The heart is a dream.
The soul is the dreamer.
God is the Reality-Bridge
Between the heart-dream
And the soul-dreamer.

936

Greatness likes to sit.
Goodness likes to stand.
Selflessness likes to serve
   the world
While sitting and while standing.

937

When the talkers begin to listen
To the Inner Pilot,
This world will be flooded
With God-lovers and
   God-servers.

938

God loves our small jokes,
But He never likes our big jokes.
Our biggest joke is:
God does not need us.

939

God does not want me to be
A slave to my every desire.
He wants me to be
A master-fulfiller of every
   promise.

940

Every morning
God's Compassion-Eye descends
And helps me fly
To far horizons of
   self-transcendence.

941

In my outer life,
God is His Compassion-Eye.
In my inner life,
God is His Inspection-Eye.

MY CHRISTMAS-NEW YEAR-VACATION-ASPIRATION-PRAYERS

942

My mind,
Do not dare to delay
My heart's blooming.

943

Every day
My Lord pilots my life-boat
Between the shore of my
    heart's tears
And the shore of my soul's smiles.

944

Each time I offer my heart-tears
To my Lord Supreme,
He immediately comes one
    step closer
To my life.

945

Each time I offer my life-smiles
To my Lord,
He immediately grants me a visa
To enter into a new country
In His universal Life.

946

My Lord,
I would like to remain
Eternally a server of Yours,
And I do not want to become
Your Eternity's partner.
"My child,
Then your heart will be empty
Of My Love,
Your life will be empty
Of My Concern
And your breath will be empty
Of My Satisfaction.
My child,
If you become My partner,
Then you will take so much
Of My world-transforming
    responsibility."
My Lord, forgive me.
I shall abide by Your Request.

947

Each self-giving life
Is a very special God-emissary
Here on earth.

948

The inner life
Is a blissful dream.
The outer life
Is a painful reality.

949

Like my soul,
I must become
A bliss-discoverer
And
A doubt-invader.

950

My aspiration is not a substitute
For God-manifestation.
My meditation is not a substitute
For God-manifestation.
My constant God-oneness-life
Is an infallible substitute
For God-manifestation.

951

We must sing
All our God-manifestation-songs
While paving
Our golden life-road.

952

My heart's God-obedience-flower
Must forever last.
My life's God-obedience-hour
Must forever last.
My mind's God-obedience-tower
Must forever last.

953

Every day
I must self-givingly bend
    and kneel
Before the Will
Of my Absolute Lord Beloved
Supreme.

954

Only one thing is needed—
A oneness-heart—
For peace to bloom and blossom
On the lap of Mother Earth.

955

My mind wants to interpret
All my dreams.
My heart wants to love
All my dreams.
My soul wants to fulfil
All my dreams.

956

In my outer life,
My Lord wants me to be
His inspiration-voice.
In my inner life,
My Lord wants me to be
His aspiration-choice.

MY CHRISTMAS-NEW YEAR-VACATION-ASPIRATION-PRAYERS

957

My day I begin
With my
    God-obedience-nectar-drink.
My night I begin
With my
    God-surrender-nectar-drink.

958

My aspiration-sunrise-shore
Is inside my heart,
And nowhere else.

959

Our God-gratitude-road
Is absolutely safe,
And it is never
Overcrowded.

960

When I am in my mind,
My mind gives me what it has:
Sighs.
When I am in my heart,
My heart gives me what it is:
Delight.

961

My Lord compels me
To sleep.
He promises
To remain awake.

962

My faith clears my way
To God's Palace.
My love shortens my way
To God's Palace.

963

I take most valuable lessons
From my past failures.

964

Real forgiveness
Does not remember
The past.

965

My heart-tears
And my soul-smiles
Are discovering everything
That my Lord has kept hidden
From me.

966

The hour of struggle
Is powerful.
The hour of victory
Is blissful.
The Hour of God
Is Godful.

967

I love.
That means I am ready to trust.
I trust.
That means I am not sure
Whether I shall love or not.

968

My Lord tells me
That there is only one safe place
For me,
And that place
Is His Heart-Home.

969

When God is in my heart,
I start the race.
When I am in God's Heart,
I complete the race.

970

My soul is asking me
Not to be afraid
Of the unknown tomorrow,
For my soul is already there.

971

The Golden Boat
Has just arrived.
I must go
Immediately.

972

I love to fly
On the blue-gold wings
Of my selfless God-service.

973

When the heart speaks to you,
Take it as an infallible
And invaluable truth.

974

God's Forgiveness-Power
Has shattered
All my mind-boundaries.

MY CHRISTMAS-NEW YEAR-VACATION-ASPIRATION-PRAYERS

975

Cheerfully and sleeplessly
I must cultivate
The art of a oneness-heart.

976

Each divine thought
Is a new God-fulfilment-promise
Of my heart.

977

My Lord,
The fragrance of
Your Compassion-Eye
Is all I need
To become a choice instrument
Of Yours.

978

My Lord Beloved Supreme
Gives me His tearful Eye
And sorrowful Heart
To carry with me
When I go back
To my old desire-land.

979

Sincerity-prayers succeed.
They do not fail.

980

O seeker,
You are such a fool!
How do you expect your
    mind-forest
To be without desire-thorns?

981

My God-Friend
Has been indefinitely waiting
For my desire-friends
To leave me permanently.

982

Selfless service is the
    golden bridge
Between this world of aspiration
And the world of
    God-realisation.

983

Alas,
When will I be able to meet
With my divine tutor,
My soul?

984

God's Compassion-Eye
And His Forgiveness-Heart
Know what I do and what I have
    become,
Yet His Love for me
Is always on the increase.

985

I may not know
What God's Eye looks like,
But I do know God's Heart
Unmistakably plus perfectly.

986

At long last,
Today I have given up
My God-disbelief-profession.
I have now seen
My life's real teacher:
My illumination-soul.

987

My Lord,
May my longing
For Your Smile, Compassion,
Love and Affection
Be sleepless and breathless.

988

My Lord tells me
That my heart must not miss
Even a single opportunity
To be in His Presence.

989

My Lord tells me
That He will meet me
At every point
Where my meditations
And my actions
Are inseparable.

990

Unless I have convinced myself
That I am a supremely
    chosen child
Of my Master,
My Goal shall perpetually remain
A far cry.

991

God is always ready and eager
To remove the veil
That exists between Him and me,
But alas,
I enjoy watching the veil.

MY CHRISTMAS-NEW YEAR-VACATION-ASPIRATION-PRAYERS

992

My Lord tells me
That He definitely wants me
   to have
Indomitable courage and
   strength,
But He wants to walk, march,
Run and sprint
All the time ahead of me
To reach the Goal.

993

My Lord,
I love You beyond measure!
"My child, I never thought
That you would be a perfect
   stranger
To truth.
If you really love Me,
Then you will leave
All you have and all you are
In My safe Hands."

994

Alas, it is too late
For me to ask God
Where I can find Him,
When it will be the right time
And how I can please Him.
Now my desire-bound life and I
Can tell my Lord only this:
"O Lord, we love You."

995

My mind must live
In prayers.
My heart must live
In meditations.
Only then shall I be able to have
A full life of God-Beauty
And God-Fragrance.

996

My Lord tells me,
"My child,
Do not reverse the truth.
Dive deep within.
My Dictates are not binding you.
It is you who are binding
   My Dictates
And delaying My manifestation
Here on earth."

997

My Lord,
Why am I so ungrateful to You?
I clearly see that
Your Heart is drawn out
   towards me
To shelter me
And be my strongest support.

998

I must be the winner
In the race of life—
I must!

999

My Lord tells me,
"My child,
When your enemies hinder you
In every way imaginable,
Cultivate faith in Me.
I shall be with you,
In you and totally for you."

1000

If I do not care
To manifest my Lord's Light
On earth,
Why should He liberate me
From the bondages of time?

1001

I have come to learn
That my own sincerity-heart
Is a source of tremendous energy
And vitality
In my spiritual life.

1002

O my inner faith,
You are the only one
To enable me to withstand
All the attacks
Of my stark adversaries.

1003

My Lord says to me,
"My child, do not give up,
Do not give up!
I am coming, I am coming!
I am coming to you as a Beacon
In your ignorance-night."

1004

Do not doubt,
Do not hesitate!
Your God-fulfilment-promise
You will be able to carry through
To completion.

1005

Weakness-multitudes
Soulfully confessed
Are immediately forgiven.

MY CHRISTMAS-NEW YEAR-VACATION-ASPIRATION-PRAYERS

1006

God's Love is not only
For a few selected seekers.
It is definitely available
To all.
Needless to say,
You and I are included.

1007

God's special Blessings
Are not beyond our reach.
It is His genuine desire
That we all receive
His special Blessings
Directly from His own Hand.

1008

Time is short, very short.
Our uppermost concern
Has to be God-fulfilment
Here on earth.

1009

God says to me,
"My child,
Just give Me once and for all
What you are:
Ignorance-life.
I shall, in return,
    immediately give you
The abundance of My own Life:
Beauty, Light, Delight,
Perfection and Satisfaction."

1010

I give God
An iota of my love.
God gives me
His entire Life
And His very Breath.

1011

God says to me,
"My child, true,
You have gone astray.
But do I not have Love-Power
To draw you back?
Lo, you are back
And once more safe
Inside My Heart-Home."

1012

When God's Voice
Is my only choice,
He in no time bridges
The longest gap
Between my life and His Heart.

1013

I have completely forgotten God,
But God tells me that His Heart
Is still sleeplessly occupied
With me and my life.

1014

My Lord Beloved Supreme
    tells me,
"My child,
You can doubt Me if you want to,
But you will never be able
    to doubt
My Love."

1015

My Lord of infinite Compassion
Says to me,
"My child,
You express your wild hostility
Towards Me
And I accept it gladly.
I know that is your way of life.
My child,
Since I gladly accept
What you give Me,
Can you not accept
What I have to offer:
My Love, My Concern,
My Compassion and
    My Forgiveness?"

1016

When I meditate
Solely on God's Victory,
I go far beyond
The confines of time.

1017

Ignorance-night I have.
Wisdom-light I need
To enrich my life
Divinely and ceaselessly,
And God is all ready
To fulfil me.

MY CHRISTMAS-NEW YEAR-VACATION-ASPIRATION-PRAYERS

1018

God says to me,
"My child,
If you light your heart-candle,
I shall take care of your
    darkness."

1019

The body says, "I can sleep."
The vital says, "I can strangle."
The mind says, "I can fight."
The heart says, "I can love."
The soul says, "I can watch
And send my report to God."

1020

God says that He has seen me
Countless times,
And I am still the same.
Next time He wants to see me
With a new mind, a new heart
And a new face.
If I fail Him,
He may never give me
Another chance.

1021

When my mind
Wants to speak to God,
God says to my mind,
"You are too close!
Go back at least
One hundred metres.
Do not worry—
I have two very big Ears.
I shall be able to hear you
Very easily."

1022

When my heart
Wishes to speak to God,
God says to my heart,
"My child, why do you have
    to stand
So far away?
Am I a stranger?
Come, come very, very close
    to Me.
The nearer you come,
The better for both of us
To hear each other."

1023

God's Eye
Examines all and sundry,
With no exception.

1024

God's Heart
Examines only
The chosen few.

1025

My mind thinks
It knows everything
About God.
My heart feels
It has to learn everything
About God
From God Himself.

1026

My Master tells me
That if I want to become
A perfect disciple of his,
Then he expects cheerful
    surrender
And not forced surrender
To His God-oneness-will.

1027

I must reach
The summit
Of my God-surrender-ecstasy.

1028

Alas,
All my meetings with my mind
Are always noisy, unproductive,
Worthless and useless.

1029

I feel lonely
Only when my God-Friend
Is not beside me.

1030

God's Compassion-Eye
Is always ready to greet
The seeker in me.

1031

God's Satisfaction-Heart
Is always ready to embrace
The divine lover in me.

1032

The mind's self-doubt-blows
Are extremely powerful
And unthinkably destructive.

MY CHRISTMAS-NEW YEAR-VACATION-ASPIRATION-PRAYERS

1033

The smiles of my soul
Are my heart's
Heaven-climbing hopes.

1034

My God-devotion-heart
Steers my life-boat
To the Golden Shore
Of the ever-transcending
    Beyond.

1035

The insecurity
Of my inner life
Is the madness-thunder
Of my outer life.

1036

My Lord Supreme has
    blessed me
With an aspiration-road
Which is at once ageless
And endless.

1037

My soul-bird is teaching me
How to fly far above
The streaming tears of my heart
And
The brooding fears of my mind.

1038

My Beloved Lord's
Most inspiring and most
    energising
Long-distance calls
Are cordless and wordless.

1039

May my heart
Be a galaxy
Of God-blossoming dreams.

1040

To maintain our inner poise,
We must give equal value
To success and failure.

1041

My unconditional
    aspiration-heart
Is a luxury
I have received from
God's Compassion,
Affection, Love and Bliss.

1042

My heart urges me
To love God.

1043

My soul compels me
To serve God.

1044

God pleads with me
To remember Him
Sleeplessly and self-givingly.

1045

Alas,
My mind
Is shockingly heartless.

1046

Alas,
My heart
Is helplessly homeless.

1047

Alas,
My life
Is unthinkably godless.

1048

Everything deceives me
Save my aspiration-heart-tears.

1049

The moment my
    God-obedience-heart
Stops functioning,
My earth-existence becomes
A colossal failure.

1050

To lose
A childlike heart
Is to miss
A God-Heart-Smile.

MY CHRISTMAS-NEW YEAR-VACATION-ASPIRATION-PRAYERS

1051

The beauty
Of the earth-planet
Is extremely inspiring.

1052

The duty
Of the earth-planet
Is extremely surprising.

1053

The outer world
Loves
Quick motion.

1054

The inner world
Loves
Intense aspiration.

1055

Every day
Is a holiday
For my God-surrender-life.

1056

I climb up
And sit at the very top
Of my hope-mountain.

1057

I climb down
And become
My promise-fulfilment-fountain.

1058

Alas,
My body chooses
The lethargy-life.

1059

Alas,
My vital chooses
The hesitation-mind.

1060

Alas,
My mind chooses
The impatience-vital.

1061

To my great joy,
My heart chooses
God's Protection-Feet.

1062

O Pilot of the New Year-Boat,
Do give my heart a new hope,
My life a new promise
And me a new assurance
That You are going to take me
To Your Golden Shore.

1063

O my mind,
I beg of you,
Please leave your old life behind—
Please!

1064

O my heart,
I beg of you,
Please cry more for humanity—
Please!
And please smile more at God—
Please!

1065

I know, I know,
God's Compassion-Eye—
For this my heart lives.

1066

I know, I know,
God's Forgiveness-Heart—
For this my life lives.

1067

I know, I know,
God's full manifestation
    on earth—
For this I live.

1068

God Himself feeds the genuine
    seekers
Every day.
Therefore, their aspiration-hearts
And their service-lives
Are becoming stronger and
    stronger
Every day.

MY CHRISTMAS-NEW YEAR-VACATION-ASPIRATION-PRAYERS

1069

Self-importance—
Dangerous, dangerous!
I must shun it
Once and for all.

1070

The heart never questions,
Never doubts God's Presence
In each and every life
And each and every death.

1071

My Lord,
I promise I shall not delay
My unconditional
Surrender-life-existence on earth
Any more.

1072

A God-searching mind
Must embody
Sincerity.

1073

A God-aspiring heart
Must embody
Intensity.

1074

A God-serving life
Must embody
Integrity.

1075

To see my Lord smiling,
Even for a fleeting moment,
I am prepared to cover
The length and breadth
Of the world.

1076

My Lord Supreme tells me
That He does not stop enjoying
The exquisite fragrance
Of my gratitude-heart-tear-
   garland.

1077

I know and I feel
That my Lord Beloved Supreme
Has an everlasting Love
For me.

1078

God does not hide anything
From me.
Because of my blind eyes,
I do not see
What He does for me
Self-givingly and sleeplessly.

1079

God blesses me
Out of the Bounties of His
Heart.
Alas, where is my
    receptivity-heart,
Where?

1080

If we want to walk
Every day
In the newness of life,
Then we must have enthusiasm
In our mind
In abundant measure.

1081

Every morning and evening
My Lord tells me
Only one thing:
Not to do,
But to be.

1082

God expects
The deepest affection-portion
From my aspiration-heart,
And no,
Never some random portion.

1083

The days are short.
My desires are endless.
O climbing aspiration-flames,
Where are you?
In your absence
I am helpless,
I am hopeless,
I am useless.

1084

I search
For my inner food:
Life divine.

1085

An insecurity-mind-plant
Rapidly grows.

1086

An impurity-life-river
Dauntlessly flows.

MY CHRISTMAS-NEW YEAR-VACATION-ASPIRATION-PRAYERS

1087

God-manifestation on earth
Entirely depends
On humanity's genuine love
For God.

1088

A faultless heart
Is possible,
But not
A faultless life.

1089

The human in us
Sleeplessly needs
Self-mastery.

1090

The divine in us
Breathlessly needs
God-discovery.

1091

How can God tame
My unruly earth-existence-life
If I every day blame God
Consciously and deliberately?

1092

My life needs nothing
From the future.
It needs everything
From the immediacy of today.

1093

Every day, without fail,
My Lord Himself breathes
My gratitude-heart-tear-breath.

1094

Desire-journey ends
In the land of nowhere.

1095

Not to entertain
My mind, my vital and my body,
But to enlighten my life
I came into the world.

1096

The beauty of my prayer
And the fragrance of my
   meditation
Are carrying me
To my Lord's Heart-Home.

1097

My heart's
Devotion-temple
Is my life's
Pole-star.

1098

Look forward,
My life!
Never, never look back
At the sad failures
Of the past.

1099

I must hold myself
To the absolutely highest
God-satisfaction-standard.

1100

I must brighten my mind,
Deepen my heart
And strengthen my life.

1101

Be fully prepared!
Lo and behold,
The unparalleled
    opportunity-train
Is come.

1102

God tells me
That God-Satisfaction
Is my birthright.
I have only to claim it,
The sooner the better.

1103

I must find my inner road
Myself,
Or I must beg God
To make one for me.

1104

Every divinely blooming thought
Becomes
A supremely blossoming
    experience.

1105

My prayers and meditations
Are answered
Not when I am begging God,
But when I am loving
And serving God.

MY CHRISTMAS-NEW YEAR-VACATION-ASPIRATION-PRAYERS

1106

God's Protection-Shelter-Home
Is for all human beings,
Whether they are aspiring
Or desiring.

1107

I unmistakably see
That my desire-mind-cloud-sky
Is clearing.

1108

May my gratitude-heart
Expand and expand
In every direction.

1109

When my meditation
Is very deep,
I breathe in perfect rhythm
With my Beloved Lord Supreme.

1110

He who has never visited hell
Will never be able
To appreciate, admire,
Adore and love Heaven
Most adequately.

1111

Only the helpless tears
Of my heart
Are given the chance
By my Lord Supreme
To take a short-cut
To His Heart-Home.

1112

Every morning
The very first thing I do
Is to offer my
    gratitude-heart-tears
To my Lord Beloved Supreme.

1113

A God-surrender-life means
A life of ever-blossoming
God-Delight.

1114

My Lord tells me
That He will make me
A blue-gold star
In His Heart-Sky
If I meditate soulfully
And self-givingly.

1115

Yesterday my Lord gave me
The lightning speed of
   inspiration.
Today my Lord gives me
The lightning speed of aspiration.
Tomorrow my Lord will give me
The lightning speed of
   self-offering.

1116

God comes to my
   surrender-angel
Inside my heart
On tiptoe
With His infinite Joy
And infinite Pride.

1117

Every day our inner faith
Needs newness-joy
To grow into
The Fulness of God.

1118

Every morning my heart and I
Hoist our Supreme Lord's
Victory-Flag.

1119

There is nothing
That a hope-heart
Cannot achieve.

1120

Alas,
I fool myself miserably
By thinking that I know
Who I truly am.

1121

I must replace the pleasure-life
Of my outer world
With the heart-joy
Of my inner world.

1122

God proudly smiles at my mind
When He sees that it has
Even an iota of peace.

1123

If I really want peace
In my life,
Then I must not busy myself
With what others do and say.

MY CHRISTMAS-NEW YEAR-VACATION-ASPIRATION-PRAYERS

1124

To be perfect in my outer life,
I must harmoniously live
With my inner
God-aspiration-heart.

1125

A famous life
Is no match
For a God-Pride-heart
And a God-faithfulness-life.

1126

To see my
    Lord Beloved Supreme
Smiling,
I am ready to sacrifice everything
In my life.

1127

I must not postpone
Even for a single day
My unconditional surrender
To God's Will.

1128

Not what the mind says,
But what the heart feels
I must immediately believe
And accept.

1129

My heart's soulful
Devotion-skill
Is my life's momentous
Enthusiasm-thrill.

1130

A devotion-heart
That has intensity
Is of paramount importance.

1131

A doubting mind
Can influence other minds,
But never an aspiring heart.

1132

Every morning I receive
My Lord's Blessing-Rain
With my gratitude-heart-tears.

1133

My heart-breath descends
From my Lord's
Transcendental Delight.

1134

I must multiply
My heart's sweetness
And my life's oneness.

1135

When the Hour of God strikes,
Do not delay!
Just run your fastest
To your final Destination.

1136

Every morning
Prayerfully, soulfully and
    blissfully
I fly on the wings
Of my God-love.

1137

Do not mind
If you fall.
Only allow God
To lift you up again.
He is all ready
To do you this big favour.

1138

In the marketplace of life,
Nothing is essential
And nothing is permanent.

1139

Sweet is God's
Compassion-Eye.

1140

Sweeter are God's
Affection-Arms.

1141

Sweetest is God's
Fondness-Heart.

1142

The mind gives millions of
    reasons
Why it does not want to accept
    God
As its Creator.

1143

The heart says,
"I cannot live without God
Even for a fleeting moment.
No reason-snare
Can ever catch me."

MY CHRISTMAS-NEW YEAR-VACATION-ASPIRATION-PRAYERS

1144

I need
An ever-progressing
God-gratitude-life.

1145

A God-eagerness-heart
Feeds on only
Now.

1146

My Lord says to me,
"My child,
I am infinitely more interested
In your aspiring heart
Than in your life's
Mighty achievements."

1147

I desperately and sleeplessly need
Enthusiasm-thrill
In my dry mind.

1148

God says to me,
"My child,
I want to reverse the game.
My only desire is this:
From now on,
You will be indulgent to Me
And not to yourself."

1149

In each century,
God-realised souls
Can be counted
On the fingertips.

1150

To smile at God
Is a seeker's
Very first requirement.

1151

I dearly love
My God-adoration
And
My God-manifestation-
    convictions.

1152

Do not enjoy your friendship
With your unaspiring mind.
You will be a dejected
And rejected God-devotee.

1153

When we please God
In His own Way,
He accepts us as true members
Of His inner Family.

1154

Aspiration
Is the transcendence-assurance
Of our previous achievements.

1155

God-criticism-acceptance
In our spiritual life—
Not only unacceptable,
But also unpardonable.

1156

God the Forgiveness-Heart
And
God the Compassion-Eye
Pick us up
After each fall.

1157

To protect
His supremely chosen children,
God is God's
Round-the-clock Concern.

1158

Hope
Is a supreme necessity-quality
In our God-aspiring life.

1159

My God-oneness-heart
Is earth's representative
To Heaven.

1160

My purity-heart-friend
Tells me what to do
To please God
All the time.

1161

My divinity-soul-friend
Teaches me how to become
A supremely choice child
Of my Lord Beloved Supreme.

MY CHRISTMAS-NEW YEAR-VACATION-ASPIRATION-PRAYERS

1162

My Compassion-flooded Lord
Tells me:
"Not the distance travelled,
But the destination reached."

1163

I badly failed God
In my God-aspiration-
    examination.
Is it not surprising?
No!
Is it not shocking?
Yes!

1164

Every morning my Lord,
God the eternal Beggar,
Comes to me
For my two sincerity-eyes
And one purity-heart.

1165

I live in between
My life's soulful sobs
And my heart's blissful throbs.

1166

Today my heart is awakened
To the beauty and fragrance
Of a oneness-world.

1167

I have zero tolerance
For those who constantly
Find fault
With my Lord Beloved Supreme.

1168

Alas,
Whenever I look for my mind,
I find it in the grip
Of God-ingratitude.

1169

The mind has no time
For God's Tears.
The heart gives its whole life
To be inseparably one
With God's Tears.

1170

At every moment
We must be careful!
Ruthless and baseless
Worries and anxieties
Invade our lives
When we enter into
Our mind-jungles.

1171

"Nothing remains the same for
   long."
Not true!
My unconditional
God-surrender-life
Always remains the same.

1172

My Lord,
How will I recognise You
If or when You come to see me?
"My child,
You will be able to recognise Me
Easily
From your ecstasy-flooded
Heart-throbs."

1173

When we are aspiring
For divine qualities,
There is no such thing
As too much.

1174

When we greedily crave
For earthly possessions,
Each possession can decrease
Our God-hunger.

1175

If you think and feel
That you are working extremely,
Extremely hard,
Just think of the Old Man
Upstairs in Heaven.
Your embarrassment
Shall beggar description.

1176

Today's God-adoration
Invariably tomorrow
Becomes God-destination.

1177

All my prayers
And all my meditations
Have only one secret desire
Inside them:
God-fulfilment in God's own
   Way.

MY CHRISTMAS-NEW YEAR-VACATION-ASPIRATION-PRAYERS

1178

To my greatest joy,
Every day my God-oneness-heart
And my man-oneness-life
Are expanding.

1179

To fulfil our heart's
Every divine need,
God Himself
Comes down.

1180

In the doubting and suspecting
Mind-jail,
It is extremely difficult
For the seeker-heart
To survive.

1181

The mind-newspaper
Carries only accidents,
Catastrophes, crimes,
Obscure and impure news.

1182

The heart-newspaper
Carries only the news
About the Supreme Lord,
About the cosmic gods
And goddesses
And about the archangels
And angels.

1183

Each moment
Comes to our aspiration-heart
With a new
    God-fulfilment-dream.

1184

Today is the day for me
To step out of my mind's
Self-imposed insecurity-prison.

1185

Every morning and evening
I am mesmerised
By God's Self-Transcendence-
Vision-Beauty-Eye.

1186

The mind lends.
The heart gives.
The body and the vital
Do not give
And do not take.

1187

God is extremely proud of
    Himself
And extremely proud of me
When He sees my life
In between His Friendship
And His Partnership.

1188

My Lord,
I cannot stop thinking of You,
Although I may not think of You
All the time
Either highly or gratefully.

1189

There is a constant battle
Between God's Pride in me
And my own disappointment
With my life.

1190

Invincible faith
And nothing else
A seeker needs
In his spiritual life.

1191

The moment we enter
Into God's Boat,
He promises us
In His own inimitable Way
Smooth sailing
On His Oneness-Fulness-Sea.

1192

My Lord tells me
That real spirituality
Has nothing to do
With idle and useless curiosities.

MY CHRISTMAS-NEW YEAR-VACATION-ASPIRATION-PRAYERS

1193

My Lord,
Do tell me,
How long can You ignore
The streaming tears
Of my broken heart?
"My child,
There shall come a time
When I shall be able to prove to
    you
That My Kindness is always
    flooded
With My Wisdom-Light."

1194

Spirituality's heart-home
Is absolutely the wrong place
For those who are craving
For world-supremacy.
Spirituality's heart-home
Is absolutely the right place
For those who are longing
Only for God-intimacy
And God-oneness.

1195

My gratitude-heart-tears
Do not fall down.
They just fly up
High, higher, highest
To my Lord's Heart-Home.

1196

My Lord,
Do give me the capacity
To devour the dust of Your Feet
Speedily and completely.

1197

My heart's sobbing whispers
Reach my Lord's Heart
With lightning speed.

1198

I wish to find my life
In between my
    aspiration-intensity
And my Lord's
Compassion-Immensity.

1199

God comes
Closer and closer
To my heart-tears.

1200

God becomes
Dearer and dearer
To my life-smiles.

1201

Alas,
Why do I live
In my unlit mind-cave,
And not
In my fully illumined
   heart-home?

1202

In the morning
God examines
My mind's purity
And my heart's beauty.

1203

In the evening
God examines
My life's tolerance
And patience.

1204

In the morning
I soulfully gather
Hope-petals.

1205

In the evening
I prayerfully sow
Surrender-seeds.

1206

My Lord's soulful Eye
Shelters my heart-beauty
And my soul-fragrance.

1207

At night
My Lord wants me to count
The unconditional love-moments
That I had during the day.

1208

Insecurity and pride
Have the same source:
Ego.

1209

My Mother India tells me:
"Silence, my son, silence!
Silence in your inner life,
Silence in your outer life."

1210

My Mother India tells me:
"My son,
Sail your heart-boat, sail.
Do not use your mind-volcano
To assail,
Do not — never!"

MY CHRISTMAS-NEW YEAR-VACATION-ASPIRATION-PRAYERS

1211

My Mother India tells me:
"My son,
Power is not the answer.
Compassion is not the answer.
Even forgiveness is not the
  answer.
God's Vision-Eye-Fulfilment
Is the answer, the only answer."

1212

My Mother India tells me,
"My son,
The world-crisis will be over
Only when the strength of the
  mind
Cheerfully embraces
The power of the heart,
And only God knows
When and how it will happen.
But it will definitely happen,
In the very, very, very, very
Distant future.
Until then,
All God-seekers of the world
Must pray sleeplessly
And meditate breathlessly
Only for God's Victory."

1213

I must blame myself
And not the world
For not taming
My undivine mind.
I must blame myself
And not the world
For not feeding
Regularly, cheerfully, proudly
My God-hungry heart.

1214

We all must be careful,
Very careful!
The patience of the world-soul
Is wearing thin, very thin.

1215

I want my life to revolve only
Around God-made yoga.
Yoga means union,
Union with God,
Union with God's Will.

1216

I love and fulfil
The silence-whisper-messages
Of my soul.

1217

My imagination-mind,
Wake up, wake up!
Sleep no more.
My aspiration-heart,
Climb up, climb up!
Delay no more, delay no more!
My dedication-life,
God Himself is watching.
Be careful, be careful!

1218

My Lord has commanded
Hope, enthusiasm,
     encouragement,
Promise and fulfilment
To accompany me wherever I go.

1219

My Lord,
What does prayer do?
"My child,
Prayer makes and keeps
Your heart-day bright."

1220

My Lord,
What does meditation do?
"My child,
Meditation makes and keeps
Your mind-night illumined."

1221

My Lord,
What does gratitude do?
"My child,
Gratitude makes and keeps
Your heart sweet and pure."

1222

My Lord,
What does surrender do?
"My child,
Surrender makes you feel
That you are absolutely Mine,
And also your surrender makes
     Me feel
That I am absolutely yours."

1223

My Lord, what shall I do
With my stark enemies?
"My child, if you really love Me,
If you really need Me,
Then you will have nothing,
Nothing, nothing to do
With your enemies."

MY CHRISTMAS-NEW YEAR-VACATION-ASPIRATION-PRAYERS

1224

My Lord, some friends
Who have betrayed me
And are no longer with me,
And some friends who are
Still with me
But mix with them
And talk with them
And receive wild and absurd
    gossip
And spread it all around:
What shall I do with them?
"My child, your time on earth
Is extremely precious.
Throw them out of your heart,
Throw them out of your mind,
And throw them out of your life
Immediately.
You do not need
These so-called friends."

1225

My Lord, please, please tell me
Who are my real enemies?
"My child, your real enemies
Are those who are
Ingratitude incarnate."

1226

My Lord Beloved Supreme,
When do I give You utmost joy?
"My child,
When you claim only Me
As your own, very own."

1227

My Lord Beloved Supreme,
When do I give You utmost pain?
"My child,
When you tell me unthinkable
    things,
Such as you are worthless,
You are hopeless
And you are useless."

1228

My Lord Beloved Supreme,
Am I really worthy of You?
"My child,
Have you nothing better to do
Than to hurl an insult at me?
I am your Creator.
You are My creation.
It is My bounden Responsibility
To mould you and shape you
In My own Image.
You have just to love Me
    unreservedly
And, if it is possible,
    unconditionally.
Be happy. Remain happy.
Your zenith-perfection-life
Is My sole Responsibility."

1229

My soul is a perpetual
God-manifestation
And
God-satisfaction-promise-hunger.

1230

My outer success
Takes a very, very long time
To reach my Lord's
Heavily burdened Ears.

1231

My inner progress
Sooner than at once
Reaches my Lord's
Eager Ears.

1232

My Lord,
Do You ever get tired?
"My child, I do.
I get tired when I read
The lengthier than the lengthiest
Complaint-list from My children
Against My creation."

1233

My Lord Beloved Supreme,
Out of Your infinite Bounty,
You have made me
A mountain-success.
Now I pray to You to make me
A fountain-progress.

1234

My Lord Beloved Supreme,
Today I have a volley of
    questions.
"My child, I am all ready."
My Lord,
Where does my obedience stand
In my spiritual life?
"My child, your obedience
Is your pre-school course."
My Lord,
Where does my love stand
In my spiritual life?
"My child, your love
Is the kindergarten course."
My Lord,
Where does my devotion stand
In my spiritual life?
"My child, your devotion
Is the primary school course."
My Lord,
Where does my surrender stand?
"My child, your surrender
Is your high school course."
My Lord,
My unreserved surrender,
Where does it stand?
"My child,
Your unreserved surrender
Is your college course."
My Lord,
My unconditional surrender,
Where does it stand?
"My child,
Your unconditional surrender
Is your university course."
My Lord,
Where does my sleepless,

MY CHRISTMAS-NEW YEAR-VACATION-ASPIRATION-PRAYERS

breathless
And unconditional surrender
   stand?
"My child,
That is your PhD course."

1235

My Lord,
When I exploit Your indulgence,
What happens to me?
"My child,
You are the one to feel and know
What happens when you exploit
My indulgence."
My Lord,
We all talk about self-indulgence.
What actually is self-indulgence?
"My child,
Self-indulgence drastically
   reduces
The God-oneness-dream-
   capacity."

1236

My Lord,
Will I ever be able to please You
In Your own Way?
"My child,
You will be able to please Me
In My own Way
Only when you live on earth
Only for me,
And not for your doubting,
Criticising, suspecting, torturing
And annihilating mind."

1237

A birthday
Is the blossoming
Of a new
Consciousness-delight-dream.

1238

The world demands
The very best from me.

1239

My Lord desires
To have
Everything of mine.

1240

The final and last choice
Has to be made here and now.
No more chances
Shall be granted.

1241

Not my outer belief,
But my inner faith
That decides who God is,
Where God is
And what God actually expects
From my life.

1242

The outer success
Reaches the fleeting
Pride-crown-destination.

1243

The inner progress
Reaches the abiding
Happiness-throne-goal.

1244

What we have
Is a false outer smile.
What we need
Is a sincere inner cry.

1245

An open mind
Is a very rare achievement.
A God-surrender-life
Is a God-achievement.

1246

I must examine
The beauty and fragrance
Of my own happiness-heart
Before I offer them
To humanity's heart.

1247

My knowledge-light
Is the quantity-beggar.
My wisdom-delight
Is the quality-chooser.
My Lord Supreme tells me
Not to worry.
He will gladly take care of
The beggar in me
And the chooser in me.
I just have to love Him only
And need Him only.

1248

To me, the highest height
Is not the happiest privilege,
But the greatest and heaviest
Responsibility.

1249

My Lord has chosen
My utterly insignificant life
To accomplish the impossible:
The full manifestation of God
Here on earth.

1250

If my life really desires
To be a God-server,
Then God's Heart will be
My life's untiring supplier.

MY CHRISTMAS-NEW YEAR-VACATION-ASPIRATION-PRAYERS

1251

I measure my life-boundaries.
My Lord counts only
My heart-garden-flowers.

1252

There are God-doubters.
There are God-believers as well.
Who can prevent me
From being a God-believer,
And who can prevent me
From being a God-lover,
A God-server
And, finally, a God-manifester?

1253

In God's Eye
I am never insignificant.
In God's Heart
I am eternally and infinitely
More significant
Than I can ever imagine.

1254

My life-book begins with
The God-aspiration-chapter
And ends with
The God-realisation-chapter.

1255

The heart has another name:
Aspiration.
The mind has another name:
Suspicion.
The vital has another name:
Restlessness.
The body has another name:
Idleness.
Life has another name:
Uncertainty.
Man has another name:
Complexity.
The soul has another name:
Observer.
God has another Name:
Forgiver.

1256

My Lord blessingfully whispers.
Alas, I pay no attention.
My soul compassionately
    whispers.
Alas, I pay no attention.
My heart lovingly whispers.
Alas, I pay no attention.

1257

My mind speaks to me.
I immediately obey.
My vital speaks to me.
I proudly obey.
My body speaks to me.
I lovingly obey.
Alas, when shall I stop
Obeying them, when?
Alas, when shall I be
The choice instrument
Of my Lord Supreme, when?

1258

In this life
I need only one qualification:
God-obedience.

1259

Only one thing
I shall never, never, never desire:
God-disobedience.

1260

My God-obedience
Is my God-closeness.
My God-disobedience
Is my God-aloofness.

1261

My God-satisfaction
Asks my God-obedience
To run side by side with it
All the time.

1262

My God-defiance
Bravely marches along the road
That has no goal.
My God-disobedience
Proudly follows my
    God-defiance.

1263

We cannot merit
God's Transcendental
    Consciousness
And His Universal
    Consciousness,
But we can inherit and do inherit
His Transcendental
    Consciousness
And His Universal
    Consciousness.

MY CHRISTMAS-NEW YEAR-VACATION-ASPIRATION-PRAYERS

1264

My outer beauty
Attracts and welcomes
All the hostile forces
   of the world.
My inner beauty
Frightens and transforms
All the hostile forces
   of the world.

1265

If I am a real God-lover,
Then I must always remember
That God the Power infinite
Is my constant helper.

1266

I love God.
This may be an iota of truth.
God loves me.
Indeed, this is the bloom of truth,
And this is the blossom of truth.

1267

I dare and dare to say
That my Lord and I
Love each other intensely
And care for each other
   immensely.

1268

God wants only
The selflessness-hearts
To broadcast His most glorious
Life-Activities here on earth.

1269

God tells me that spirituality
Is not something fanatic,
Fantastic, eccentric and idiotic,
But really realistic and idealistic.

1270

My prayers and I
Together
Climb and climb.

1271

My meditations and I
Together
Dive and dive.

1272

My life is absolutely safe
Only when I can remain seated
At the Feet of my Lord Supreme.

1273

The inner worlds
And the outer world
Are clashing and crashing
   together.
Yet my Beloved Lord Supreme
Has kept me
Absolutely unshaken.

1274

Alas,
In an unknown and
   mysterious way,
We cherish our endless
Worries and anxieties.

1275

In the battlefield of life,
My Lord has granted
   my heart-tears
The supreme victory
Over the darkest ignorance-night.

1276

Only inside the heart of silence
Does God give us
His Nectar-flooded Smile.

1277

My Absolute Lord Supreme,
I love You, I really do,
But the Cosmic Game
That You play with me
Is so confusing.

1278

"My child,
I love you, I really do,
But the earthly game
That you play with Me
Is so uninspiring."

1279

I prayerfully offer my
   Lord Supreme
The streaming tears of my heart.
My Lord Supreme blessingfully
Offers me
The beaming Smiles of His
Heart.

1280

The mind, the vital and the body
Ruthlessly attack
The poor and pure heart,
But they eventually
And deplorably lose.
Why?
Because God always
Takes the side of the heart.

MY CHRISTMAS-NEW YEAR-VACATION-ASPIRATION-PRAYERS

1281

This morning
My Lord Absolute
Compelled me to discard
My long-cherished
   ignorance-mask.

1282

I am the owner
Of sincerity-weakness-tears.
God is the Owner
Of Forgiveness-Divinity-Smiles.
God is commanding me to barter
My tears for His Smiles,
And I immediately obey.

1283

O Heaven, do accept
What I have to offer:
My prayers.
O earth, do accept
What I have to offer:
My service.

1284

Spiritually my soul is fully grown
Precisely because for centuries
My soul has been sowing
God-Smiles and God-Ecstasies
In every heart.

1285

My outer life loves
The success-dance.
My inner life loves
The progress-song.
I love my Lord's
Victory-Banner.

1286

My only desire is to obey
My Lord Absolute Supreme
All the time
With a flower-pure heart.

1287

God tells me that
I do not need His Permission
Before I trust others,
But I do need
His express Permission
Before I distrust others.

1288

In the spiritual life,
To see humanity
Without the heart of beauty
And purity
Is the height of stupidity.

1289

A caring heart
Is a daring glory.

1290

My life and I
Faithfully follow
The tears
Of my ever-climbing heart.

1291

There is a sure way
To make oneself happy,
And that way is to bury the past
In oblivion-cave.

1292

The aspiring heart
Is always an open door
To a new God-hope
And a new God-promise.

1293

Alas, it is not God,
But it is I
Who have forsaken myself.

1294

There are many paths to reach
The God-Summit-Heights.
Each path is absolutely right
In its own way.
But my heart and I have chosen
The path of love, devotion
And surrender.

1295

Our heart-aspirations
And
Our life-dedications
Are very carefully examined
By God Himself
Before He allows us to live
In His Infinity's Heart-Home.

1296

At last,
At the very peak,
I discover what I seek.

1297

O friendship-flower,
O friendship-flower,
Do not wither,
Do not wither.

MY CHRISTMAS-NEW YEAR-VACATION-ASPIRATION-PRAYERS

1298

Come what may,
Come what may,
My heart must pray,
My heart must pray.

1299

No dead end,
No dead end.
Just a bend,
Just a bend.

1300

My Lord gives me
A new lesson
At every hour
So that my heart can be
His Beauty's flower.

1301

God is not an iron rod,
God is not an iron rod.
Let us all go quickly,
Go to the Shelter of God.

1302

Meditation, meditation,
Meditation:
My God-preparation,
My God-preparation.

1303

No prayer, no prayer,
No prayer:
Life is an ignorance-lair.

1304

No meditation, no meditation:
Life is an utter imperfection.

1305

Sound
Is man-cheering.
Silence
Is God-becoming.

1306

Life-river flows.
Patience-tree grows.

1307

Life is a thunder-gong.
Death is a silence-song.

1308

My life-story
Is painful.
My heart-song
Is Godful.

1309

What is peace?
The absence of selfishness.
What is bliss?
The presence of oneness.

1310

Wake up, my mind,
Wake up
To our Lord's
Sweetness-Presence-Smile.

1311

God's nationality
Is a Self-Transcendence-Vision-
 Reality.

1312

God feels me
Only when
My heart kneels.

1313

My bleeding heart-tears
Are my alarm clocks
To put an end
To my ignorance-slumber.

1314

My soul-smiles whisper,
And I arrive at God's Heart-Door
Always on time.

1315

Only a God-obedience-life
Receives from God
His real Reward:
His Heart of Infinity.

1316

My tears and my smiles
Have created my human life.
My God-promises
And my God-fulfilments
Are creating my divine life.

1317

Meditation means
The beginning of
A God-becoming-life.

1318

Meditation-sun shines
Around the clock
Throughout Eternity.

MY CHRISTMAS-NEW YEAR-VACATION-ASPIRATION-PRAYERS

1319

Peace-dreamers
Are
Heart-givers.

1320

God warns us inwardly
Long before darkness comes
    down
Upon our lives.

1321

O my ignorance-mind,
You can cherish your proud
    opinions,
But I shall cherish only
My God-union-heart-hunger.

1322

God never misses an opportunity
To tell the aspiration-hearts
That He is all for them.

1323

My convictions
Are always founded upon
God-Opinions.

1324

God wants only
My gratitude-heart-tears
To introduce me to Him.

1325

If everybody knew
How unconditional at
    every moment
God truly is,
This world would have become
The Garden of Eden.

1326

O seeker,
Do not forget
That curiosity-attacks
Can be extremely dangerous.

1327

My fame
Is fleeting.
My God-surrender-joy
Is everlasting.

1328

Nothing is incurable—
No, not even the wild suspicions
Of the mind.

1329

I must wake up
And join my heart's
Sleepless cries for God.

1330

No matter what others think
   of me
Or say about me,
I shall always take the side
Of my aspiration-heart.

1331

A true God-lover
Is, indeed,
A true God-manifestation-light-
   Hero-warrior.

1332

An aspiration-heart
Is always in search of
A worry-free life.

1333

God has a very special plan
For me.
I must not allow my mind
To indulge in useless
   expectations,
Worries and anxieties.

1334

Every day I must practise
My God-surrender-songs
At least for ten minutes.

1335

As I treasure
My God's Forgiveness-Smiles,
Even so, He treasures
My gratitude-tears.

1336

Some seekers do not pray
   and meditate
Even once a week.
Therefore the sages and the seers
Of the hoary past
Are horrified
At their aspiration-forgetfulness
And aspiration-negligence.

1337

Finally my prayerful life
Is becoming a unique
God-gratitude-heart-beauty-
   fragrance.

MY CHRISTMAS-NEW YEAR-VACATION-ASPIRATION-PRAYERS

1338

May this be my last message
To Your Eye, my Lord:
That I shall obey Your Eye only.

1339

May this be my last message
To Your Heart, my Lord:
That I shall love Your Heart only.

1340

May this be my last message
To Your Feet, my Lord:
That I shall devour
The dust of Your Feet only.

1341

In a very slow measure,
I give to God
What I have.

1342

In a sudden rapture,
God gives to me
What He is.

1343

When God came to him
For the first time,
God saw his heart
Fast asleep.
Therefore, God went back
To His celestial Abode.

1344

When God came to him
For the second time,
His mind rejected God.

1345

When God came to him
For the third time,
His vital ignored God.

1346

When God came to him
For the fourth time,
His life criticised God.

1347

When God came to him
For the fifth time,
He asked God
Why He continued coming.
He asked God if God was a
    beggar
Or a robber.

God said to him,
"My child,
I am neither a beggar
Nor a robber.
I just cannot help seeing you,
For you are My Divinity's
Self-Transcendence-Dream."

1348

It is only when
My heart flies and flies and flies
In Infinity's skies
That God shows me
Where lies the path
Of His Immortality's Smiles.

1349

When I pray,
I can touch God's Feet.
When I meditate,
I can feel God's Heart.

1350

God wants
My self-discipline-life
To mingle
With His proudest Smile.

1351

My mind wants to be
The God-knower.
My heart wishes to be
The God-lover.

1352

My God-dependence-joy
Has no equal.

1353

My mind carries yesterday's
Failure-bondage.
My heart carries tomorrow's
Victory-garland.

1354

The finite power
Challenges.
The infinite Power
Embraces.

MY CHRISTMAS-NEW YEAR-VACATION-ASPIRATION-PRAYERS

1355

Earth is a stranger
To Heaven's ceaseless Smiles.
Heaven is a stranger
To earth's helpless tears.

1356

God's golden Heart
Descends.
Man's broken heart
Ascends.

1357

When my mind
Salutes God,
He immediately plays
His Rhapsody-Flute.

1358

God's Greatness
Puzzles and blinds me.
God's Goodness
Cradles and nestles me.

1359

May a gratitude-flower
Be found
In each heartbeat
Of mine.

1360

Mine is a heart
Of eagerness.
God's is a Breath
Of Closeness.

1361

O my stupid mind,
How long are you going to enjoy
Negativity's torrential rain?

1362

God says to my heart,
"My child, I have a beautiful
    story
To tell you."
My heart says to God,
"Father, I have a soulful song
To sing for You."
"My child, My story
Is all about your previous life
When you were My
    fondness-lamb."
"My Father, my song
Is all about my immediate future
When You will make me
Your inseparable
    oneness-heart-hero."

1363

Mine is a greedy mind
For God's constant
Outer attention.

1364

Mine is a hungry heart
For God's ceaseless
Inner Compassion.

1365

For my life's outer success,
I depend one hundred per cent
On God's Compassion-Eye.

1366

For my life's inner progress,
I depend one hundred per cent
On God's Forgiveness-Feet.

1367

For my life's inner cries
And outer smiles,
I depend one hundred per cent
On God's Satisfaction-Heart.

1368

May my heart's burning
    aspiration
Go a very long way in awakening
The God-sleeping human lives.

1369

The great men
May often badly fail us
In our high expectations
Of their life-conduct.
But the good men
Can never, never fail us
In awakening, inspiring
And aspiring in and through us
For us to reach our destined
Goal.

1370

For the mind,
God-surrender
Is a totally new approach.

1371

O God-seekers and God-lovers,
Let us join
God's Oneness-
    Victory-Drum-March!

MY CHRISTMAS-NEW YEAR-VACATION-ASPIRATION-PRAYERS

1372

Let me be sincere to myself
At least once:
Since I joined the spiritual path,
I have come to know myself
Infinitely better.

1373

My faith in my Master
Shall definitely conquer
All my doubts
In any context.

1374

My Lord's blessingful Requests
Do not believe in tomorrow.
They believe only
In here and now.

1375

My life's
God-fulfilment-willingness-
    dictionary
Does not house the word
"Impossibility".

1376

Three real enemies
We all have:
Hesitation, procrastination
And frustration.

1377

The core of spirituality
Is at once our inner choice
And outer voice.

1378

A true seeker is he
Who is always cheerfully
    committed
To God-satisfaction-dreams.

1379

My prayer is my Lord's
Protection-umbrella.

1380

My meditation is my Lord's
Protection-fort.

1381

My proud mouth loves to preach
All the time.
My soulful hands love to practise
All the time.

1382

The outer voice may speak
Many languages.
The inner voice speaks
Only one language:
The language of the heart.

1383

May my life once again become
A child's
Purity-sweetness-flooded heart.

1384

Mine is a God-bestowed vision,
Far beyond
The misty self-doubt-mountains.

1385

Unconditional surrender
Is a springboard
To Divinity's lofty heights.

1386

My mind does not dare to
   bring me
Torturous doubt-waves
Any more.

1387

God's inner Name
Is Compassion.
His outer Name
Is Concern.

1388

The more I can love the world,
The sooner I shall be able
To forgive the world.

1389

Every morning my
   Lord Supreme
Invites me to be with Him
During His Delight-
   Chariot-Ride.

1390

I must not forget
That each wrong desire
Has a strangling grip.

MY CHRISTMAS-NEW YEAR-VACATION-ASPIRATION-PRAYERS

1391

Each good thought
Has two long-stretched
Sheltering arms of light.

1392

A meditation-life
Is the only escape
From the dire bondage of time.

1393

God's inner Tears
And His outer Smiles
Protect His favourite children
Every day.

1394

My Lord,
Only to You my sleepless life
And my breathless heart
Shall remain open.

1395

My Lord proudly chooses
My unconditional surrender-life.

1396

God tells me
That my purity-heart
Is by far the best shrine.

1397

God tells me
That my smiles have made Him
Extremely, extremely strong.

1398

God comes to me and tells me,
"My child, let us measure
Sincerely and proudly
Each other's heart."

1399

My sincere concern
For the poor world
God deeply appreciates and
    admires.

1400

O my heart,
Once you start repeating
My Lord's Name,
Never, never stop!

1401

Today I am under very strict
   orders
From my Lord Beloved Supreme
To remain happy and cheerful
At every moment.

1402

My life-boat
Has reached the Golden Shore
At my Lord's ambrosial Feet.

1403

Finally
God has some good news for me:
He is telling me
That I shall not fail Him
Any more.

1404

A heart-ride-elevator is needed
To meet with our
   Beloved Supreme
At the topmost floor.

1405

Every morning without fail
I must sing
A God-satisfaction-song.

1406

My prayer-connection
With my Lord Supreme
Is extremely sweet.

1407

My meditation-oneness
With my Lord Supreme
Is permanently delightful.

1408

A sublime meditation
Means an exploration
Of the heart-depth.

1409

If God asks me twice
To do something,
Then I am not
A true God-lover.

1410

Our mind is apt to replay
All our Himalayan blunders.

MY CHRISTMAS-NEW YEAR-VACATION-ASPIRATION-PRAYERS

1411

Our heart is apt to keep
In secrecy supreme
All our God-pleasing deeds.

1412

God is God's highest Hope
For every sincere seeker.

1413

God's loftiest Pride I become
Only when I am in love
With everything about God.

1414

My heart-tears
Embody my soul's
Ecstasy-thrill.

1415

To a purity-mind,
Real meditation
Is as simple as breathing.

1416

I have peace of mind
Only when I see everything
From God's point of view.

1417

God's big Ears
Are extremely fond of
My little prayers.

1418

A simplicity-life embodies
God's abundant Light
And Delight.

1419

Every morning
During my meditation
God visits my heart-home,
And many, many celestial beings
He brings with Him.

1420

My God-gratitude
Is at once
My heart-expansion
And my life-revelation.

1421

The body does not fly any flag.
The vital flies its own flag.
The mind flies its own flag.
The heart flies God's Flag.
The soul does not fly any flag,
For God has chosen the soul
To be His own Flag.

1422

The outer running
Begins on the road
And ends on the road.
The inner running begins
Inside the silence-heart,
And it continues
Along Eternity's Road.

1423

In the outer life,
Time's deadline exists.
In the inner life,
Time has no deadline.

1424

False tears
God sooner or later forgives.
Real tears
God immediately accepts
And forever treasures.

1425

When my body, my vital,
My mind and my heart
Are absolutely pure,
All the galaxies most beautifully
And most powerfully revolve
In my Infinity's Eye.

1426

God the Sound
Feeds
My soaring prayers.

1427

God the Silence
Feeds
My diving meditations.

1428

My outer frame
May not be beautiful,
But the Real in me,
My Lord Supreme,
Is extremely beautiful.

MY CHRISTMAS-NEW YEAR-VACATION-ASPIRATION-PRAYERS

1429

My body may not be strong,
But inside my body
The real power,
The Power Absolute,
Dwells.

1430

Do not look at my eyes
If you need anything from me,
But look at my heart.
You will get everything
From my heart.

1431

My Lord,
I sleeplessly long to be
Your breathless slave.

1432

It is high time for me
To come out of my mind's
Darkness-confusion-
    hesitation-cave.

1433

God powerfully clasps
My heart of gratitude
To His own Heart of Pride.

1434

Every day we please
Our ego-lord.
Alas, how rarely we please
The Pilot of our own life-boat.

1435

May my heart's hope-sun
Never set.

1436

No God-loving heart
Can ever be short
Of oneness-supplies.

1437

My heart loves God
In His infinite
And ever-changing moods.

1438

I must immensely enjoy
My heart's millions of pluses
And vehemently reject
My life's hundreds of minuses.

1439

My Lord's Compassion-Smiles
And my heart's aspiration-tears
Eagerly, lovingly and
    self-givingly
Work together.

1440

Every day my heart and I
Desperately long for a glimpse
Of our Lord's Feet.

1441

O my mind,
Now that you are extremely pure,
I am so proud of you!
Please do not allow yourself to
    be fouled
By stark ignorance any more.

1442

A self-giving life
Always basks in the sunshine
Of God's Paradise-Presence.

1443

When I go far beyond the domain
Of my earth-bound mind,
God immediately stops the clock.

1444

At times God may close
His Ear to me,
But He never closes
His Eye to me.

1445

I shall never allow
The beauty of my
    aspiration-heart
To fade.

1446

No anxiety, no worry
Can ever perturb
A God-surrender-life.

1447

My sleepless God-devotion-heart
Does not allow doubt-fog
To cloud my horizons.

1448

This morning my Lord Supreme
Came to me and said,
"My child, I am now making you
A permanent member
Of My Universal Heart-Society."

MY CHRISTMAS-NEW YEAR-VACATION-ASPIRATION-PRAYERS

1449

My outer race-victory-smile
Makes God
Enormously happy.

1450

My inner race-victory-smile
Makes God
Boundlessly proud of me.

1451

O my God-pleasing readiness,
Willingness and eagerness-life,
Wake up, wake up!
Sleep no more!

1452

The misuse of God's Compassion
Extinguishes our heart's
Heaven-climbing flames.

1453

God does not mind
When I tell Him
Whatever is on my mind.
He does not mind
Even when I ruthlessly
Speak ill of Him.
But He does mind
When I think ill of myself.

1454

Each self-giving act
Expedites our inner journey
To God's Heart-Home.

1455

In the spiritual life,
There is only one
Unpardonable blunder:
Ingratitude.

1456

My heart's gratitude-sweetness
God incessantly
And breathlessly drinks.

1457

My Lord Beloved Supreme,
When will You be compassionate,
Close and intimate to me again?
"My child, right now!
This is the right time—
This very moment."

1458

Alas, my heart's purity-moon
Does not recognise me and
    my life
Any more.

1459

Only in my silence-heart
My soul-bird sings.

1460

The Hour of God has struck.
Humanity once more
Is going to open its heart-garden.

1461

Affection ascends.
Attachment descends.

1462

My mind multiplies everything
Incorrectly.
My heart unifies everything
Perfectly.

1463

Each aspiration-cry
Is
A God-discovery-attempt.

1464

Each meditation-depth-attempt
Is rich
With God-realisation-promise.

1465

The mind has endless questions.
The heart has only one question:
"Am I really pleasing my
　　Lord Supreme
In His own Way?"

1466

God's Compassion-Eye
And His Forgiveness-Heart
Are showing my life-boat
The Golden Shore.

1467

I pray to God
To give me the capacity
To live in the soulfulness of my
　　heart
And in the Fulness of His Will.

1468

To make the fastest progress
In my spiritual life,
I need a mind watchful,
A heart soulful
And a breath Godful.

MY CHRISTMAS-NEW YEAR-VACATION-ASPIRATION-PRAYERS

1469

Every day
I must devotedly nourish
My God-willingness-life-plant.

1470

The perfection of a seeker's life
Is a gradual hill
And a throbbing thrill.

1471

My life's story
Shall eventually end
In my Lord's loftiest Glory.

1472

My Lord Supreme tells me
That every day
He requires only four persons:
The dreamer in me,
The seeker in me,
The lover in me and
The server in me.

1473

We can overfeed ourselves easily,
But we can never overfeed
Our Lord Supreme
With our love, devotion and
   surrender.

1474

My only task
Is to accelerate the hour
Of my ego's demise.

1475

The transcendental Love
Blooms.
Lo and behold,
The universal Peace
Blossoms.

1476

Everything that I receive
During my deepest meditation
Is handmade by Heaven.

1477

Determination-volcano
I have.
Patience-sea
I need.

1478

My Lord Supreme,
Your Forgiveness-Heart
Has given my life
Not only a new beginning,
But also a real meaning.

1479

An unimaginable silence-thrill
We can enjoy
Only when our mind
Is absolutely still.

1480

At every moment
My Beloved Supreme is
    devouring
My happiness-eye-smiles
And my sadness-heart-tears.

1481

My God-surrender-delight
Is the polestar
Of my life.

1482

Fastest I am able
To sail my life-boat
Precisely because
My God-gratitude-heart
Is full of silver tears.

1483

The heart
Of every real God-seeker
Is God-obedience.

1484

My heart and I
Bow and bow and bow
To everything
That my Lord blessingfully says
And compassionately does.

1485

A true seeker
Spends all his time
On God's Needs
And does not spend even a
    second
On his own needs.

1486

Perfect perfection
Is not a mental hallucination.
Perfect perfection
Is a distant tomorrow's realisation
In every aspect of life.

1487

My God-surrender-life
Is the only proper way
For me to aspire.

MY CHRISTMAS-NEW YEAR-VACATION-ASPIRATION-PRAYERS

1488

Nobody
Can ever complete
The inner education.

1489

We all must develop
An intense and immense
Attraction to God.

1490

Each seeker
Is an unhorizoned dream
Of God's Vision-Eye.

1491

A lion-heart is indispensable
To win
Life's battle-victory.

1492

Sleepless and breathless tears
Show us the shortest way
To the highest Heaven of delight.

1493

The desire-bound human beings
Suffer from chronic
Doubt-afflictions.

1494

Every day
I make a bold attempt
To extinguish my life's
Desire-fire.

1495

My utter desire-failure
Was the very beginning
Of my aspiration-success.

1496

My soul's inner poise
I apply
In every disturbing situation.

1497

May my heart remain
Always hungry
For oneness-happiness.

1498

God's Silence-Eye
Is
The world-awakening bell.

1499

God never demands
More than I can give Him
Cheerfully.

1500

Our response to God's
Compassion-Eye-Invitation
Has to be compulsory
And not voluntary.

1501

I must climb up
The mountain-summit
Of God-worship.

1502

Our negativity-mind
Has to be crushed
At every moment.

1503

Every morning my heart feels
That my soul and my
     Lord Supreme
Are having most serious
And most intimate conversations.

1504

The greatest joy and the
     highest pride
I get
Only when I see my heart-tears
Are self-givingly mingling
With the golden dust of my
     Lord's Feet.

1505

Even a moment
Of our unconditional surrender
To God's Will
Brings us very close to God.

1506

Today I have utterly destroyed
My mind's
     God-disobedience-tree—
Root and branch.

MY CHRISTMAS-NEW YEAR-VACATION-ASPIRATION-PRAYERS

1507

Let my life's only motto be
Aspiration—
Sleepless aspiration
And breathless aspiration.

1508

May my Lord's absolute Victory
In my life
Be imminent.

1509

Every morning I receive
Most beautiful Smiles
From God's Transcendental Eye.

1510

Every evening I receive
Most powerful Blessings
From God's Universal Heart.

1511

God Himself
Proudly beats
My surrender-victory-drum.

1512

God's Vision-Eye
Is the home
Of all my sweet dreams.

1513

God's Compassion-Affection-
    Love-Embrace
Is for all,
Born and yet unborn.

1514

My life-road is absolutely clear
Only when I faithfully listen
To the dictates of my
    aspiration-heart.

1515

The mind does not believe
In God-gratitude,
But the heart does—
It always does.

1516

When my heart-bird sings,
God immediately stops
Whatever He is doing.

1517

God tells me
That my God-devotion-magnet
Is not only most powerful,
But also most beautiful.

1518

The ego does not want to die,
No matter what happens.
The soul does not want to give up
Its God-manifestation-promise,
No matter what happens.

1519

When my heart-tears
Send an invitation
To my mind,
Even my mind does not dare
To ignore.

1520

May every day
My earth-existence
Feel a very close connection
With God's Heart-Home.

1521

My aspiration-heart
Responds only
To tomorrow's rainbow-dawn.

1522

God's Name-repetition
Embodies all my prayers
And all my meditations.

1523

My heart-tears
Come from my soul's
Beginningless journey.

1524

My life-smiles
Come from my soul's
Endless journey.

1525

From time immemorial,
This world of ours
Has been in bondage-night.
Alas, we have no idea
When it will be able to celebrate
Its independence-delight.

MY CHRISTMAS-NEW YEAR-VACATION-ASPIRATION-PRAYERS

1526

No God-dream
Can ever be empty.

1527

The love of the heart
Blooms.
The oneness of the soul
Blossoms.

1528

In the morning
My Beloved Supreme
Is lovable and adorable.
In the evening
My Absolute Supreme
Is incomparable and
   approachable.

1529

My Lord Beloved Supreme,
Please, please stop
Your separation-game!
Can You not see
That my eyes are crying
And my heart is bleeding for
You?

1530

May my God-service-joy
Forever remain
Unparalleled.

1531

The divine in us
Loves God-dictation.
The human in us
Loves man-quotation.

1532

The Compassion-Eye
Of my Lord Beloved Supreme
Every morning clears the road
For my life's progress-chariot.

1533

Just yesterday
I was helpless and hopeless.
But today my Lord,
Out of His infinite Bounty,
Has made my heart useful
And my life fruitful.

1534

God is asking me
To make my pure devotion-dream
A sure manifestation-reality.

1535

When I am without God,
My mind and I collect
    destruction-facts.
When I am with God,
My heart and I act and act
    and act
Lovingly, devotedly,
Self-givingly and breathlessly
For a new creation,
Empty of darkness.

1536

A sweet surrender-life-joy
Discovers Eternity's Light
And Infinity's Delight.

1537

The beauty of love,
The fragrance of devotion
And the sweetness of surrender
Are unimaginably exquisite.

1538

My wild
God-unwillingness-disobedience-
    extinction-hour
Is fast approaching.

1539

God desires my life to be
His Lotus-Heart-Home.

1540

There are countless things
    on earth
For us to feed,
But alas, why do we feed
Our desire-hunger-fire
That burns our God-aspiration,
God-dedication
And God-manifestation-life?

1541

I must not make
My Lord's Golden Boat heavier
With my expectation-frustration-
    heavy weights.

1542

At long last
My age-old ignorance-prison
Is in flames.

1543

The Master teaches his disciples
How to hear
God's Silence-Footsteps.

MY CHRISTMAS-NEW YEAR-VACATION-ASPIRATION-PRAYERS

1544

By virtue of my prayers,
I increase immensely
My life-beauty.

1545

On the strength of my
    meditations,
I increase measurelessly
My heart-fragrance.

1546

The morning-devotion-breath
Of my heart
Awakens me and carries me
To the Heart-Home
Of my Lord Supreme.

1547

I must not do anything
Without having permission first
From my God-oneness-heart.

1548

My third eye sees everything.
My third eye knows everything.
My third eye becomes
    everything.
My third eye is everything.

1549

Every day
I must bask in the sunshine
Of my God-gratitude-heart.

1550

My eyes are wide open,
But alas,
My heart is fast asleep.

1551

The beauty of my tears
Is in my God-adoration.

1552

The fragrance of my smiles
Is in my God-surrender.

1553

My Lord Beloved Supreme
Will not allow me to know
What failure truly is.

1554

My mind doubts
My extraordinary capacities,
Yet I love my mind.
My wild vital kicks me day
    and night,
Yet I love my wild vital.
My body does not obey me,
Yet I love my body.
My Lord Supreme loves me,
Cares for me and protects me,
Yet I do not love my
    Lord Supreme.

1555

God is at once
The sweetest Dream
Of my heart
And the farthest Reality
Of my eyes.

1556

We can succeed
In transforming the world
Only with our love-smiles
And sympathy-tears.

1557

I ply my life-boat
Between
Earth's solemn duty-shore
And
Heaven's ambrosial
    Beauty-Shore.

1558

Heaven's Nectar-Smiles
Bring us down.
Earth's heart-tears
Return us.

1559

My life-blood
Secretly embodies
All my prayers.

1560

My heart-breath
Silently embodies
All my meditations.

1561

In the inner world
I am a joy-living heart.

MY CHRISTMAS-NEW YEAR-VACATION-ASPIRATION-PRAYERS

1562

In the outer world
I am a joy-giving life.

1563

My life begs and begs
My soul
To keep its eyes closed.

1564

My soul begs and begs
My life
To keep its heart open.

1565

Long ago
I far transcended
All my expectation-barriers.

1566

Peace on our lips
We all have.
Peace in our hearts
We all sadly need.

1567

No limit
To what my love, devotion
And surrender can do,
Not only for me,
But also for the entire world.

1568

Keep singing, keep singing!
God will soon be arriving.

1569

If I continue calling,
My life will blossom
And my Lord Supreme
Will smile, sing and dance.

1570

The exquisite bliss
Of my God-surrender-life
Nobody on earth
Can hamper.

1571

My Master's tears and smiles
Are the only members
Of my heart-family.

1572

The desiring mind
Is apt to brood.
The aspiring heart
Is apt to bleed.

1573

God's Compassion-Eye
　intervenes
Between
Man's Himalayan blunders
And his well-deserved
　punishment.

1574

God's Compassion-Confidence
　in me
Is my only
Competence-victory.

1575

My Lord,
Your ceaseless Tears I see
Not only in my heart,
But also in every heart.
My Lord,
Your Nectar-Smiles I see
Nowhere, nowhere, nowhere.

1576

I give my Lord Supreme
Unimaginable joy and pride
When I am able
To steal His Compassion-Eye
And His Forgiveness-Heart.

1577

To protect me
From the undivine forces,
My Beloved Supreme
Has kept His Eye and His Heart
As my sentinels at my heart-gate.

1578

Every moment is a golden
　opportunity
For me to love and serve
The tears and the smiles of
　the world.

1579

I must disregard and discard
What my mind thinks of me
And says about me.

MY CHRISTMAS-NEW YEAR-VACATION-ASPIRATION-PRAYERS

1580

I do not go to the sky-moon—
I go to my heart-moon
For it to inspire me
And inundate me
With Infinity's Peace and Bliss.

1581

I have many desires,
But my Lord has only one:
My constant happiness.

1582

Day and night
My soul is helping me
To discount all my worries
And anxieties.

1583

God loves
My very, very short-distance
   prayers
And not
My ultramarathon-distance
   prayers.

1584

God's unseen Hand
Most lovingly
And most compassionately
Takes my hands
To show me the way
To the Golden Shore.

1585

My greatness depends on
The acceptance of the world.
My goodness depends on
The Love and Concern
Of my Beloved Supreme.

1586

Every morning and every evening
My complete God-surrender-life
Is cradled
By the beauty and the fragrance
Of Heaven.

1587

I must keep my heart's love
And my life's gratitude
Always together.

1588

Love shows the road.
Devotion walks on the road.
Surrender takes love and
　　devotion
To the Destination.

1589

I write my Lord's biography
With my shallower than the
　　shallowest
Book-knowledge.

1590

My Lord writes my biography
With His ever-increasing
　　Heart-Tears
And
With His ever-increasing
　　Soul-Smiles.

1591

I must become a perfect stranger
To ignorance-sleep
So that I can grow into
A God-lover
Of the highest magnitude.

1592

The human in me
Has only one task to perform:
Awake!

1593

The divine in me
Has three tasks to perform:
Bravely march forward,
Sleeplessly climb upward,
Breathlessly dive inward.

1594

Silence is God's
Secret and sacred
Man-Enlightenment-Whisper.

1595

Humanity's life
Is nothing but
A fragile faith in God.

1596

My outer suffering
Is
My inner courage-builder.

MY CHRISTMAS-NEW YEAR-VACATION-ASPIRATION-PRAYERS

1597

My inner suffering
Is
My outer eye-opener.

1598

Patience
Is the most sublime progress
In disguise.

1599

The real Master is chosen
By the real seeker in us,
And not by the mind — never!

1600

God has repeatedly told me
That He is interested
Only in what I am doing,
And not what I am saying.

1601

There was a time
When I had a volley of questions,
But now I have only one
    question:
Do I have a real God-hunger?

1602

When I pray,
I pray with my upward eyes
To see my Lord's Eye.

1603

When I meditate,
I meditate with my inward heart
To sit at my Lord's Feet.

1604

During my deepest meditation,
I hear my Lord Beloved Supreme
Secretly whispering:
"My child, you were born to be
My Eternity's Greatness,
My Infinity's Goodness
And My Immortality's Fulness.
My child, this message
Is not only for you,
But it is for each and every
Creation of Mine."

1605

God's Compassion-Eye-
    Inspiration
Is
My Godward journey's start.

1606

God's Tears
Wake my heart.
God's Smiles
Shake my life.

1607

My aspiration
Means the beginning
Of my God-oneness-cry and
    smile.

1608

My Lord Supreme,
Will You be able to believe me
When I say that I love You
Infinitely more than I love
    myself?

1609

To love others
Before we love ourselves
Is, indeed,
A very rare achievement.

1610

God knows and sees
That my heart is very rich
In world-concern.
Therefore He has made me
A supremely chosen instrument
Of His Heart.

1611

My creativity-beauty
Comes from my Lord's
Activity-Fountain.

1612

The beauty and profundity
Of my heart-tears
Only my Master deeply values.

1613

When I try to keep a secret
From God,
He terribly suffers
From my utter stupidity.

1614

I must admit,
In all sincerity,
That God has smiled at me
Infinitely more times
Than I have cried for Him.

MY CHRISTMAS-NEW YEAR-VACATION-ASPIRATION-PRAYERS

1615

Every day
My soul's fragrance-delight
Is intensifying
My heart's aspiration-cry.

1616

My desire-life,
It is getting late!
Go to sleep, go to sleep!

1617

My aspiration-heart,
It is getting late!
Wake up, wake up!

1618

The hesitation-mind
And the insecurity-life
Love to live together.

1619

I must shun two things —
Self-doubt and
    world-indifference—
To make the fastest progress
In my spiritual life.

1620

Since we human beings have
    created
The darkest night of the world,
It is our bounden duty to
    illumine
The darkest night of the world.

1621

God's Mind-Philosophy
Is Forgiveness.
God's Heart-Song
Is Forgiveness.
God's Life-Story
Is Forgiveness.

1622

Only my heart-microscope
Can measure the distance
Between my life-tears
And my death-smiles.

1623

Each day
Is a Power-Sun-
    Revelation-Manifestation
Of God.
Each night
Is a Compassion-Moon-
    Revelation-Manifestation
Of God.

1624

Compassion
Is the success-secret
Of the higher world.

1625

Love
Is the success-secret
Of the inner world.

1626

Smile
Is the success-secret
Of the outer world.

1627

Surrender is the fastest highway
That leads us
To the Transcendental Heights.

1628

Wherever we go,
We must carry with us
Our heart's aspiration-flames.

1629

Only my God-gratitude-heart-
    tears
Enable me to fly
In the sky of Infinity.

1630

God gets tremendous Joy
And Satisfaction
When He is able to sail His
    Dream-Boat
In my life's devotion-river.

1631

The mind does nothing
For God,
Yet it expects Love from God
All the time.

1632

This world of ours will be perfect
Only when our God-service-life
Is constantly on the march.

1633

God is extremely happy to see
That His Immensity
And my intensity
Are sleeplessly growing together.

MY CHRISTMAS-NEW YEAR-VACATION-ASPIRATION-PRAYERS

1634

Spirituality
Is a breathless
Self-transcendence-adventure.

1635

My world-improvement-
    service-joy
Is more precious to God
Than anything else.

1636

My meditation-time
Is my Lord's
Only resting-hour.

1637

My Lord and I deeply enjoy
Our mutual appreciation:
My Lord tells me
That my heart-tears
Are inimitable.
I tell my Lord
His Eye-Smiles
Are inimitable.

1638

I must and I must discover,
As soon as possible,
The key to my Lord's Heart-
    Home.

1639

Nothing human in me
Exists any more.
I have become today
A supremely choice instrument
Of my Lord Supreme.

1640

God's Heart
Is in each moment.
God's Eye
Is in each movement.

1641

No more my aspiration-heart
Shall suffer
From God-separation-pangs.

1642

May every morning
My aspiration-heart-garden
Produce a most beautiful
God-gratitude-rose.

1643

The disobedience of the mind
Is a very, very old story.
The obedience of the heart
Is a most soulful song
That has neither beginning
Nor end.

1644

My Beloved Supreme,
Out of His infinite Bounty,
Tells me that my entire life
Is a most powerful song-bridge
Between humanity's tears
And Divinity's Smiles.

1645

Today my heart
Is a meditation-plant.
Tomorrow my life
Shall become a
 Heaven-climbing tree.

1646

The only way to free oneself
From the mind's prison
Is to forgive others.

1647

Hesitation, doubt and fear
Leave me
Only when I stay
On the God-navigated course.

1648

Like my Lord Beloved Supreme,
I also must take
A full-time service:
Loving unreservedly
And unconditionally
Each and every human being.

1649

My meditation-depth
Is my Lord's
Ecstasy-Height-Pride.

1650

My Lord's
Compassion-Concern-
 Heart-Door
Never has any lock.

1651

Our mind-maladies
Can be cured
Only by repeating constantly
God's sacred Name.

MY CHRISTMAS-NEW YEAR-VACATION-ASPIRATION-PRAYERS

1652

Morning devotion-singers
Give tremendous joy
To their Lord Supreme.

1653

Music of the heart-tears
And heart-smiles
Is bound to thrill
All sincere seekers of the world.

1654

Every morning
I pray to my Lord Supreme
To bless me
With a rainbow-heart-
 beauty-smile.

1655

Just yesterday
My Lord Beloved Supreme
 scolded me
Most powerfully.
He said, "My child,
You must take
 My express Permission
Before you do something
Or say something important."

1656

When I give God
More than I promised,
He gives me
Seven transcendental Smiles.

1657

Dreams come true
Only if we dearly love them
And proudly treasure them.

1658

Humanity is not interested
In the light.
It is interested only
In the power-supremacy.

1659

My acceptance of spirituality
Is neither my obligation
Nor my responsibility,
But a golden opportunity
To love God and be loved by
 God.

1660

Life has no dead end.
Life carries the promise
Of endless progress-delight.

1661

When my mind is happy,
Everything is pure.
When my heart is happy,
Everything is perfect
And everybody is perfect.
When I am happy,
My Lord Supreme
Immediately embraces me.

1662

My Lord, may I offer You
A true story?
"No!"
My Lord, may I offer You
A beautiful poem?
"No!"
My Lord, may I offer You
A soulful song?
"No!"
My Lord, may I offer You
My gratitude-heart-tears?
"Yes, yes, yes!
My child, start offering."

1663

The songs of my voice
Are pure and sweet.
The songs of my heart
Can touch God's Feet.

1664

The self-mastery-education
Nobody can ever complete.

1665

To pay even the slightest
    attention
To my insecurity-life
Is the height of my stupidity.

1666

I always approach
My Lord Beloved Supreme
On my bended knees
And not just with my
    folded hands.

1667

Every morning
I place my sincerity-heart-tears
And my sincerity-heart-smiles
At the Feet of my Lord Supreme
Before I enter into my
    meditation.

1668

My Lord Beloved Supreme
Himself
Uses
My God-devotion-heart-magnet.

MY CHRISTMAS-NEW YEAR-VACATION-ASPIRATION-PRAYERS

1669

My constant God-dependence
Is the safest and surest
God-discovery-road.

1670

My God-aspiration-questions
And answers of the past
Are of no avail.
My God-aspiration-questions
And answers of the future
Are simply ridiculous.
My God-aspiration-questions
And answers of my present life
Are of supreme importance.

1671

My Lord,
My only prayer to You
Is this:
Do continue to remain
Fully in charge of my life.

1672

Every morning
I become
My heart's God-worshipping joy.

1673

Each happy thought
And each happy feeling
Gives me the strength
Of a roaring lion.

1674

Delight
Is bound to permeate
A God-surrender-heart.

1675

Spirituality alone succeeds
In giving the God-seekers
A God-oneness-home.

1676

Be brave, divinely brave,
Supremely brave!
Do not surrender
To despair.

1677

Kneeling prayers
Receive immediately
Illumining Smiles
From God's Eye.

1678

Every morning
I memorise four soul-stirring
And heart-elevating Messages
From my Lord Supreme.

1679

God wants my life to be
The beauty of my heart
And
The fragrance of my soul.

1680

My only need
Is what my Lord
Blessingfully gives me.

1681

Each new moment
Is a new bloom
Of my aspiration-heart.

1682

My Lord tells me
That my God-gratitude-heart
Is my promise-fulfilled life.

1683

God tells me
That the surrender of my mind
Is His prized possession.

1684

My desire abruptly closes
My heart-door.
My aspiration slowly, steadily
And unerringly opens
My heart-door
And keeps it open.

1685

The Golden Age has decided
Not to sleep any more.
It is about to wake up
To illumine the world
Once again.

1686

Falsehood
Is sensation.
Truth
Is compassion.

MY CHRISTMAS-NEW YEAR-VACATION-ASPIRATION-PRAYERS

1687

Falsehood
Is fearless.
Truth
Is deathless.

1688

Falsehood
Ultimately fails.
Truth
Sleeplessly sails.

1689

Falsehood
Attracts.
Truth
Rejects.

1690

My Lord Supreme Himself
Proudly hoists
My obedience-flag.

1691

No streaming heart-tears,
No express God-Arrival.

1692

God's Compassion-Eye
Visits
My sleeping body.

1693

God's Pride-Head
Visits
My serving life.

1694

God's Delight-Heart
Visits
My surrendering breath.

1695

My God-thoughts dream and
    dream
Inside the silence
Of my sweet and deep sleep.

1696

My God-actions
Are invited by God Himself
To fly and fly
In His Infinity's Sky.

1697

God is not displeased
With my feeble weakness-body.

1698

God is extremely displeased
With my strong, bold and wild
Disobedience-vital.

1699

God is at once
A Compassion-Teacher
And an Illumination-Student.

1700

The beauty of a devotion-heart
And the fragrance of a
  surrender-breath
Are the supremely choice
  Blessings
From the Unknowable.

1701

Alas,
There is not a single day
That our doubting minds
Do not torture us
And our Lord Beloved Supreme.

1702

I love my soul-commands—
I really do!

1703

I love my heart-whispers—
I really do!

1704

I am not a singer,
But the angels come and sing
  for me.
Why?
Because they have been asked
By my Lord Beloved Supreme.

1705

I am not a seeker,
But the cosmic gods come and
  bless me.
Why?
Because they have been asked
By my Lord Beloved Supreme.

1706

My Lord's Feet
Beckon
My prayer-tears.

MY CHRISTMAS-NEW YEAR-VACATION-ASPIRATION-PRAYERS

1707

My Lord's Heart
Beckons
My meditation-silence.

1708

We must not anticipate.
At God's choice Hour,
God will definitely
Do the needful.

1709

Those who pray
For a world-oneness-heart
Are the harbingers
Of tomorrow's golden dawn.

1710

My hope-heart-bloom
Takes me to God.

1711

My promise-soul-blossom
Brings God to me.

1712

All that lives
Is my heart's beauty.
All that dies
Is my mind's ugliness.

1713

One forgiveness-prayer-tear
Can stand against
Ten serious blunders.

1714

We can not only practise
    meditation,
But also can become
The Inner Pilot of meditation.

1715

My thought can be displeased
With God,
But my feeling cannot.

1716

When I talk to God,
Man becomes jealous.
When I talk to man,
I receive a very powerful
    Embrace
From my Lord Supreme.

1717

Life is a golden opportunity.
The sooner we realise it,
The better.

1718

My self-transcendence is blessed
By Eternity's Silence,
Infinity's Sound
And Immortality's Delight.

1719

My God-revelation
Is the beauty of my realisation.
My God-manifestation
Is the fragrance of my realisation.

1720

The tears of my heart
And the smiles of my soul
Are the Footsteps
Of my Lord Beloved Supreme.

1721

My hope-heart
Starts.
My promise-breath
Completes.

1722

My mind
Never wants to change.
It is I who have to force
My mind to change.

1723

Heaven is not infinite miles
Above my head.
Heaven is right here,
Deep inside my
    God-gratitude-heart.

1724

God's Desire and my desire
Have the same goal:
Love.

1725

How can my limited mind
Ever experience
The beauty and majesty
Of my Absolute Lord Supreme?

1726

Nothingness and Infinity
Are the two shores
Of God's Life Universal.

MY CHRISTMAS-NEW YEAR-VACATION-ASPIRATION-PRAYERS

1727

To my greatest surprise,
I seek freedom
And yet I love captivity.

1728

Alas, we all are in love
With a real stranger-thief:
Ignorance.

1729

In vain
Death, the finite,
Tries to hide
Life, the Infinite.

1730

The acceptance of Light
And the rejection of darkness
Must be done
With utmost sincerity,
Willingness and eagerness.

1731

My heart is no more mine.
My heart is all Yours,
My Lord Beloved Supreme.
"My Heart is also no more Mine,
My sweetest child.
It is all yours,
Yours it was,
And yours it will forever be."

1732

My Lord,
My prayers
Do not touch Your Heart.
My meditations
Do not touch Your Heart.
My cries
Do not touch Your Heart.
My tears
Do not touch Your Heart.
What else can I do, my Lord?

"My sweet child,
Patience, patience!
Wait for My choice Hour."

1733

Never give up hope!
Hope ultimately succeeds.

1734

The unlit man
Is his mind.
The illumined man
Is his heart.
The perfect man
Is his soul.

1735

Fight against mankind—
You are a fool.
Fight against yourself—
You are a saint.

1736

My life belongs
To my faith.
My faith belongs
To God.

1737

Each pure thought
Is a strong bridge
To cross
To God's Heart-Home.

1738

I wish to be
A God-loving heart
And not
A world-interesting man.

1739

Forget the past.
Guide and lead the present.
Tomorrow's golden dawn
Will bless you and embrace you.

1740

Oneness from Above
Is sure illumination.
Oneness from below
Is sweet devotion.

1741

Only the aspiring heart
Has the capacity to bury itself
In the ambrosial Lap
Of its Beloved Supreme.

1742

Only the unconditional
God-surrender-seekers
Receive very special lessons
From their Beloved Supreme.

MY CHRISTMAS-NEW YEAR-VACATION-ASPIRATION-PRAYERS

1743

The unaspiring mind-land
Is a dangerous place.

1744

My life's greatness
Has badly failed to please God.
My heart's goodness
Has sadly failed to please God.
My sleepless gratitude-heart-tears
And my breathless
    surrender-life-smiles
Have unreservedly pleased God.

1745

My prayer-life began
With begging.
My prayer-life now is singing
Only God's Glories.
My prayer-life shall end
With surrendering my all
To the Will of my
    Beloved Supreme.

1746

God is a strange matter
With the arid intellectuals.
My Lord, do give me
A simplicity-life and
    a purity-heart
To sing always
Your Victory-Songs.

1747

Self-lovers and self-servers
Are to be found all-where.
God-lovers and God-servers
Are extremely rare achievements.

1748

Nobody can ever dare
To take away from me
My God-Touch-Thrill.

1749

Morning begins.
I begin to pray.
God begins to give.
In silence supreme
He gives me His All.

1750

When my mind thinks of God,
God lightens
My life-burdens.

1751

When my heart prays to God,
God removes
All my life-burdens.

1752

When I meditate on God,
God says to me,
"My child,
All your burdens
Are self-imposed."

1753

My sweet Lord,
May the sound of Your Footfall
Frighten my doubting mind.
May the sound of Your Footfall
Awaken my sleeping heart.
May the sound of Your Footfall
Enlighten my serving life.

1754

My Beloved Lord,
Today I have nothing to spare.
"My child,
Come, come closer to Me!
Empty your heart.
I have everything
To share with you."

1755

In the morning I sing
With the blissfully
    ascending waves
Of my heart-sea.

1756

In the evening I sing
With the peacefully
    descending waves
Of my heart-sea.

1757

My Lord Beloved Supreme,
Today You have made me
Immeasurably happy
By allowing my heartbeat
To mingle, sing and dance
With the golden dust
Of Your golden Feet.

1758

I know, I know,
My heart-tears for God
Will never be lost
In the dust of the earth.

1759

O my mind-doubts,
I shall not cherish you any more!
You must leave me alone.

1760

O my heart-fears,
I shall not shelter you any more!
You must leave me alone.

MY CHRISTMAS-NEW YEAR-VACATION-ASPIRATION-PRAYERS

1761

O my life-weaknesses,
I shall not carry you any more!
You must leave me alone.

1762

Once more
I have won back my
   heart-kingdom
From the hostile forces.
From now on
My heart-kingdom and I
Shall forever remain together.

1763

My Lord,
Your Flute has stolen
The tears of my heart.

1764

"My child,
Your songs have stolen
The Smiles of My Eye."

1765

God's choice Hour
Has struck.
His Hunger-Heart
Has devoured my devotion-life.

1766

This morning
My Lord said to me,
"My child, if you once more weep
At your unworthiness,
Never shall I visit you!
As I claim you
To be My All,
Even so, you must claim Me
To be your All."

1767

My Lord,
Please tell me
When Your Hour will strike
For You to place Your Feet
Inside my crying and
   bleeding heart.

1768

Ignorance-sleep
Attacks us
With no warning.

1769

Like my heart,
I must make my mind,
My vital and my body
Always available
To my Beloved Supreme.

1770

My Lord,
This time when You enter
Into my heart,
Please bring with You
Your Enthusiasm
And Dynamism infinite.

1771

Each God-lover
Is a direct instrument of God
For God's full manifestation
Here on earth.

1772

My Lord Supreme has graced me
With His divine Presence,
But alas, I am not ready
To race against ignorance-night
And win the supreme Victory
For my Lord Supreme.

1773

My Lord never disappoints me.
It is my expectation-cleverness
That disappoints me.

1774

True,
I cannot sprint,
I cannot run,
I cannot march,
I cannot walk,
But I can easily crawl
Towards my
    Lord Beloved Supreme.

1775

God's long Stories
Awaken me.
God's beautiful Poems
Charm me.
God's soulful Songs
Thrill me.
God's Tears and Smiles
Perfect me and fulfil me.

1776

When I go to God
As a beggar,
He immediately closes
His Eyes and Ears.

1777

When I go to God
As His own child,
He immediately stands up,
Blesses me and embraces me.

MY CHRISTMAS-NEW YEAR-VACATION-ASPIRATION-PRAYERS

1778

Wisdom-light
Is giving and giving.
Ignorance-night
Is self-styled and
    self-multiplying.

1779

God does not appreciate
My shyness.
He appreciates
My openness.

1780

Earth needs
God's Descent.
Heaven needs
God's Consent.

1781

My immediate
And eternal need
Is God-fulfilment
In God's own Way.

1782

Every second,
Many, many, many God-seekers
Are pleasing God in His own
    Way.
How I wish I could be
One of those fortunate ones!

1783

God-worshippers
And
God-lovers
On any path
Are my only
Divine brothers and sisters.

1784

Like my soul,
How I wish I could spend
All my time
Only with my
    Lord Beloved Supreme!

1785

To realise God, reveal God
And manifest God here on earth
Is the birthright
Of a selfless God-lover.

1786

The day my Lord
Cannot come to see me,
He sends His Heart to me.

1787

The day my Lord's Heart
Cannot come to see me,
He sends His Eye to me.

1788

The day my Lord's Eye
Cannot come to see me,
He sends His Ear to me
To receive messages
From my soul, heart,
Mind, vital and body.
In this way, every day
My Lord keeps
A very, very special connection
With me.

1789

Every morning
My Lord's Heart
Says something very nice
To His Eye
About me.

1790

God-believers are, indeed,
God's happiness-harbingers
To mankind.

1791

Disappointment,
I do not know you
And I do not want to know!

1792

When we run
On the aspiration-track,
God says to us,
"My children, no slow speed
Is allowed!"

1793

No impurity-bite
When we pray.
No mind-intrusion
When we meditate.

1794

God tells His seeker-children
That without the climbing
Aspiration-flames
From their hearts,
They will never be able
To satisfy Him in His own Way.

MY CHRISTMAS-NEW YEAR-VACATION-ASPIRATION-PRAYERS

1795

When I am able to offer
Even an iota of satisfaction
To my Lord Beloved Supreme,
My heart immediately gets
Throbbing joy.

1796

Forgiveness
Is the only real happiness
That lasts.

1797

To become a happiness-fountain,
I must forgive those
Who ruthlessly hurt me
Every day.

1798

My Lord,
Today I am praying to You
To think of me
And work in and through me
To the fullest.

1799

My Lord,
You have taught me
Many, many, many things
Right from my very birth.
Only two more things
Please teach me:
How to have tears in my heart
When I pray to You
And how to have poise in
    my heart
When I meditate on You.

1800

My Lord says to me
That from today
Until I breathe my last,
He will decide for me
And choose for me
My life's "yes" and "no".

1801

To my soul
My Lord has given the capacity
To be a maker of bliss,
My heart, to be a maker of peace
And me, a maker of gratitude.

1802

Every day
I must give myself
The time I need
To please my Lord Supreme,
Not only when I am fully awake,
But also when I am dreaming.

1803

I must not enjoy any more
Unrealistic expectations
In my life.

1804

Every morning
My Lord's Compassion-Eye
Comes to me
To guide and lead me
On the golden path ahead.

1805

Today I shall have to be
My true self
So that my Lord can use me
In a very special way.

1806

If my love of God
Is genuine,
Then I cannot have
Burdening anxieties.

1807

If I cannot forgive myself
For all the blunders
That I have made over the years,
Then how can I proceed?
How can I ever dream
Perfection-dreams?
Move, I must, forward.
Fly, I must, upward.
Dive, I must, inward,
To be once more
What I truly am
And shall forever remain.

1808

What am I doing?
I am powerfully discarding
My cluttering mind-thoughts.

1809

What am I doing?
I am remembering
That God and I were
Once upon a time
One heart in two bodies.

MY CHRISTMAS-NEW YEAR-VACATION-ASPIRATION-PRAYERS

1810

What am I doing?
I am most devotedly
Listening to God.
He is telling me
What His Transcendental Self
And His Universal Self do
In order to feed humanity's
Birthless and deathless hunger.

1811

O my cradling hopes,
You I love,
You I need.

1812

O my twinkling dreams,
You I love,
You I need.

1813

O my blossoming realities,
You I love,
You I need.

1814

O my ascending God-tears,
O my descending God-smiles,
You I love,
You I need.

1815

Every little thing
That my Lord does for me
Thrills me, my heart,
My very existence.

1816

Every morning and evening
God blesses and embraces
His surrender-lamb-seekers.

1817

My Lord proudly loves
My staunch obedience-life.

1818

Every day without fail,
My Lord and I deeply enjoy
Our tears-and-smiles-moments
    together.

1819

My soulful heart
Sleeplessly and self-givingly
Pays attention
To all God's Needs and Wants.

1820

My Lord deeply and profusely
Inhales my tearful and cheerful
Gratitude-heart-incense.

1821

O my proud disobedience-mind,
Be careful!
God is secretly watching.

1822

God's every Hope, every Dream
And every Promise
Have become
My extremely intimate friends.

1823

When this world of ours
Was first born,
There was only one thing:
Delight, Infinity's Delight.

1824

I do not mean to be
A God-attention-beggar,
But, unfortunately or fortunately,
I am.

1825

Each new moment
Is a new
God-search-joy.

1826

We dream
Of many, many things,
But God dreams only
Of our devotion-heart-tears.

1827

Time immediately disappears
When my Lord Beloved Supreme
Appears before me.

1828

Morning proudly takes me
To my heart's
    silence-temple-shrine
To meditate.

1829

Evening peacefully takes me
To my Lord's Heart-Home
To meditate.

MY CHRISTMAS-NEW YEAR-VACATION-ASPIRATION-PRAYERS

1830

Each time I meditate,
My Lord reveals to me
A new heart-world.

1831

My aspiration-heart-sunrise
Gives my Lord joy
Far beyond my imagination.

1832

My heart lives only
For the Beauty and Fragrance
Of my Lord's Closeness-Heart.

1833

My outer life
Heavily leans
On God the Duty.

1834

My inner life
Sleeplessly and breathlessly relies
On God the Beauty.

1835

I felt God's Forgiveness-Heart
Long before I saw it.

1836

My choice:
Either God's Nectar-Feet
Or my pride-head.

1837

Neutrality is not
Wisdom-light.
Neutrality is
Weakness-foolishness.

1838

My Lord,
Will the long, very long years
Of my utter helplessness,
Hopelessness and uselessness
Be ever over?

1839

Hope-heart definitely blossoms.
It blossoms only
At God's choice Hour.

1840

The binding mind
Has to be either illumined
Or blinded.

1841

God's Compassion-Eye
Eagerly devours
The sincere seeker's
Himalayan blunders.

1842

When oneness
Embodies everyone,
Fulness it becomes.

1843

There are many
Secret and sacred ways
To enter into God's Heart-Home.
The seeker can play the role
Of the chooser.

1844

Face and brave your arch-enemy
With the beauty and fragrance
Of your God-smiling heart.

1845

My Lord tells me
That if I start
To like and love myself,
Then He will like me and love
   me more,
Infinitely more.

1846

Not my own efforts,
But my Lord's
   unconditional Love
Has made me
What I am now.

1847

Man plays.
God watches and suggests.
His Suggestions end in vain.
God plays.
Man sleeps and sleeps.

1848

God cares.
He cares sleeplessly for us.
To believe in Him,
We need a daring heart.

1849

Do not hesitate.
Meditate.
God Himself is going to open
His Heart-Gate
And leave it wide open for you.

MY CHRISTMAS-NEW YEAR-VACATION-ASPIRATION-PRAYERS

1850

My courage
Lies in my tolerance.
In my tolerance,
God's Pride in me looms large.

1851

Prayer-life is protection.
Meditation-life is illumination.
Service-life is liberation.
Surrender-life is satisfaction,
God's Satisfaction and my
    satisfaction.

1852

An intensity-heart
Is an immense
God-fulfilment-capacity.

1853

All my mind's doubt-threats
Are being devoured
By my mounting
Aspiration-heart-flames.

1854

Today my soul
Is in full control.
Therefore, today I must succeed
In the battlefield of my life.

1855

In Heaven,
We see Paradise.
On earth,
We make Paradise.

1856

My dreams
Are my heart-wings.
My reality
Is my soul-bird.

1857

I am the possessor
Of two dreams:
God-quest-dream
And
Ignorance-conquest-dream.

1858

My soul-life
Is oneness.
My heart-life
Is vastness.
My earth-life
Is God-manifestation-fulness.

1859

God wants my patience
And perseverance
To draw His Victory-Chariot.

1860

My Lord, I miss You.
"My child, I miss you too."
My Lord, I love You.
"My child, I love you too."
My Lord, I need You.
"My child, I need you too."
My Lord,
Will I ever be able
To become like You?
"My child,
That is My only Dream,
My only Dream,
My only Dream.
I want you to be like Me,
Another God."
My Lord,
Will I be happy then?
"My child,
That I do not know
And I do not want to know."
My Lord,
Will I be miserable then?
"My child,
That I do not know
And I do not want to know."

God, my Lord, my Father,
My Eternity's All,
Such being the case,
I do not want to be another God.
You remain what You
    eternally are
And please allow me to remain
What I am.
I want to mingle
With the dust of Your Feet
Throughout Eternity.

1861

Absurd to think and feel
That we take a great risk
While serving God the man
And man the God.

1862

I am divinely and supremely
    brave.
That means my enemies
Have either surrendered
Or are about to surrender.

1863

The only purpose of my life
Is to grow world-oneness-plants
Inside my
    aspiration-heart-garden.

MY CHRISTMAS-NEW YEAR-VACATION-ASPIRATION-PRAYERS

1864

Be quiet.
God the Justice-Light
Is watching you.
Be quiet.
God the Compassion-Height
Wants to whisper something
Extremely important to you.

1865

I want to be
A corrected man.
God wants me to be
A perfected God.

1866

The outer world
Values power.
The inner world
Values time.

1867

My eyes are afraid of
World-darkness.
My body is afraid of
My soul's light.

1868

My outer journey
Is the shortest breath.
My inner journey
Is Eternity's Breath.

1869

A new friend
Is a new blessing
From Above.

1870

An old friend
Is made of
God's gold Heart.

1871

An eternal friend
Is a constantly self-giving heart
From the Unseen.

1872

The only Friend
Both in Heaven and on earth
Is my Lord God,
The Unknowable.

1873

In our spiritual life,
Patience is
The success-harbinger.

1874

In our spiritual life,
Surrender is
The progress-precursor.

1875

I trust.
Therefore I last
And I outlast.

1876

My happiness does not
    depend on
My possessions.
My happiness does not
    depend on
My renunciation.
My happiness entirely
    depends on
My constant, cheerful and eager
    oneness With God's Will.

1877

In theory,
We all have gladly surrendered
To God's Will.
In reality,
It is shockingly false.

1878

Alas,
I think of God
Only when my desire-hunger
Ruthlessly tortures me.

1879

I love God
Not because God loves me
Infinitely more.
I love God
Precisely because
I am extremely, extremely
And extremely fond
Of His inescapable Love-Net.

1880

My heart
Shall no more remain
A short-lived God-hunger.

MY CHRISTMAS-NEW YEAR-VACATION-ASPIRATION-PRAYERS

1881

God's Face
May at times be invisible,
But His Heart
Is always visible.

1882

God's Closeness
Is my life's fulness-smile.

1883

Alas, God's Heart
Is a sleepless Tear for me.

1884

Doubt is dangerous,
And self-doubt
Is infinitely more dangerous.

1885

By nature, man is not
A God-Conversation-
    attention-ear.

1886

My heart's solemn promise
To God
Is my aspiration-return.

1887

My God-unwillingness
Does not become me.

1888

Today I am my heart's
Aspiration-candle.
Tomorrow I shall become
    my soul's
Illumination-sun.

1889

My mind never opens.
God's Eye never closes.

1890

I need only one thing:
I need a tireless
God-surrender-heart.

1891

When God's Compassion-Eye
    appears,
My sufferings start to disappear.

1892

When God's Forgiveness-Heart
   appears,
My sufferings completely
   disappear.

1893

Heaven's Beauty
And earth's duty
I equally love.

1894

Heaven's Beauty
Awakens my heart.

1895

Earth's duty
Energises my life.

1896

Oneness and fear
Are perfect strangers
To each other.

1897

My Lord,
May I come close
To Your Feet?
"No, My child,
I want you to come close
To My Heart."

1898

Even the abysmal abyss
Has more light
Than our conscious and
   deliberate
God-disobedience.

1899

No God-loving meditation
Can ever be an escape
From the world.

1900

My constant self-offering
To the world
Is a local call
To my Lord Beloved Supreme.

MY CHRISTMAS-NEW YEAR-VACATION-ASPIRATION-PRAYERS

1901

My hesitant self-offering
To the world
Is the longest-distance call
To God.

1902

My mind is determined
To possess the world.

1903

My soul is determined
To address the world.

1904

My heart is determined
To caress the world.

1905

I am determined
To become the world.

1906

God the Eye beckons me.
God the Heart speaks to me.
God the Breath embraces me.

1907

When God the Eye
Beckons me,
I offer my heart's gratitude-tears.

1908

When God the Heart
Speaks to me,
I offer my life's gratitude-smiles.

1909

When God the Breath
Embraces me,
I become the flood
Of oneness-gratitude-delight.

1910

Who is safe in today's world?
No, not even multibillionaires,
Needless to say
The poorer than the poorest.

1911

Who is safe in today's world?
Not he who is wallowing
In the supremacy-pleasures
Of unbounded power.

1912

Who is safe in today's world?
He who is endowed
With God's Protection-Assurance
Here, there and all-where.

1913

What do I learn from
    God's Tears?
I learn from God's Tears
That He has infinite concern
    for me.

1914

What do I learn from
    God's Smiles?
I learn from God's Smiles
That He has confidence in me
In measureless measure.

1915

My Lord, please tell me,
Why am I so unkind to You?
Why, why?
Why do I keep You waiting
    for me
For Eternity?

1916

"My child, if you come to Me
Even beyond Eternity's Eye
    and Heart,
I shall not mind,
As long as you come to Me,
Enter into My Heart
And become the Beauty of
    My Dream
And the Duty of My Reality."

1917

God tells me
That He is not at all worried
About my transformation,
Since He has no fixed schedule
    for me.

1918

O ignorance-night,
I am not afraid of conversing
    with you,
But I am terribly afraid
Of your unthinkable vibration
That indefinitely lasts.
I am preparing myself
To conquer your vibration-power,
So that I can inundate my
    Mother Earth
With Infinity's Delight.

MY CHRISTMAS-NEW YEAR-VACATION-ASPIRATION-PRAYERS

1919

No more
My mind's outer eye!
No more
My mind's outer ear!

1920

From now on,
My heart's inner eye and
    inner ear
I shall immediately welcome
And eternally treasure.

1921

In the small hours of the morning
God comes to me
Not to preach, not to teach,
But to love me, my entire being.

1922

God comes to me in the evening
Not to bless, not to smile,
But to examine my love, devotion
And surrender.

1923

God comes to me at night
Only for one thing:
He comes to dream in and
    through me
His Infinity's Dream.

1924

When I run forward,
I easily receive God's Smile.
When I climb upward,
I more easily receive God's Smile.
When I dive inward,
I most easily receive God's Smile.

1925

My meditation
Is my God-invocation
In the heart of my silence-smile.

1926

My meditation
Is my animal life-purification.
My meditation
Is my human life-transformation.
My meditation
Is my divine life-manifestation.

1927

No mind-emptiness,
No heart-oneness,
No God-fulness.

1928

My streaming heart-tears
Strengthen my prayer-life.

1929

My beaming soul-smiles
Lengthen my silence-meditation.

1930

My madness-mind
Challenges God.

1931

My gladness-heart
Embraces God.

1932

God is all the time crying
For the illumination
Of the doubting and
   suspecting mind.

1933

The doubting and suspecting
   mind
Is spying all the time on God
To discover some imperfection
   in God.

1934

My Lord tells me
That every eager effort
Of my heart
He deeply values.

1935

An intense God-love
Means a desire-conquered life.

1936

Alas,
The fleeting moments of my life
Are empty of God's Light.

1937

God's Flute
Awakens my heart.
God's Gong
Awakens my mind.
God's Drum
Awakens my life.

MY CHRISTMAS-NEW YEAR-VACATION-ASPIRATION-PRAYERS

1938

I have millions of flowers
In my heart-garden,
But I love the silence-flower
Infinitely more than any
   other flower.

1939

Detachment— not out of shock,
But out of wisdom-light—
Permanently lasts.

1940

A God-unwillingness-mind
Is, indeed,
A real God-failure-life.

1941

What I sleeplessly need
Is a Heaven-ascending heart.

1942

My Lord,
Every day my love increases for
   You.
How is it that Your Love for me
Does not increase even once
   a year?
"My child,
I really do not know
How to answer your question."

1943

My Lord,
Please, please free me
With Your Compassion-Eye.

1944

My Lord,
Please, please, please bind me
With Your Affection-Heart.

1945

When I arrive
At my Lord's Palace,
He immediately embraces me
Most fondly and most proudly.

1946

When my Lord arrives
At my cottage,
I immediately place myself
At His Feet
And devour the dust of His Feet.

1947

My heart's gladness
And my life's sadness
Both hear my Lord's choice
Voice.

1948

Impossibility-accomplishments:
This is what my Lord
Every day expects from me.

1949

Each time I prayerfully cry
Or soulfully smile,
My Lord invites me
To enter into
His Heaven-Heart-Garden.

1950

The divine Grace
Comes down from Above
Not when I want it,
But only when I desperately
   need it.

1951

Not God's Eye,
But God's Heart takes the timing
In all our Heavenward races.

1952

A gratitude-God-lover
And a devoted God-seeker
Are God's most favourite
   children.

1953

God has a very big Desire:
His Desire is to see me happy
Twenty-four hours a day.

1954

What is my mission?
My mission is the outer
   manifestation
Of my Lord's inner Vision.

MY CHRISTMAS-NEW YEAR-VACATION-ASPIRATION-PRAYERS

1955

Heaven is nowhere else
Save and except
In my
Lord's Compassion-flooded Eye.

1956

My aspiration-heart's
Most favourite task:
My God-prayer-tear-cries.

1957

Rotating worries and anxieties—
Alas,
This is what the human mind is.

1958

No 'why', no 'how',
No 'when', no 'where'—
My life's God-surrender is.

1959

Alas,
When will we realise
That our doubts
Are our mind-made products?

1960

My Lord's Love-Bridge
Spans my aspiration-cries
And my dedication-smiles.

1961

From now on,
No information-collection-mind,
But aspiration-ascension-heart.

1962

Division
Is the self-promoter.
Union
Is the God-prompter.

1963

The unaspiring mind
Is an over-hasty
Judgement-pronouncer.

1964

When my self-dedication
Is absolutely unconditional,
My aspiration-cry skyrockets.

1965

Only the prayerful
    receptivity-hearts
Are able to watch
God's hundreds of miracles
    every day.

1966

My Lord must come first.
My Lord must come last as well,
And in between
There must be none.

1967

A sleepless,
Self-giving life
Is all sunshine.

1968

My Lord Supreme tells me
To practise every day
Forward sprinting,
And never, never
Backward sprinting.

1969

My aspiration-heart
Is determined today
Not to allow the mind
To walk along
The godless shore.

1970

My Lord, do capture me!
Can You not see
Each and every breath of mine
Is for You, only for You?

1971

God and I barter every day
My gratitude-tears
And His Pride-Smiles.

1972

My Lord loves to hear from me
My heart-songs
For hours and hours.

1973

My Lord has no time
To hear even one story
Of my life.

MY CHRISTMAS-NEW YEAR-VACATION-ASPIRATION-PRAYERS

1974

Humanity's total transformation
Is only a local train,
And can never be
An express train.

1975

I devour the dust
Of my Lord's Feet.

1976

My Lord devours the sands
Of my life's
Never-ending mistakes.

1977

O seeker,
Be always on the alert!
At every moment
Try to please God in His own
Way.
His Compassion-Eye
May not visit you again.

1978

My oneness with the Will
Of my Lord Beloved Supreme,
Alas,
Is still at the beginning stage.

1979

God gives me His Heart-Breath
Far beyond my necessity.
Needless to say,
I deserve it not in the least.

1980

My aspiration-heart
Is not brittle.
Therefore,
It cannot be broken.

1981

Darkness cannot surround us
If we can ever develop
True love of God.

1982

Although it is a most painful task,
We must accept
The inevitable.

1983

We must not think
Of escaping our past,
But we must dare
To challenge the past
And go far, far beyond
The domain of the past.

1984

Every day, early in the morning,
My Lord Himself enters into
My heart-garden
And collects all my prayerful,
    soulful
And beautiful heart-blossoms.

1985

At every moment I must and
    must
Soulfully pray to God
To illumine the darkness
Of my ignorance-night.

1986

God tells my aspiration-heart
Immediately to devour
All my desires,
For they can at any moment
Attack my aspiration-heart
And destroy it totally.

1987

May my enthusiasm-heart
Be not only dauntless,
But also sleepless and breathless.

1988

God calls it
My delight-heart-fountain.
I call it
My Lord's unconditional
Compassion and Love-Mountain.

1989

If the tears of our hearts
Are sincere,
Then God will definitely keep us
Inside His
    Compassion-Protection-
Perfection-Satisfaction-Ring.

1990

My God-obedience-boat
My Lord always
Blessingfully and proudly keeps
On the right course.

1991

A prayerless heart
Is, indeed,
A hopeless and useless life.

MY CHRISTMAS-NEW YEAR-VACATION-ASPIRATION-PRAYERS

1992

The gratitude-heart
Is absolutely necessary
To live upon this whole earth.

1993

Aspiration-life begins
The God-discovery-adventure.

1994

Unless I make my Lord happy,
How can I be really happy?

1995

My heart's each new God-song
Is a forward step
Towards my Lord's Heart-Home.

1996

I am my life's
Inner tears.
God is His inner Heart's
Unending smiles.

1997

Nothing is as charming,
Illumining and fulfilling
As my inner boat-ride
With my Lord Supreme.

1998

God's Compassion-Eye
Is always desperately eager
To keep the genuine seekers
    happy.

1999

With His own Hands
Our Lord Supreme feeds
His unconditionally
    surrendered Children.

2000

A complete surrender-life
Means a oneness-dance
Of God and the seeker.

2001

Aspiration-life means
Countless
God-fulfilment-opportunities.

2002

All my devotion-heart-letters
God's Heart immediately reads
And His Hands immediately
    fulfil.

2003

The mind
Is the strength
Of only one individual.

2004

The heart
Is the power
Of multitudes.

2005

I must walk, march, run and
    sprint
Behind my
    Lord Beloved Supreme,
For He knows
Where He is taking me.

2006

God surrenders to me.
God says to me,
"My child, I have been leading
    you
For centuries after centuries.
Now I feel you can lead Me."

"My Lord,
You must always lead me.
The child has always to follow
The Father.
Please do not break
    Your Cosmic Law
For me."

2007

Life needs courage,
Courage invincible.
Heart needs oneness,
Oneness universal.

2008

Eternity is within.
Infinity is without.
Immortality is at once
Within and without.

2009

Man in general:
A self-motivated plan.

2010

Ultimately, self-importance
Becomes homeless—
Nowhere to go.

MY CHRISTMAS-NEW YEAR-VACATION-ASPIRATION-PRAYERS

2011

God has only one message
For me:
"Up, up, My child!
To the very top, My child!
Stop not
Until the Goal claims you
And your all."

2012

Do not think unnecessarily,
Do not think!
Your mind will completely
    be covered
With ink.

2013

God says to me,
"My child,
Seek Me, seek, seek!
Your heart's tears and cries
Are still very weak."

2014

Alas, alas, alas!
My life knows how to sleep,
My heart knows how to weep,
And I know how to cry and sigh
In vain.

2015

I know, I know
Whom only I owe
For my ignorance-conquest-
    Victory-smile:
He is none other than
My Inner Pilot.

2016

My Lord's
    Heart-Village-Invitation
Is the greatest privilege
And deepest delight
Of my life.

2017

Who saddens the Heart
Of my Lord Beloved Supreme?
Not me, not me, not me!
Who gladdens the Heart
Of my Lord Beloved Supreme?
Me, me, me!

2018

O foolish mind,
Do not dare to fight
With the Omnipotence-Silence!

2019

Silence embodies,
Reveals and manifests
God's Transcendental Dream
Upon earth.

2020

Life is Eternity's
Silence-journey
Towards Infinity.

2021

God says to me,
"My child,
If you are ready to be responsible
For your today's life,
Then I shall be fully responsible
For your entire future life."

2022

Do not try to inform the world
Who you are.
Just try to reform the world
With the tears of your heart.

2023

Each soulful prayer
Touches God's Feet.

2024

Each deep meditation
Enters into God's Heart.

2025

God has made me
His Divinity's partner,
Not because my mind
Is extremely powerful
And not because my heart
Is extremely beautiful,
But because I am of Him
And I am for Him.

2026

As long as my Lord Supreme
Knows and sees
That my heart-cries are sincere,
I do not have to prove anything
To the world.

2027

Every day my God-surrender-life
Has to increase in beauty
    and purity
If I really want God to love
    me more
And ever more.

MY CHRISTMAS-NEW YEAR-VACATION-ASPIRATION-PRAYERS

2028

When I think
Of my Lord Supreme,
He is His Power infinite.

2029

When I pray
To my Beloved Supreme,
He is His Compassion infinite.

2030

When I meditate
On my Absolute Supreme,
He is His Satisfaction-Heart
  infinite.

2031

God is His Immortality's
Hope-Dream and
  Promise-Reality
For His full Manifestation
In each human being upon earth.

2032

My love of God
Must immensely increase
From this very moment.

2033

My God-Feet-devotion
Must immensely increase
From this very moment.

2034

My God-heart-surrender
Must immensely increase
From this very moment.

2035

With my aspiration-cries
And my dedication-smiles,
I am desperately trying
To make up for lost time.

2036

My Lord's Compassion-Eye
Loves to play all the time
With the tears and smiles
Of my heart.

2037

My Lord Beloved Supreme
Is extremely fond
Of my heart-whispers.

2038

My Lord wants
The beauty of my smiles
To be invincible.

2039

My Lord wants
The fragrance of my tears
To be indestructible.

2040

God begs my doubting mind
To mingle
With my aspiring heart.
He also tells my aspiring heart
Not to worry.

2041

Every single God-seeker
Embodies
God's Vision-Fulfilment-Eye.

2042

The desire-life
That I once stupidly chose
I am now wisely
Casting aside.

2043

Each moment I can apply
For my conscious ascent
To the highest.
Alas,
What prevents me,
If not my unwillingness-mind?

2044

Every day
My Lord Beloved Supreme
Drinks and drinks and drinks
From my
   gratitude-heart-fountain.

2045

My Lord is always eager
To receive the tears
Of my heart.

2046

Sooner or later
We needs must journey
Towards the Unknowable.

2047

My joys know no bounds
When I am
My heart-country-traveller.

MY CHRISTMAS-NEW YEAR-VACATION-ASPIRATION-PRAYERS

2048

We must realise
That the river of time
Does not wait
For anyone.

2049

To my greatest joy,
Inside my Lord's Heart-Garden
My gratitude-heart-flowers
Keep growing and growing.

2050

O my mind,
I am begging you
To come with me only once
Into the silence-world.

2051

I must never, never suffer
From a broken heart-relationship
With my Eternity's
    Beloved Supreme.

2052

Alas,
Most of us love
Only emergency prayers.

2053

My Lord, chain me!
Chain my heart, chain my life
And chain my all
To Your Compassion-flooded
Will.

2054

May my life's
God-surrender-shrine-worship
Be fulfilled
In this lifetime.

2055

My Lord,
As long as You care
For my heart-garden,
I shall not mind
If You do not care
For my mind-jungle
And my life-market.

2056

With every God-gratitude-breath
Of mine,
I come closer and closer
To my Lord Supreme.

2057

My Lord,
You have endless Names,
But I call You
And I shall forever call You
By only one Name:
Forgiveness.

2058

God tells me
That He secretly and
    proudly treasures
My prayer-life
And my meditation-heart.

2059

The sleepless and selfless
Heart-giver
Expects no return.

2060

The earth-time ticks and ticks
To awaken me.
The Heaven-time beckons
And beckons me
To raise me high, higher, highest.

2061

Who is my Mother Earth,
If not a ceaseless flood
Of God-Tears?

2062

Who is my Father Heaven,
If not an ocean
Of God-Smiles?

2063

God quickly comes
To the seeker
Who does not claim anything.

2064

God proudly comes running
To the seeker
Who lovingly, devotedly
    and soulfully
Claims God.

2065

I wish every step of my life
To be guided
By the Compassion-Eye
Of my Lord Beloved Supreme.

MY CHRISTMAS-NEW YEAR-VACATION-ASPIRATION-PRAYERS

2066

God is exceedingly
And equally pleased
With my sleepless heart-tears
And my breathless soul-smiles.

2067

What was I doing?
I was repeating and chanting
God's Forgiveness-Name.

2068

What am I doing?
I am repeating and chanting
God's Compassion-Name.

2069

What will I be doing?
I will be repeating and chanting
God's Inspiration,
    Encouragement
And Enthusiasm-Names.

2070

Centuries ago
I started devouring
The golden dust
Of my Lord's Feet,
And I have not stopped
Even for a fleeting moment.

2071

Since my Lord
Does not think of my future,
Why do I have to think
Of my future?
Do I not know
That my future is eternally safe
In my Lord's Hands?

2072

Alas,
Very few people enjoy
Walking along life's
Transformation-road.

2073

When my heart suffers,
My soul comes
With an overwhelming flood
Of sympathy.

2074

Move away, my mind!
My God wants to enter
Into my heart.

2075

How can a seeker
Succeed
Without his faith-breath?

2076

Self-doubt is, indeed,
The very beginning
Of a dangerous self-threat.

2077

May my heart
Always remain enraptured
By God's Sweetness-Eye.

2078

Every day we should increase
Our love-devotion-
    surrender-speed
On our God-fulfilment-road.

2079

Alas,
I do not know how and when
I have lost contact
With my Beloved Supreme.

2080

When I cry,
I see myself above earth.
When I smile,
I see myself below Heaven.

2081

My aspiration-mountain
And my dedication-fountain
Must work together.

2082

My life,
Continue to pray!
My heart,
Continue to meditate!
Ignorance-forces before long
Will retire and surrender.

2083

My love, my devotion
And my surrender
Have only one Source:
My Lord's Compassion-Eye.

2084

Where is God?
God is just behind me,
Watching me very carefully.

2085

What is God doing?
God is merrily dancing
Inside my singing.

MY CHRISTMAS-NEW YEAR-VACATION-ASPIRATION-PRAYERS

2086

God's Will
Is not my master.
God's Will
Is my Eternity's partner.

2087

Our prayers
Inch by inch
Take us to God's Feet.

2088

Our meditations
Mile by mile
Take us to God's Heart.

2089

As we want to be loved
By God,
God also wants to be loved
By us—
Even more so.

2090

Hard to believe,
But it is true:
God loves not only
My aspiration-heart,
But also
My recreation-life.

2091

Mother Earth
Dearly loves
Her running children.

2092

Father Heaven
Proudly loves
His meditating children.

2093

Mother Earth expects
Smile-lustre
From her children.

2094

Father Heaven expects
Peace-hunger
From His children.

2095

Be neither a clever seeker
Nor a stupid seeker.
Publicly you smile;
Privately you sigh.

2096

All sincere seekers
Agree on one thing:
We need God the Love
More than God the Power.

2097

My singing heart
Is God's proud Eye.

2098

There was a time
When I was a lover
Of God's Feet,
But now I am a devourer
Of God's ambrosial Feet-dust.

2099

Sleepless self-giving
Knows no equal.

2100

The mind thinks
That it can easily live
Without God's Love.

2101

The heart feels and knows
That it cannot live
Even a fleeting second
Without God's Love.

2102

My Lord's Compassion-Eye
And my heart-cries
Can never be separated.

2103

My Lord tells me
That He does not want
To hear from me
My sad news and bad news
Any more.

2104

God's Pride-Eye
And my love-heart
Celebrate elaborately
Our mutual arrivals.

2105

Insecurity-heart disappears
Only when
God's Compassion-Eye appears.

MY CHRISTMAS-NEW YEAR-VACATION-ASPIRATION-PRAYERS

2106

My heart-tears
Have a free access
To my Lord's Smile-Eye.

2107

Outwardly God does not tell me
What He thinks of my visits
To His Heart-Home,
But inwardly He does.
I know it, I can feel it—
It is all His blessingful Love
And Joy.

2108

The mind
Does not love God.
The mind
Does not need God.
It enjoys only
Its self-importance.

2109

I have only one desire:
I wish to be
A breathless, heart-diving
God-lover.

2110

Today I am determined
To do everything
In God's own Way.

2111

To have purity,
The seeker has to feel
That he is a child
Of the Eternal Now.

2112

If you are searching for God
With a genuine thirst and hunger,
Then God will without fail
Appear before you.

2113

My life is in between
God's Compassion-Arms
And His Forgiveness-Heart.

2114

God's Will does not operate
In a doubting mind.
God's Will operates only
In a self-giving life.

2115

It is far beyond the capacity
Of the mind
To think that God
Is all Forgiveness.

2116

The heart feels
That God is sleepless
And unconditional Forgiveness.

2117

Shut up, my mind!
My heart and I are ready
To fly
On our aspiration-wings.

2118

Alas,
When God gives talks
On surrender,
The number of the seekers
    present
Is disappointing.

2119

A gratitude-heart
Is a very rare reality.

2120

God-closeness depends upon
The brightness and sincerity
Of our smile.

2121

My gratitude-heart
And my surrender-life
Are both needed
To fulfill God's Dream on earth.

2122

My soul allows my heart
To talk to God
Only on one condition:
My heart has to speak to God
Only about God.

2123

God wants my inner experiences
To guide my outer life.

2124

My life
Without fail
Tremendously improves
When I inspire others.

MY CHRISTMAS-NEW YEAR-VACATION-ASPIRATION-PRAYERS

2125

My heart
Makes the fastest progress
When it establishes its
   oneness-delight
With the entire world.

2126

Move not backward!
Stark ignorance-night
Will once more tempt you
And devour you.

2127

Move forward!
God's Compassion-Eye
And God's Affection-Heart
Are beckoning you.

2128

God loves me
Not because I also love Him.
God loves me
Because I am ready,
I am willing
And I am eager
To love Him.

2129

The human
In each human being
Always thinks differently.

2130

The divine in us
Always thinks
Exactly the way
God wants us to think.

2131

The child-heart-loser
With tremendous difficulties
Makes his spiritual progress
Inch by inch.

2132

He who has not lost
His child-heart
In his spiritual life
Is surprised by his own
Unimaginable progress.

2133

When I doubtfully think
That God loves me,
God immediately
Sheds tears of sorrow.

2134

When I unmistakably feel
That God loves me,
God's Eye immediately
    starts swimming
In His Infinity's Ocean of
    Delight.

2135

I tell the world
That God dearly loves me.
The world asks me,
"Where is the proof?"

2136

When the world tells me
That God loves the world,
I tell the world,
"I need no proof,
For God has repeatedly told me
That loving
Is the only thing He knows."

2137

My happy heart
Is the only thing
That my Lord wants to have
From me.

2138

Every thought—
Encouraging or discouraging—
Has a magnetic power.

2139

My Lord has a very special Love,
Affection and Fondness
For the heart-blossoms
Of my life.

2140

Do not try to escape your past.
Challenge and conquer your past
Once and for all,
So that you can march forward,
Dive inward and fly upward.

2141

Every day we must say
Our God-surrender-prayers
Early in the morning
And in the evening.

2142

My God-gratitude-thrill
Can never be described.

MY CHRISTMAS-NEW YEAR-VACATION-ASPIRATION-PRAYERS

2143

May I be the possessor
Of an enthusiasm-heart
And a sleepless prayer-life
To please my Lord
At every moment.

2144

My heart,
You must give your undivided
    attention
To the soul
When the soul comes down
To give you God-lessons.

2145

Out of His infinite Bounty,
My Lord has taken me away,
Far beyond the domain
Of confusion-mind-
    darkness-night.

2146

Desire needs us
Desperately.
Aspiration we need
Sleeplessly.

2147

If I do not aspire,
I shall not be able to conquer
My ego's
    self-advertisement-pride.

2148

A God-crying heart
I am—
Two God-smiling eyes as well.

2149

Be a self-giver
Before you become a
    God-dreamer.
Be a God-dreamer
Before you become a God-lover.

2150

All our heart-progress-days
Shall be garlanded
By God Himself.

2151

To be an atheist
Is easier
Than believing in God.

2152

To believe in God
Is easier
Than thinking of God.

2153

To think of God
Is easier
Than praying to God.

2154

To pray to God
Is easier
Than loving God.

2155

To love God
Is easier
Than obeying God.

2156

To obey God
Is easier
Than having a sleepless
God-oneness-meditation.

2157

To meditate on God
Is easier
Than pleasing and fulfilling God
All the time.

2158

To please and fulfill God
Is easier
Than becoming a
    God-representative
On earth.

2159

To become a God-representative
Is easier
Than manifesting God
Throughout the length and
    breadth
Of the world.

2160

To manifest God all-where
Is to put an end
To the Cosmic Game
Of comparison.

MY CHRISTMAS-NEW YEAR-VACATION-ASPIRATION-PRAYERS

2161

Dream-lover
I was.

2162

Action-believer
I now am.

2163

Self-giver
I shall become.

2164

God-knower
My Ultimate Goal is.

2165

I can have true love of God
If I can go far beyond the
    frontiers
Of all man-made
And man-prophesised religions.

2166

Self-doubters
Are bound to be
Their inner happiness-losers
Plus their goal-destroyers.

2167

Each seeker
Has to face ignorance-night
Undaunted.

2168

Do not take the world
As a meaningless, useless
Object-display.

2169

Take the world
As God's full
Manifestation-Promise-Land.

2170

My Lord,
I have very powerfully clasped
Your Feet.
No ignorance-force
Can dare to take me away.

2171

The real spiritual life
Is a one-way
Progress-delight-road.

2172

Each heart
Is
A God-singing song.

2173

The Compassion-Eye
Of my Beloved Supreme
Thunders
At my disobedience.

2174

I must pay all attention
To the beauty of God's Creation
And not indulge
In my self-creation.

2175

I really love to take shelter
Under the Sovereignty-Sky
Of my Beloved Supreme.

2176

To my greatest joy,
My God-manifestation-
   hope-flood
Is coming back.

2177

Physical hunger-nourishment
Is needed
To sustain the body.

2178

Spiritual hunger-nourishment
Is indispensable
If God is to be realised.

2179

Do not retire!
If you retire,
God's Pride
Will not hire you.

2180

The mind
Cannot come out of
The fact-factories.

2181

The heart
Can easily cross far beyond
The fact-boundaries.

MY CHRISTMAS-NEW YEAR-VACATION-ASPIRATION-PRAYERS

2182

God tells me
That He treasures
My happy heart's
Gratitude-blossoms.

2183

A child-heart is always eager
To play life's
Transformation-satisfaction-
 game.

2184

My intense prayers
Soar high,
Very high.

2185

My profound meditations
Roar,
Triumphantly roar.

2186

Each sincere prayer
Is a newness-smile
Of my life.

2187

Each deep meditation
Is a soulfulness-song
Of my heart.

2188

I dearly love
My God-worship.

2189

God proudly loves
My God-partnership
And God-friendship.

2190

Each good thought
Of mine
Is a rainbow-beauty.

2191

Each dedicated service
Of mine
Is my God-satisfying duty.

2192

Gratitude
Never takes anything
For granted,
But ingratitude does.

2193

Love
Is never afraid
Of fear.

2194

Fear
Is always afraid
Of love.

2195

Every day I want my life
To be a most soulful
God-surrender-song.

2196

Peace and love
Shelter each other
And fulfil each other.

2197

Sweetness
Is the most powerful strength
Of the heart.

2198

When I look for silence,
I find silence
Inside my soul.

2199

When I look for my soul,
I find my soul
Inside my silence.

2200

Each God-seeker
Is a special breath
Of God's Heart.

2201

Each God-seeker
Is a special flower-beauty
And fragrance
In God's Heart-Garden.

MY CHRISTMAS-NEW YEAR-VACATION-ASPIRATION-PRAYERS

2202

Each God-seeker
Is a special player
In God's Cosmic Drama.

2203

Each God-seeker
Is chosen by God Himself
To be a song of His Heart
For the perfection of humankind.

2204

The spiritual life
Is an endless
God-discovery-adventure.

2205

I am now going back
To my childhood's
Bliss-flooded mornings.

2206

God lovingly and proudly
   preserves
All my heart-songs
In His own Heart-Safe.

2207

My love of God
Is building a new hope-temple
And making a new
      promise-shrine.

2208

My desire-life has received
A very short-lived Blessing
From God.

2209

My aspiration-heart has received
An everlasting Blessing
From God.

2210

Hope
Knows no fear.

2211

Hope dares to blossom
Even inside the abysmal abyss.

2212

A seeker's hope-heart
Gladdens God's Heart
Most significantly.

2213

Hope secretly feeds
And strengthens
Promise.

2214

God the Supreme Artist
Has given me another chance
To make my face, eyes and heart
Exceedingly beautiful.

2215

To avoid God,
Either consciously
Or even unconsciously,
Is to enter into the chasm
Of nothingness.

2216

The mind becomes old
And withered,
But the heart can remain young
Forever.

2217

God wants my love for Him
Lovingly, soulfully and
   self-givingly
To encircle the globe.

2218

A child-heart knows not
How to doubt
God's Affection.

2219

No matter how undivine we are,
God's Compassion-Funds
Never run low.

2220

If you want to be
Close to God,
Then eagerly learn
As many things as possible
About God.

2221

Each thought
Is the creator
Of a new experience.

MY CHRISTMAS-NEW YEAR-VACATION-ASPIRATION-PRAYERS

2222

When a seeker fails,
God takes the full blame.

2223

Alas,
In vain God expects
More love and more gratitude
From mankind.

2224

True,
My life-boat is slow,
But it is extremely reliable.

2225

My mind-library houses
Neither God-written books
Nor books written about God.

2226

Wisdom and age
Do not depend on each other.

2227

The difference between
   infant seekers
And adult seekers:
Infant seekers love God
Only from the heart;
Adult seekers love God
This moment from the heart,
Next moment from the mind
And the following moment
From the physical consciousness.

2228

My life must become
The beauty
Of my soul's smile.

2229

My God-aspiration,
God-dedication and
   God-absorption
Have to be sleepless.

2230

I light my God-heart-candle
With my devotion-breath.

2231

Every day
My heart collects Compassion
And Forgiveness-Flowers
From my Lord's Heart-Garden.

2232

When I measure God's Blessings
With my mind,
I only add more miseries
To my life.

2233

When I measure God's Blessings
With my heart,
My life is inundated
With bliss.

2234

God-dreamers
Will eventually be
God's Victory-announcers.

2235

God-dreamers
Know no obstacles.

2236

I am not afraid of storms,
For God
Is my life's Boatman.

2237

I must bloom
Where my Lord plants me,
And nowhere else.

2238

When I am a member
Of the outer world,
I myself
Make all my decisions.

2239

When I am a member
Of the inner world,
God not only makes
All my decisions,
But also gladly and proudly
Executes them.

2240

God does not want me
To be
An invisible life.

MY CHRISTMAS-NEW YEAR-VACATION-ASPIRATION-PRAYERS

2241

God wants me
To be
An indispensable heart.

2242

Courage is needed
For the outer victory.

2243

Unconditional surrender
To God's Will
Is needed
For the inner victory.

2244

Everybody has
An absolute secret.
Mine is an open secret:
I know the Will
Of my Lord Beloved Supreme.

2245

Always the inner cries
And the inner tears
Have to be kept
In good health.

2246

Sound
Is extremely eager
To be heard.

2247

Silence
Is majestically eager
To raise the consciousness
Of the world.

2248

I have come to learn
At long last
That there is nothing as fragile
As my self-confidence.

2249

Alas,
Humanity is blindly speeding
Towards dire uncertainty.

2250

I have heard, I have heard
The clarion call
Of my Transcendental Self—
I have heard, I have heard.

2251

For the God-lover,
Impossibility
Is just a dictionary word.

2252

My mind
Has an urgent message
For God:
From now on,
My mind will listen
To my heart.

2253

To attend Heaven-school,
The seeker must get
A compassion-certificate
From Mother Earth.

2254

My heart has discovered
That God, my Lord,
Is
An ever-transcending Newness.

2255

Meditation
Does not believe in
Man-delivered information.

2256

Meditation means
The beauty and fragrance
Of the fast-revealing
    illumination.

2257

The joys
Of the Heaven-Kingdom
I have.

2258

The sorrows
Of the earth-planet
I am.

2259

Mine is a God-gratitude-song
That is perpetually sung
By my heart.

2260

Unity
Begins the Cosmic Game,
Multiplicity
Continues the Game,
And this Game never ends.

MY CHRISTMAS-NEW YEAR-VACATION-ASPIRATION-PRAYERS

2261

Two things are infinite:
My mind's ignorance-night
And
My heart's God-delight.

2262

Two things are eternal:
My crying heart
And
God's smiling Eye.

2263

Two things are immortal:
God's Vision
And
God's Compassion.

2264

Success is
Action-pride.

2265

Progress is
An ever-transcending
Destination.

2266

Success is
Capacity-supremacy.

2267

Progress is
Heart-ecstasy.

2268

Pray
Like a child.

2269

Meditate
Like a yogi.

2270

When God cries,
I remember immediately
All my mistakes.

2271

When God smiles,
I forget
All my good deeds
And bad deeds.

2272

Inch by inch,
Minute by minute,
I shall try to dive into
My Lord's fathomless Heart.

2273

When God hears
That I am on His side,
I please Him
More than anything else —
So says God.

2274

When God walks
Among us,
Our hearts become
Infinity's Fragrance.

2275

When God the Beauty
Blessingfully enters into
My eyes,
My entire being becomes
Not only beautiful,
But also blissful.

2276

If we try to please humanity,
Even in a thousand ways,
We sadly fail.

2277

When we try to please God,
Even in a single way,
We please Him
Sooner than at once.

2278

My heart of silence
Is full of
God-Messages.

2279

To go a little higher
Is to see God a little better
And be a little closer.

2280

My Lord Supreme sings
    and sings
The glories of my
    willingness-mind
And eagerness-heart.

MY CHRISTMAS-NEW YEAR-VACATION-ASPIRATION-PRAYERS

2281

My mind desires
Independence-pride.

2282

My heart desires
God-dependence-peace.

2283

I desire
God-satisfaction-delight.

2284

My humility
Is the secret
Of my God-closeness.

2285

My life and I
Shall be simpler and simpler
Every single day
To please our Lord Supreme.

2286

My heart and I
Shall be sweeter and sweeter
Every single day
To please our Lord Supreme.

2287

My Lord and I
Shall be dearer and dearer
Every single day
To perform our respective tasks.

2288

My Lord tells me
That my
  God-gratitude-heart-tears
And my
  God-gratitude-heart-smiles
Are His strong, stronger
  and strongest
Hero-warriors.

2289

My Lord Supreme has asked
My aspiration-heart-flames
To buy only a one-way ticket
To His Heart-Home.

2290

My Beloved Supreme tells me
That as long as He can claim
  my heart
As His personal property,
He does not have to worry
About my life.

2291

My Heaven
Is my ever-blossoming
God-gratitude-heart.

2292

If you do not love your soul
    dearly,
Your life is bound to be estranged
From your bountiful soul.

2293

No human being is fated
To live in stark ignorance-night
Forever.

2294

O ignorance-night,
No matter how powerful you are,
You will not be able to uproot
My aspiration-heart-tree.

2295

The mind
Asks questions.
The heart
Immediately answers.

2296

The heart
Asks questions.
The mind
Speedily disappears.

2297

The disobedience-mind
Was summarily punished
By God Himself.

2298

My mind sleeps and sleeps,
Endlessly sleeps.

2299

My heart keeps awake
To hear the
    pindrop-silence-arrival
Of my Lord Supreme.

2300

When God asks me my name,
I tell Him that my name is
God-gratitude-heart-fragrance.
God blesses me
With an unending Smile.

MY CHRISTMAS-NEW YEAR-VACATION-ASPIRATION-PRAYERS

2301

A God-cry
Reaches
A new horizon.

2302

No aspiring heart
Should ever allow the invasion
Of the doubting mind.

2303

Our love of our Master
Inspires our Master immensely
Plus immeasurably.

2304

The soul-music
Can easily silence
The mind-turbulence.

2305

For the fulfilment of the divine
    actions
In our outer life,
Inner poise is of paramount
    importance.

2306

Our surrender-lives
Are the perfect manifestations
Of our Master's
Earth-transformation-promises.

2307

My Master
Is my most sincere
Happiness-beggar.

2308

God's burning Flame-Tears
My mind forgets
Sooner than at once,
But my heart—
Never, never, never!

2309

Every day
God invites and welcomes
My gratitude-heart
With open Arms
And soul-stirring Smiles.

2310

God is the real Lover
Of my constantly new start
To arrive at new horizons.

2311

The outer beauty
Gladdens
The human in us.

2312

The inner beauty
Awakens
The divine in us
To the Heights of the Absolute.

2313

May my life be untiringly
The singing glow
And the dancing flow
Of my heart.

2314

Alas,
We do not care
For our inner light to illumine us,
But we care
For the outer light
That puzzles and dazzles us.

2315

The divine seeker
Hungers only
For the timeless Dream of God.

2316

The Cosmic Game
Does not break anything.
It only builds everything.

2317

The mind-cave
Is empty of light.

2318

The heart-cottage
Is inundated
With silence and peace.

2319

The loud sound
Of the earth
I love.

2320

The silver silence
Of Heaven
I need.

MY CHRISTMAS-NEW YEAR-VACATION-ASPIRATION-PRAYERS

2321

My heart desires to be
The lover and worshipper
Of God
The ever-transcending Dreamer.

2322

My Lord,
Do You think
I will always be able
To love You?
"My child,
Do you think
I will ever be able
To forget you?"

2323

My Lord,
Do You think
I will ever be able
To fulfil You?

2324

"My child,
You can and you shall
Fulfil Me,
Because I am the secret Doer
And you are the outer enjoyer."

2325

My Lord takes care
Not only of my divine qualities,
But also of my undivine qualities.

2326

My Lord takes care
Not only of my success-mind
And progress-heart,
But also of my failure-life.

2327

My Lord takes care
Not only of my soul's
Strengthening smiles,
But also of my life's
Tearing fears.

2328

My Lord loves
My body's baby steps
And my soul's giant steps
Equally.

2329

I love
My Lord's Thunder-Kicks
More than I love
My Lord's Sweetness-Heart.
Why, why, why?
Because I desire
The fastest progress.

2330

I love
My Lord's Volcano-Eye
More than I love
My Lord's soft and tender
    Caresses.
Why, why, why?
Because I desire
The fastest progress.

2331

Now that I am at the Lotus-Feet
Of my Lord Supreme,
My desire-life has come
To a complete and permanent
    halt.

2332

Today I am so happy
Precisely because
My age-old stubborn mind
Is running towards
My Lord's Heart-Home.

2333

Today I am so happy
Because my heart-tears
And God's Heart-Smiles
Are singing and dancing together.

2334

Today I am so happy to see
That my infinite Lord
Has chosen my finite life
To play with Him.

2335

Nobody knows
Which came into existence first:
Love or the heart.

2336

May my aspiration-heart-river
Run, singing,
Towards the Ocean Unknowable.

2337

May my dedication-life
Fly, dancing,
Towards the Skies Unknowable.

MY CHRISTMAS-NEW YEAR-VACATION-ASPIRATION-PRAYERS

2338

The tears of my heart
Are always ascending
Towards Heaven.

2339

The smiles of my soul
Are always descending
Towards the earth.

2340

God has chosen
His Cosmic Eye
To be the sole Conductor
Of His Cosmic Orchestra.

2341

My devotion-tears
My Lord Supreme enjoys
As His most delicious feast.

2342

My cheerfulness-temptation
God cannot resist.
He comes running
To grab it!

2343

My God-gratitude-heart
Is, indeed, a fact,
Not a legend.

2344

God created each human being
In a unique way
So that He can be pleased
By each human being
In a unique way.

2345

My Lord Supreme
Takes His Compassion-Exercises
Twenty-four hours a day.

2346

Love the world
And serve the world
Unconditionally.
You will be the golden bridge
Between today's world
And the years ahead of you.

2347

My Lord,
It is Your flaming Breath
Inside my heart
That is keeping me alive
Here on earth.

2348

No more shallow promises,
My Lord!
This time I am determined
To fulfil my promise.
I shall please You at every
    moment
In Your own Way.

2349

The silence of the mind
Embodies
The Power of the Infinite.

2350

A wasted moment
Is the very beginning
Of my failure-life.

2351

I was the worst possible fool.
I took my Lord's
Compassion-flooded Eye
For granted.

2352

Each and every surrender-breath
Of my heart
Prayerfully watches my Lord
Smiling, singing and dancing.

2353

My sleepless surrender
To God's Will
Must never falter,
Never!

2354

Every morning and every evening
My Beloved Supreme
    sumptuously feeds
My aspiration-heart
And my dedication-life
To strengthen them
So that they can perform
Their respective tasks
Most successfully and most
    gloriously.

MY CHRISTMAS-NEW YEAR-VACATION-ASPIRATION-PRAYERS

2355

The difference between
God's Eye and God's Heart
Is this:
God's Eye promises;
God's Heart fulfils.

2356

God-Existence
In my life
Is my heart's faith-flame.

2357

Silence speaks.
Silence speaks
Very, very quietly.

2358

Silence listens.
Silence listens
Very, very carefully.

2359

As the prison door
Of my doubting mind
Is wide open,
Even so the Heart-Door
Of my Lord Supreme
Is sleeplessly and completely
   open.

2360

My heart-bird flies and flies
And then encircles
My soul-sky.

2361

My mind knows
How to impose
Limitation-boundaries.

2362

My soul and I know
How to smash asunder
All the limitation-boundaries
Created by the mind.

2363

Newness glows
In God's Eye
Breathtakingly.

2364

Fulness grows
In God's Heart
Sempiternally.

2365

I place
My God-gratitude-heart-garland
At my Lord's Lotus-Feet.

2366

My Lord picks up my garland
From His Feet
And puts it around my neck
With His Transcendental Smile
And Pride.

2367

This morning
My Inner Pilot said to me,
"My child,
Let your heart and My Heart
Exchange their gratitude-beauty,
Gratitude-fragrance
And gratitude-delight."

2368

Today the talker in me
Has surrendered completely
To the God-server in me.

2369

Today something absolutely new
Must take place
In my spiritual life.

2370

Today my soul, my heart,
My mind, my vital,
My body and I
Together must do something
Unprecedented.

2371

Today without fail
I shall make God,
My only Master-Lord,
Happy in His own Way.

2372

An endless
Desire-darkness-life
I was.

2373

A sleepless and breathless
Aspiration-light-heart
I now am.

2374

God does not want to know
What I do
As long as I keep His Vision-Eye
In each and every action of mine.

MY CHRISTMAS-NEW YEAR-VACATION-ASPIRATION-PRAYERS

2375

Readiness, soulfulness,
Willingness, eagerness and I
Have decided to make oneness
Our team captain.

2376

If God thinks I can,
Then definitely I can.
I must do it!
Lo, I have done it:
My God-surrender
   unconditional.

2377

My mind,
Do you really want to be happy?
Then start thinking,
Start doing,
Start becoming
Only in God's own Way.

2378

Today
I have completely liberated
   myself
From the fetters
Of my doubting and suspecting
   mind.

2379

Today I am swimming
In the sea of delight,
For I am able to run
At long last
The full length
Of my Lord's commanding Will.

2380

My God-hungry eyes,
I deeply love you.

2381

My God-hungry heart,
I desperately need you.

2382

Beautiful
When my Lord's Eye
Beckons me.

2383

Blissful
When my Lord's Heart
Beckons me.

2384

Godful
When my Lord's Feet
Beckon me.

2385

God's Compassion-Eye
Most carefully watches
My sleeping heart,
My sleeping mind,
My sleeping vital and
My sleeping body.

2386

Smiling, singing and dancing,
My Lord meets with
My surrender's every need.

2387

My outer God-obedience-life
Garners
Abundant inner wealth.

2388

My inner God-obedience-heart
Feeds and nourishes unreservedly
My outer life.

2389

My Lord dances
His Ecstasy-Dance
When my heart's inner day
Begins to break.

2390

O God-obedience-sky,
My aspiration-heart-flames
Are climbing fast, very fast,
To reach you
And be an inner member
Of your family.

2391

From the higher worlds
The spiritual Masters,
Out of their infinite bounty,
Come down to visit me,
Bless me most powerfully,
Speak to me most affectionately
And appreciate my God-service
To humanity
Most unreservedly.

2392

I must fulfil
The needs of my soul—
I must!
What are the needs of my soul?
My sleepless God-hunger
And my breathless God-service.

MY CHRISTMAS-NEW YEAR-VACATION-ASPIRATION-PRAYERS

2393

The desire-life-stories
Are extremely painful.

2394

The aspiration-heart-songs
Are exceedingly haunting.

2395

I love and bow to,
I bow to and love the
    God-seekers
Who are infinitely more
    advanced
Than I am
In the spiritual life.

2396

My heart, my mind,
My vital, my body and I
Are fully prepared
To be unconditionally
    surrendered
God-instruments.

2397

Our heart-days
Are
Our God-promise-
    fulfilment-days.

2398

No rest
After God-realisation.
No rest
Even after God-manifestation—
God comes with a new Dream.

2399

God-realisation
Is not an impossible task—
No, not even
The most difficult task.
So says my soul to my mind.

2400

To be a supremely chosen
    instrument
Of God
Has to be the aim
Of each and every God-seeker.

2401

Nothing forever remains the
    same.
This darkest night of my mind
Shall pass—
I know, I know.

2402

I do not pray to God
To weaken my enemies.
I pray to God
To illumine them.

2403

God wants me to build
A special Heaven
For me and my
    oneness-heart-friends
Here on earth
And nowhere else.

2404

No heart
Is too weak
To receive Love
From God.

2405

No life
Is too insignificant
To love
And serve God.

2406

The mind's proudest verdict:
God does not know
What the mind does.

2407

The heart's humblest opinion:
God not only knows
What the heart does
In every detail,
But also inspires the heart
To do everything
Lovingly, soulfully
And self-givingly.

2408

My heart-breath
Secretly and sacredly treasures
My sleepless love of God
And my breathless service to
    God.

MY CHRISTMAS-NEW YEAR-VACATION-ASPIRATION-PRAYERS

2409

My Lord Supreme
Is not at all interested
In listening to my life's
Worthless and useless stories,
But He is extremely eager
To hear my heart-songs
And also extremely eager
To watch my life's
Surrender-dance.

2410

I use my vision-eye
When I am in
The inner world.

2411

I use my mission-heart
When I am in
The outer world.

2412

My Lord,
Please, please, please
Do not allow
My gratitude-heart-flower
Ever to fade!

2413

When I most sincerely pray,
My Lord says to me,
"My child,
You are, indeed,
My Beauty's child."

2414

During my very deep meditation,
God comes to me and says,
"My child,
You are, indeed,
My Duty's hero-warrior."

2415

Love and serve.
Love God the Creator;
Serve God the Creation.
Your life-breath
In God's Heart-World
Will never cease.

2416

I am eagerly waiting for the day
When my God-love,
My God-devotion
And my God-surrender
Will be in full bloom.

2417

My new inner name
Is
God-Blessing-abundance.

2418

My new outer name
Is
God-surrender-ecstasy.

2419

To God,
Nothing is more important
Than my tearful heart
And my blissful eyes.

2420

To increase my love of God
Every day
Is the only way for me
To live divinely on earth.

2421

My mind and I —
When we depend on each other,
We miserably fail.

2422

My heart and I —
When we depend on each other,
We invariably succeed.

2423

My God-obedience
Is my God-given
Golden flute-melody-life.

2424

My God-disobedience
Is the thunder-drum-sound
Cherished by the hostile forces.

2425

My ego-mind
Tries to overrule
My soul's solemn
Judgement-light-utterances
In vain.

2426

My Master reveals
The unseen God to me
At the very right moment.

MY CHRISTMAS-NEW YEAR-VACATION-ASPIRATION-PRAYERS

2427

I must seriously take care
Of my inner health
And my outer life.

2428

The Tears of my Lord's
Compassion-Eye
Strengthen my life
And lengthen my breath.

2429

My love, my devotion
And my surrender —
God has taken them
As His confidants.

2430

My Lord,
Do make me
Your selfless slave
To make me really happy
In this lifetime.

2431

We all must discover
The secret and sacred magnitude
Of each divine thought.

2432

God is ready to discuss with me,
Not about my past,
Not about my future,
But about today.

2433

My real homeland
Is
My God-aspiration-heart.

2434

My Lord,
Do give me another chance!
I am ready for the climb.
This time I shall not fail You.

2435

Long, long ago
You lost God.
You are now
Rediscovering Him.
God is helping you.

2436

In the spiritual life,
Every day, every hour,
Every minute
I must long for
God's inner Guidance
And God's outer Guidance.

2437

God's Compassion-Eye
Blessingfully teaches me
How to cry.

2438

God's Forgiveness-Heart
Blessingfully teaches me
How to smile.

2439

I make no mistake
When I tell the world
That I am all God's.
I make no mistake
When I tell the world
That God is all mine.

2440

My Lord says to me,
"My child,
You are totally mistaken.
You must say
That you are all God
And I am all you, only you."

2441

With every single breath,
My heart and I
Are rising towards
Our Lord Beloved Supreme.

2442

At long last
I am able to enter
Into my life's
Beauty-fragrance-inundated
    horizon.

2443

Transcendence and expansion
Work together
Happily and proudly.

MY CHRISTMAS-NEW YEAR-VACATION-ASPIRATION-PRAYERS

2444

When I offer
My life's power-of-attorney
To my Lord Supreme,
He immediately embraces me
Lovingly, powerfully and
    self-givingly.

2445

A sleepless self-giver-seeker
To humankind
Has no time for himself.

2446

During my deep meditation,
When God-ecstasy appears,
My inefficiency-life
Immediately disappears.

2447

From this moment on,
My Lord shall take His seat
Inside my stupidity-flooded
    mind.

2448

My Lord Supreme
Never says "no"
To me,
But I do say "no"
To Him.

2449

My Lord Supreme
Never doubts me,
But I do doubt Him.

2450

My Lord Supreme
Never insists—
But I do.

2451

Where do I live?
I live in between
My life's eagerness-heart
And my life's intensity-breath
To fulfil my
    Lord Beloved Supreme.

2452

Self-indulgence,
I have nothing to do with you.
I shall see you no more.

2453

Every day my Lord Supreme
Most seriously examines
My mind-purity-capacities.

2454

Every day my Beloved Supreme
Most affectionately feeds
All my necessities.

2455

Desires
Dominate my life.
Aspiration
Elevates my heart.

2456

Every morning
And every evening
I wash my Supreme Lord's Feet
With my devotion-heart-tears,
And then I kiss His Feet
Self-givingly.

2457

Determination
Of the utmost strength
Is needed
For God-realisation.

2458

I do not want to be
A book-knowledge-smart
Man.

2459

I want to be
A heart-wisdom-smart
Seeker.

2460

We all must be
Very, very careful.
Doubt can at any moment
    plunder
All our divine qualities.

2461

Faith-flower-fragrance
Is exquisite.

2462

I must make
My God-dedication-strides
Longer than the longest.

MY CHRISTMAS-NEW YEAR-VACATION-ASPIRATION-PRAYERS

2463

The mind gets tired
Right after
A very short prayer.

2464

The heart does not get tired
Even after
A very long meditation.

2465

The cyclone-violences
In various parts of the world
Can be stopped
By soulful prayers
And powerful meditations.

2466

We need a failure-ignoring
And self-doubt-shunning
    aspiration
To arrive
At our destined Goal.

2467

Today
My God-worship-shrine-heart
Is exceedingly happy and excited,
For soon
My Lord will arrive.

2468

My Lord is telling me
That all my God-dreams
Will definitely become
Reality-blossoms
At His choice Hour.

2469

A true seeker
Is a Heaven-inspired
God-messenger
On earth.

2470

God's invisible blows
Awaken
My life.

2471

God's visible blows
Expedite
My Godward journey.

2472

My Master's acceptance
Of my life
Is God-realisation guaranteed
At God's choicest Hour.

2473

God knows everything
Except one thing:
His Heart has yet to learn
How to exclude
Any human being.

2474

Humanity is either enjoying
Or suffering from
God-faith-eclipse.

2475

The Transcendental God-Height
Is only for the one-pointed
God-seekers, God-lovers
And God-servers.

2476

My Lord Supreme,
Just for a brief moment
Do show me
Your Divinity's
Absolute Splendour.

2477

Until just yesterday
Attachment and I were
Dearest friends,
But now we two have become
Perfect strangers.

2478

My pride-mind says to God,
"God, I need nothing
From You."

2479

My humility says to God,
"My Lord, I need everything
From You, only from You."

2480

Knee-bending
Is needed
To cultivate our God-devotion.

2481

Head-bending
Is needed
To nurture our God-surrender.

MY CHRISTMAS-NEW YEAR-VACATION-ASPIRATION-PRAYERS

2482

God does not want me
To remain asleep
Before His All-Compassion-Eye.

2483

My prayerfulness-heart
And my soulfulness-life
Reveal the closeness
Of my Lord's Heart.

2484

This morning
When I woke up,
I was so excited to see
That I woke up in the Heart
Of my Lord Supreme.

2485

My Lord Supreme,
May my heart follow You,
Your Eye and Your Heart
Wherever You go.

2486

My Lord Supreme,
I have only one prayer:
Do make my heart
As beautiful and pure
As the morning sunrise.

2487

My outer life
Faces the world.
My inner life
Embraces the world.

2488

Genuine and authentic
   spirituality
Knows no
Outer world-cleverness-
   compromise.

2489

Occult power
Is quite often
Drastic and volcanic.

2490

Spiritual power
Is always pure
And absolutely sure.

2491

Action, action—
Preferably heart-action—
All the time!

2492

The Temple of God abides
Inside our life-breath
And nowhere else.

2493

My Lord,
If You have a moment to spare,
I have so many things
To tell You—
Specially all about You.

2494

Every day I feel
My Lord is coming
Closer to me,
For I am constantly singing
His Victory-Song.

2495

To have more inner Blessings
From our Lord Supreme,
We must reduce
Our outer desires.

2496

At every moment
There is a flight
From earth to Heaven.
The plane does not wait
Even for a fleeting second.

2497

O come and bless me,
Infinity's Beauty
And Eternity's Duty!

2498

I must please
My Mother Earth
And my Father Heaven
With my heart's
   aspiration-mountain
And my life's
   dedication-fountain.

2499

My desire-mind
Wants to devour
My aspiration-heart.

2500

My aspiration-heart
Longs to illumine
My desire-mind.

MY CHRISTMAS-NEW YEAR-VACATION-ASPIRATION-PRAYERS

2501

Today my Lord Supreme
Is paying His
   Compassion-flooded
And much-desired Visit
To my heart-home.

2502

My God-devotion
Secretly strengthens
My outer life.

2503

My God-devotion
Sacredly deepens
My inner breath.

2504

To have spiritual experiences
Of the summit-heights
Is quite an easy task
For those who have made
Their unconditional surrender
Lovingly and cheerfully
To God's Will.

2505

My Lord,
I do not need a new face,
But I need a new heart
To love You and please You
In Your own Way.

2506

My Lord,
You have left me alone
In my mind-jungle-cave.
How cruel You are!

2507

My Lord,
It seems that
You think only of Yourself
All the time.
How cruel You are!

2508

Days have run into weeks,
Weeks into months,
Months into years,
Yet You still ignore me,
My Lord.

2509

Those who deliberately
Take the side of darkness
Verily live
In the animal kingdom.

2510

Great men come into the world
To do great things,
Mostly for themselves.

2511

Good men come into the world
Only to do good things
For the world,
And nothing for themselves.

2512

God has repeatedly told me
That He does not want
His Leadership-Command.
He wants only
My friendship-smile.

2513

When my Lord arrives,
My heart-tears
And my soul-smiles
Thrive unimaginably.

2514

O seeker,
Be not discouraged
By your repeated sad failures.
God will give you
Innumerable chances.
You are bound to succeed.

2515

Every morning
And every evening
God comes to me
To examine my purity-mind
And my hospitality-heart.

2516

My heart's devotion-progress
Is my Lord's sleepless
Desire-hunger.

2517

My God-aspiration
Eventually becomes
My God-realisation.

2518

My God-devotion
Ultimately becomes
My God-affection.

MY CHRISTMAS-NEW YEAR-VACATION-ASPIRATION-PRAYERS

2519

My God-surrender
Invariably becomes
My complete God-satisfaction.

2520

I started my spiritual journey
As a God-beggar.
Then I continued
As a God-lover, as a God-server.
Now I am continuing still
As a God-partner.

2521

When I see the sunrise,
The celestial beauty of my soul
Immediately dances before me.

2522

If you admit your failings,
God will without fail invite you
When next time He goes out
    sailing.

2523

A seeker's greatest gift to God
Is his ever-blossoming
Gratitude-heart.

2524

For all the world-problems,
The sleepless self-offering
Of each individual
Is the only answer.

2525

My God-obedience
Is my God-Protection
In my life.

2526

My God-obedience
Is my perfection-delight
In God's Heart.

2527

How I long for the red-letter day
When my Lord Supreme
Will proudly claim me
As His own, very own.

2528

For me to agree with God
Implicitly all the time
Is to keep my mind completely
    shut
And my heart unreservedly open.

2529

An outer life-adventurer
I was.
An inner life-explorer
I now am.

2530

Self-transcendence-joy
Unmistakably knows
No equal.

2531

My heart and I get much more
    joy
When we walk far behind
Our Lord Beloved Supreme
Than when we walk with Him
Side by side.

2532

Each happy thought
Disperses our mind's
Thick and dark clouds.

2533

Alas, my expectation
Quite often enters into
A frustration-abyss.

2534

"Be happy and remain happy.
Forget about your mistakes,
Even the very last one"—
So says my Lord Supreme.

2535

God's morning mirror
Is my aspiration-heart.
God's evening mirror
Is my surrender-life.

2536

God's most favourite Home
Is my ever-blossoming
Gratitude-heart.

2537

I do not need
A world-surprising, giant mind.
I need only
A simple, God-loving heart.

2538

Self-importance-pride:
No, no, no— never!
Self-transcendence-joy:
Yes, yes, yes— ever!

MY CHRISTMAS-NEW YEAR-VACATION-ASPIRATION-PRAYERS

2539

My mind-unlearning desire
And my heart-climbing aspiration
Must go together.

2540

At night
God's Compassion-Eye
   teaches me.
In the morning
God's Oneness-Heart
   examines me.

2541

The earthly races
Are for the God-seekers.
The Heavenly races
Are for the God-discoverers.

2542

Today Heaven is beckoning
My climbing heart-flames.

2543

Today I have become
My God-Breath
To sing and play
In the Heart of His Universe.

2544

Yesterday I buried
All my sorrows, cries, tears
   and sighs
In oblivion-cave.

2545

Within,
Heavenly beauty my heart is.
Without,
Earthly duty my life is.

2546

Time inspires me,
Time aspires in and through me,
Time is affectionate to me
And time is proud of me
Precisely because I most
   sincerely value
The unreserved blessings of time.

2547

Silence speaks.
Silence creates.
Silence fulfils.
Silence becomes
God's choicest Voice.

2548

Be not indifferent.
Be not different.
Be interdependent
If you really want joy
In measureless measure
From your life.

2549

My outer qualification
Is my Lord's Compassion-Eye
In action.
My inner qualification
Is my Lord's Forgiveness-Heart
In action.

2550

We must never, never indulge
In our negativity-mind,
Even for a fleeting moment.

2551

My humility is
My God-fulfilment-capacity
Far beyond my imagination.

2552

I must not delay.
Time does not wait for me.
But my Lord Supreme waits
   for me
Indefinitely, lovingly,
   self-givingly
And unconditionally.
Therefore I love my
   Lord Supreme only
And I need Him only.

2553

My life depends entirely
On God's Compassion-Eye.
God's Heart entirely depends
On my cheerful and delightful
Surrender-breath.

2554

Depression and enthusiasm
Are immediate neighbours.
I must make the right choice.
I must go immediately
And live with enthusiasm
Permanently.

2555

The outer world-recognition-
   beggars
Are failure-emperors
In the inner aspiration-world.

MY CHRISTMAS-NEW YEAR-VACATION-ASPIRATION-PRAYERS

2556

God's Compassion-exploitation
I was.
God's Compassion-distribution
I now am.

2557

Victory to my Supreme!
Victory to my Lord Supreme!
Victory to my Lord Beloved
 Supreme!
Victory to my Lord Beloved
 Absolute Supreme!
Victory, victory, victory!

2558

The soul introduces the seeker
To the Master.
The Master introduces the seeker
To the Absolute Supreme.
The Absolute Supreme
 introduces
The God-realised seeker
To humanity.
Humanity says to the
 God-realised seeker,
"Sorry, I am not ready.
You have come untimely.
You have come long before
 the hour.
You may come and visit me
 once again
After at least 200 years."
The God-realised seeker
 says to humanity,
"Amen!" and adds,
"Humanity, I love you.
Humanity, you I love.
Humanity, I shall love you
Forever and forever and forever."
Finally, the God-realised seeker
 says
To the Absolute Supreme,
"Supreme, my Supreme,
What have You done?
Supreme, my Supreme,
What have I done?"

2559

What I can do,
Poor God cannot do.
God cannot sleep.

2560

What God can do,
Poor me cannot do.
I cannot dream.

2561

Only to please my Lord,
I smile and smile
And smile.

2562

Only to please my soul,
I fly and fly
And fly.

2563

Only to please my heart,
I suffer and suffer
And suffer.

2564

Only to please my mind,
I doubt and doubt
And doubt.

2565

Only to please my vital,
I challenge and challenge
And challenge.

2566

Only to please my body,
I sleep and sleep
And sleep.

2567

Only to please my life,
I struggle and struggle
And struggle.

2568

Only to please myself,
I hide and hide
And hide.

MY CHRISTMAS-NEW YEAR-VACATION-ASPIRATION-PRAYERS

2569

Alas, God's Compassion-Eye
Is no match
For our disobedience-minds
And disobedience-lives.

2570

Each moment
Is a golden opportunity
For me
And for my God-obedience.

2571

The mind shouts.
The heart sprouts.

2572

The mind steals
From God.
The heart feels sorry
For poor God.

2573

Desire cries
Pitifully.

2574

Aspiration flies
Sleeplessly.

2575

The great life
Is not a fate-product.
The great life
Is a determination-achievement.

2576

When I concentrate,
I can feel the presence of my soul
Deep within.

2577

When I meditate,
I can speak to my soul.

2578

When I contemplate,
My Supreme Lord
Becomes extremely proud of me.

2579

I love the joy
Of my life.

2580

God loves the peace
Of my heart.

2581

No escape, no escape!
This is, indeed,
Our human life.

2582

All escape, all escape!
Freedom is, indeed,
The life divine.

2583

The outer happiness comes
Only to go.

2584

The inner happiness
Is an abiding reality.

2585

Speak ill of God;
God will forgive you.

2586

Speak ill of yourself;
The world will not care—
No, not even God.

2587

Torture and frustration
Are ruling the world.

2588

God wants only His Peace-child
To sit
On my meditation-heart-throne.

2589

The aspiration-mountain
Touches and clasps
The summit-heights of Heaven.

2590

God the Forgiveness-Heart
Indulges me.

2591

God the Justice-Eye
Teaches me and perfects me.

MY CHRISTMAS-NEW YEAR-VACATION-ASPIRATION-PRAYERS

2592

Man's life is the pendulum
Between division-night
And oneness-light.

2593

Willingly God lives
Everywhere,
But happily and proudly
    God lives
Only in the aspiration-heart.

2594

My heart and I invoke
Only the Unknowable.

2595

Alas,
I am imprisoned by the things
That I do not have.

2596

The sound of night
Can never feel
The joy of silence.

2597

Immortal
Is the silence-dream
Of the aspiration-heart.

2598

The mind touches
God's Head
To examine.

2599

The heart clasps
God's Feet
To worship.

2600

My soul-dictionary
Does not house
The word 'despair'.

2601

My Lord forgives
All my blunders
Save and except
My disobedience.

2602

My inmost Source
And my topmost Goal
Are one and inseparable.

2603

Today my soul
Has brought me and my heart
To the kingdom of Delight.

2604

My heart and I
Are God's
Love-service-blossoms.

2605

I shall rewrite my life
With my God-surrender-songs.

2606

The love of God
Is everywhere
The same.

2607

The prayers to God
Are almost everywhere
The same.

2608

The meditations on God
Are not the same
Everywhere.

2609

The realisations of God
Are not the same in every
   human being.
Some God-realised souls
Stand at the foot of the tree,
While others remain at the
   middle
Of the God-realisation-tree.
Still others reach the
   topmost branch
Of the God-realisation-tree,

2610

The emptiness of the heart
Is absolutely necessary
For a total God-acceptance,
God-realisation and
God-manifestation.

2611

The aspiration-dreams
Of the seekers
Ceaselessly ascend and ascend.

MY CHRISTMAS-NEW YEAR-VACATION-ASPIRATION-PRAYERS

2612

The realisation-realities
Of a God-realised soul
Sleeplessly blossom and blossom.

2613

My Lord,
I have only one desire:
I wish to place my head at
    Your Feet,
And my head will remain at
    Your Feet
Forever and forever.

2614

Ultimately,
Every human being has to
    surrender
To God's Will,
Willingly or unwillingly.

2615

My Lord says to me,
"My child,
You always make Me laugh.
Can you not make Me smile
Once in a while?"

2616

My Lord says to me,
"My child,
Now that you have made
Your unconditional surrender
Cheerful, complete and perfect,
Your life will be the uppermost
On My list of priorities."

2617

If I do not have
Inner peace,
I shall never be able
To make my Lord Supreme
Proud of me.

2618

Every second
Is a golden opportunity
To make my Lord
The sole Possessor
Of my inner life
And my outer life.

2619

How can I be a loser
On the battlefield of my life
If I have already claimed
My Lord Supreme
As my own, very own?

2620

As my Lord's Compassion-Eye
Thrills me,
Even so, my gratitude-heart
Thrills my Lord.

2621

During the day
I keep myself
Before my Lord's Eye.

2622

During the night
I keep myself
At my Lord's Feet.

2623

In my outer life
God is
His Compassion-Eye.

2624

In my inner life
God is
His Sweetness-Fondness-Heart.

2625

In my higher life
God is
His bright, extremely bright
Satisfaction-Smile.

2626

Yesterday
I was my own
Victory-pride.

2627

Today
I am my Lord's
Victory-Dance.

2628

To my heart's greatest delight,
Wherever I go,
My Lord's Compassion-Eye
Lights my path.

2629

Right from the very beginning
Of my spiritual life,
I saw and knew
That I had two unfailing friends:
God's Compassion-Eye
And
God's Forgiveness-Heart.

MY CHRISTMAS-NEW YEAR-VACATION-ASPIRATION-PRAYERS

2630

Every day
I desire to implore
God's Forgiveness-Heart,
But every day
God wants me to explore
His Heart-Kingdom.

2631

My Lord is taking
My aspiration-heart
Far, far beyond the horizon
Of my earthly life.

2632

My Lord's Eye
Is pulling me and pulling me
Most affectionately upward.

2633

My Lord's Heart
Is pulling me and pulling me
Most proudly inward.

2634

My Lord's Arms
Are pulling me and pulling me
Most unconditionally forward.

2635

My own inner capacities
Frighten me.
My own outer capacities
Sadden me.

2636

My Lord is telling me
That He feeds on my aspiring,
Climbing and flaming heart.

2637

To transform the world,
The God-messengers do
    bring down
The nectar-flooded Messages
From God
Most perfectly.

2638

Alas,
I do not know when and where
I shall start my gratitude-heart
To my Lord Beloved Supreme.

2639

My Lord has promised me
His Golden Shore.
Therefore, I do not mind in
    the least
Travelling through endless
Darkness-nights.

2640

My world-attachment-addiction-
    licence
Has just expired.
I shall never, never, never
    renew it.

2641

No seeker
Will ever be able to escape
From his giant ego-enemy.
The seeker must conquer
This enemy.

2642

Each seeker
Has to be endowed
With an indomitable faith
In God.

2643

Each prayer
Is a flame of my heart
Climbing towards
The highest Heaven.

2644

Each meditation
Is a unique opportunity
For me to establish
My conscious oneness
With my
    Absolute Lord Supreme.

2645

If I am not absolutely sincere
In my prayers
And in my meditations,
How can my soul set fire
To my desire-life-house?

2646

If I really want to make
The fastest progress
In my spiritual life,
My Lord's Compassion-Eye
Is bound to help me
To attempt the impossible task
And be victorious.

MY CHRISTMAS-NEW YEAR-VACATION-ASPIRATION-PRAYERS

2647

Before I pray and meditate,
My soul feeds my heart,
   my mind,
My vital and my body
With a dynamic enthusiasm
And intense eagerness.

2648

Each self-giving action of mine
Immediately becomes
A most beautiful flower
In my Lord's Victory-Garland.

2649

Each time I obey my
   Lord Supreme
Happily and unconditionally,
He comes nearer and nearer,
Proudly and triumphantly,
Towards me.

2650

First I must become
A sleepless and breathless
   God-lover.
Only then can I become
An unmistakable God-winner.

2651

Each life
Is the Beauty
Of God's Love.

2652

Each heart
Is the Fragrance
Of God's Delight.

2653

Nothing puzzles my Lord—
No, not even my
   ingratitude-mind.
But it shocks my heart
Most powerfully.

2654

My Beloved Lord says to me,
"Do not come to Me, My child,
For your perfection.
Just come to Me only
For My own Satisfaction."

2655

When I claim God
As my own, very own,
I give myself
Ten out of one hundred.

2656

When God claims me
As His own, very own,
I give myself
One hundred out of one hundred.
My Compassion-flooded
Lord Beloved Supreme
Does not agree with me.

2657

Desire kills the seeker.
Aspiration revives the seeker.
Aspiration says to the seeker,
"O seeker,
If you really love me,
Then stop loving desire!"

2658

I must stop
My life's desire-train
Immediately.

2659

I must fly
My aspiration-plane
Every day without fail.

2660

Doubt
Is world-torture.
Faith
Is God-rapture.

2661

For a true God-seeker,
Aspiration-world
Is the only world.

2662

We are promoted and honoured
In the inner world
Only when we stop expecting
From the outer world.

2663

My mind cares
Only for power—
God-Power.

2664

My heart cares
Only for the things
That are about God.

MY CHRISTMAS-NEW YEAR-VACATION-ASPIRATION-PRAYERS

2665

My desire
Is my God-lost life.
My aspiration
Is my God-found life.

2666

Alas,
My Lord is still waiting for me,
Even at the eleventh hour.

2667

All my God-dreams
Are flooded
With my God-sweetness-
 fondness-smiles.

2668

My heart hears constantly
God-Whispers:
"Go forward, My child,
 go forward!"

2669

The heart's God-devotion
And the life's God-sweetness
Are inseparable.

2670

The body binds us
Unconsciously and
 unintentionally.

2671

We bind the body
Consciously and purposely.

2672

Many, many, many times
I have come and gone.
Alas, my life is still
A God-forgetfulness-sleep.

2673

Each soul
Is a special God-Dream-Beauty
And God-Reality-Fragrance.

2674

God wants me to pave
My life-road to my destination
With the tears of my heart
And the smiles of my soul.

2675

I have come into the world
To establish my friendship
And not my lordship.

2676

In the dedication-world,
Our swift feet and our
    strong arms
Receive very special Blessings
From God.

2677

A true seeker
Feels sad and miserable
When he is away from
His God-silence-heart-home.

2678

We must cover countless miles
Of aspiration-dedication-road
Before we can arrive
At our God-realisation-
    destination.

2679

God for God's sake—
This is, indeed,
The only perfect choice
In a seeker's life.

2680

An eagerness-God-server
Gets more and more work
From God's proud Heart.

2681

My desire-fulfilment-hunger
Has finally surrendered
To my God-needs.

2682

I must focus only
On my destination,
And not on my mind-hesitation.

2683

God deliberately ignores
Our curiosity-mind-questions.

2684

We have no idea
When the time will arrive.
Time keeps it a top secret.

2685

Every seeker has the capacity
To be tall, very tall,
In inner height.

MY CHRISTMAS-NEW YEAR-VACATION-ASPIRATION-PRAYERS

2686

God does not want to remember
The names
Of proud seekers.

2687

God says to a humble seeker,
"My child,
I want you to use
My own Name."

2688

The foundation of realisation
Is unconditional surrender
To God's Will.

2689

Those who sincerely pray
Will never want to be
On their own.

2690

I came into the world
To pull Heaven down quickly
And push earth up very carefully.

2691

Every morning I meet and greet
God's Compassion-Eye
Most soulfully.

2692

Do not wait
For a new year.
Here and now
Make a fresh start
To realise God.

2693

The heart
Of a true disciple
Is always original.

2694

I do not care for
The name of a seeker,
But I do care for
The God-loving and
   God-caring soul.

2695

It is the hard-earned progress
That endures.

2696

To be independent
Of God's Will
Is an absurdity.

2697

At times
God's Silence
Is the very best answer.

2698

May my life be fed
By my heart's
Sunrise-beauty.

2699

The most effective medicine
Here on earth
Is love unconditional.

2700

Those who live in the
   desire-forest
Will not be allowed to live
In God's Heart-Nest.

2701

The outer books
Cannot cure the world.
The inner book can.
What is the inner book?
Our faith in God and
   in ourselves.

2702

God chose me
To be a lamb, His lamb,
In the inner world.
Now God is preparing me
To be a lion, His lion,
In the outer world.

2703

God wants from me
An action-answer
And not a speech-answer.

2704

Adversity can be
A unique education-helper.

2705

Do not curse the darkness-night.
Try to live always
In the Heart of Light.

MY CHRISTMAS-NEW YEAR-VACATION-ASPIRATION-PRAYERS

2706

Not when I die,
But when I dive deep within,
Will I arrive at
   God's Heart-Door.

2707

My Lord,
To my heart
You are the Lord of Compassion.

2708

My Lord,
To my mind
You are the Lord of Indifference.

2709

My Lord,
To my eyes
You are the Lord
Of ever-transcending Beauty.

2710

My Lord,
To my life
You are the Lord
Of ever-self-giving Duty.

2711

My Lord,
I worship the Beauty unparalleled
Of Your Eye.

2712

My Lord,
I worship the Fragrance exquisite
Of Your Heart.

2713

First dream and dream
And then act and act,
Ceaselessly and unconditionally.

2714

The secret facts
Must be revealed
For the betterment of the world.

2715

The sacred Truth
Must remain unknown,
If so is the Will of God.

2716

In this mortal existence,
The more we can pray,
The more we can meditate,
The sooner we shall be able
 to arrive
At the Feet of God.

2717

Nobody can estimate
How much damage
The seeker's
 disobedience-downfall
Can cause.

2718

God is personally
And compassionately concerned
About my each and every
 heart-breath
In my spiritual life.

2719

When God looks straight
Into my mind,
My mind fearfully cries.

2720

When God looks straight
Into my heart,
My heart immediately starts
Singing and dancing.

2721

An unconditional God-obedience
Is the longest stride
In our spiritual life.

2722

Speaking about God
Is good, very good.

2723

Praying to God
Is, indeed, better.

2724

Surrendering oneself
Totally and unconditionally
To God's Will
Is infinitely the best.

MY CHRISTMAS-NEW YEAR-VACATION-ASPIRATION-PRAYERS

2725

Now that my Lord is teaching me
How to deal with my defeats
And failures,
All my sorrows and all my
  sufferings
Have totally vanished.

2726

Our inner freedom-choice
Comes directly from God.

2727

God tells me
That I need no outer degrees
To become
His choicest instrument.

2728

God tells me
That my invocation
Of His Compassion-Eye
Is absolutely the highest degree
That God will give me
At His choice Hour.

2729

Whenever I forget
  God's Presence
Inside my heart,
My breath becomes
Empty of peace.

2730

My mind-prayers
Have a very, very short breath.

2731

My heart-meditations
Have a longer than the longest
  breath.

2732

When I pray and meditate
  regularly,
God comes down
And charms my eyes and
  my heart.

2733

When I do not pray and meditate
Regularly,
God's Power-Eye alarms me.

2734

At my Master's express
   command,
I have entered into
The God-manifestation-field.

2735

God does not mind
When my mind takes full credit
For our success,
But my soul and my heart
Dislike it vehemently.

2736

To shorten my doubt
And lengthen my faith,
Every day I pray
To my Lord Supreme.

2737

Each approach
To God's Heart-Home
Is special,
Plus unique.

2738

God's Promise-forgetfulness
Is a zero possibility.

2739

God's late Arrival
Is an absurdity.

2740

My mind thinks
That God's Love for my mind
Is not true.

2741

My heart feels
That God's Love for my heart
Is Truth itself.

2742

Today my Lord
Is asking my heart
To be with Him
In creating a happy world.

2743

When the time arrives,
My Lord says
That I must be with Him
While He creates
A perfect world.

MY CHRISTMAS-NEW YEAR-VACATION-ASPIRATION-PRAYERS

2744

My Lord,
I do not want to be
Your worshipper.

2745

My Lord,
I do not want to be
Your adorer.

2746

My Lord,
I do not want to be
Your lover.

2747

My Lord,
I do not want to be
Your server.

2748

My Lord,
I do not want to be
Your soldier.

2749

My Lord,
I do not want to be
Your partner.

2750

My Lord,
I want to be always
Your Compassion-Feet-dreamer.

2751

Every morning
My Lord expects from me
A great surprise.
At noon He expects
A greater surprise.
In the evening He expects
The greatest surprise.
The first surprise:
Sincere tears.
The second surprise:
Sincere smiles.
The third surprise:
Sincere surrender.

2752

God's Flute-Heart-Sweetness
Failed to transform
My life.

2753

God's Thunder-Eye-Kicks
Have transformed
My life.

2754

My prayers
Sweeten
My God-crying heart.

2755

My meditations
Awaken
My sleeping life.

2756

My God-surrender expedites
My God-journey
To my God-Destination.

2757

May each thought of mine
Embody
Rainbow-beauty.

2758

Never wait
For the next aspiration-train—
Never!

2759

O my mind,
You must not try to correct
Others' way of life.

2760

For centuries and centuries,
I depended on human beings.
From now on I shall depend
Only on my
    Lord Beloved Supreme.

2761

The higher visions
Are fast approaching
The God-lovers and God-servers.

2762

Every day God reveals Himself
In a most striking manner
To the sincere God-seekers.

MY CHRISTMAS-NEW YEAR-VACATION-ASPIRATION-PRAYERS

2763

Every day
Is a new heart-cry
Of poor Mother Earth.

2764

Any evil thought
Can extinguish
Our heart's climbing flames.

2765

I prayerfully clasp
My Lord's Compassion-Feet.

2766

My Lord
Most powerfully grasps
My earthbound life.

2767

My Lord invites me
To ride with Him
In His Heart-Car
Only when He sees that
I am no longer interested
In my ignorance-desire-life.

2768

Faith shows surrender
The way to God.

2769

The heart and hope
Are inseparable.
The soul and promise
Are inseparable.

2770

In the inner world,
A God-crying heart
Has the fastest speed.

2771

The soul translates
God's Transcendental Messages
To the heart.
The heart translates
The soul's lofty messages
To the life.

2772

God is all Love,
But alas,
God's Creation
Is empty of love.

2773

An unconditional surrender
Is the solid foundation
Of God-realisation.

2774

God looks here, there
And everywhere
To find a tear-flooded
Heart-seeker.

2775

My God-obedience
And my heart-happiness
Always stay together.

2776

My heart
Always longs to be
At my Lord's Haven-Feet.

2777

God loves to parade
The seeker's fragrance-soul
And beauty-heart.

2778

Each self-giving thought
Is a sacred heart-shrine.

2779

Self-admiration
Is quite common.

2780

God-glorification
Is quite uncommon.

2781

Today God has sent my soul
To sing and dance
On my desire-grave.

2782

God tells me
That nobody has the right
To challenge
My God-gratitude-heart.

2783

My inner God-oneness-freedom
In the midst of
Multifarious outer activities
Draws God's highest admiration.

MY CHRISTMAS-NEW YEAR-VACATION-ASPIRATION-PRAYERS

2784

God has invited me
To be always beside Him
With my unfailing love.

2785

Unless I give myself totally
To God,
How can I become
My true divine self?

2786

I did not come into the world
To prove anything.
I came into the world
To love everyone
And everything.

2787

My earthly source
Is Eternity's Joy.
My Heavenly Source
Is Infinity's Peace.

2788

I follow my heart
Lovingly.

2789

My heart follows my soul
Faithfully.

2790

My soul follows my Lord
Self-givingly.

2791

A divine traveller
Travels only at the Command
Of his Inner Pilot.

2792

Stop thinking!
The problems will
Eventually surrender.

2793

Be patient!
Adversity cannot
Forever last.

2794

O my mind,
There is no such thing
As "unlovable."

2795

To forgive those
Who wrong us
Is to gain our own
God-Satisfaction-advantage.

2796

A self-giving man
Finds himself
In the very Heart-Breath
Of God.

2797

God is never alone.
His self-giving Heart
Always accompanies Him.

2798

The fools know
Only one thing:
How to complain.

2799

The wise ones know
The real thing:
How to remain silent.

2800

God's Love-Ocean
Is only for those
Who promise to God
That He is their only aspiration,
Their only dedication
And their only realisation.

2801

God is always ready
And even eager
To help us discover
Our own uniqueness.

2802

Anything that is human
Is fleeting.

2803

Anything that is divine
Is everlasting.

2804

When there is a battle
Between truth and falsehood,
Rest assured,
The ultimate victory
Goes to the truth.

MY CHRISTMAS-NEW YEAR-VACATION-ASPIRATION-PRAYERS

2805

Alas,
Unworthiness
Secretly and cleverly
Destroys our love of God.

2806

We open our mind-door
To temptation-arrival.

2807

We open our heart-home
To God's Compassion-Arrival.

2808

If God is not sufficient
In our life,
Who else can be?

2809

God never wants
To attract seekers
By performing miracles.

2810

God wants
To attract seekers
By singing the song
Of self-offering.

2811

The mind doubts
God's Smiles.

2812

The heart devours
God's Smiles.

2813

I do not need
A free world-wandering mind.

2814

I need
A free world-loving heart.

2815

The mind is empty
Of the river-beauty.

2816

The heart is full
Of the garden-fragrance.

2817

A God-gratitude-heart
Never wastes time in thinking
Of God-Satisfaction-reward.

2818

The hour has struck
When self-transcendence-joy
Will meet with no obstruction.

2819

God's living Presence
Means
Man's ultimate transformation.

2820

Those who look for God
In a book
Will have to continue
Eternally.

2821

Those who look for God
In the heart,
God fails to hide
From them.

2822

Every morning
I thrive on God's
Compassion-Eye.

2823

During the day
I thrive on God's
Encouragement-Heart.

2824

At night
I thrive on God's
Forgiveness-Feet.

2825

Imagination expedites
God's Arrival
In our hearts.

MY CHRISTMAS-NEW YEAR-VACATION-ASPIRATION-PRAYERS

2826

My Lord,
No matter where You throw me
Out of Your Life,
I always see
That I am deep inside Your
Heart.

2827

May my aspiration-heart-sun
Never set.

2828

May my disobedience-mind-
  clouds
Be dispersed
Sooner than at once.

2829

Goodness
Always surrounds
Our hearts.

2830

The love of the heart
Is accepted
By the four corners
Of the globe.

2831

Not imperfection
But perfection
Hides deep within us.

2832

God does not want
To capture us
With His temptation-snare.

2833

God wants
To capture us
With His Eye's
  Compassion-Care.

2834

O my mind,
Why do you try
To find fault with others?
You will gain nothing,
Absolutely nothing.

2835

My heart
Has gained everything
Precisely because of
Its cheerful oneness with all.

2836

I cannot imagine
How God still has hopes
For me!

2837

My prayers
Cry and cry
To see God's Face.

2838

My meditations
Dive and dive
To feel God's Heart
And become one with God.

2839

Mind-confusion
Destroys
Our purity-hearts.

2840

Complexity and the mind
Never want to remain alone.

2841

We search for everything
But not for our spirit—
The only Real in us.

2842

Hope tells us
To look upwards.

2843

Faith tells us
To look all around.

2844

Promise tells us
To look up first
And then look down
For our God-manifestation.

2845

My Lord's Light
Is repairing my mind, vital
And body,
Which are all out of order.

MY CHRISTMAS-NEW YEAR-VACATION-ASPIRATION-PRAYERS

2846

Silence-light
Is everywhere,
All-pervading.

2847

In the morning
I hear my Lord's
Budding Whispers.

2848

During the day
I hear my Lord's
Blossoming Whispers.

2849

At night
I fulfil my Lord's
Budding, blossoming
And blossomed Whispers.
I become absolutely one
With my Lord's Will.

2850

When I choose my soul,
Only my soul,
My desire-life ceases.

2851

When I choose my heart,
Only my heart,
I feel my Lord
Is next door.

2852

When I choose my mind,
Only my mind,
I immediately become blind.
Darkness I feel all-where.

2853

My aspiring realities
Originated
In the Heart of my
    Lord Supreme.

2854

My desiring realities
Originated
Inside my mind.

2855

When I run towards my Lord
For protection,
I give my Lord's Heart
Immense joy.

2856

God most affectionately
Embraces
All our positive thoughts.

2857

God gives
A Thunder-Kick
To our negative thoughts.

2858

I am
A devoted partner
Of my soul-fragrance.

2859

I am
An affectionate partner
Of my heart-beauty.

2860

My Lord,
I am praying to You
To give me a clear path
And an easy way to go forward.

2861

O seeker,
Dive inward
Bravely.

2862

O seeker,
Go forward
Self-givingly.

2863

O seeker,
Go upward
Eagerly.

2864

The unruly mind
Is apt to destroy
My heart-blossoms.

2865

Be faithful
When you feel
That God is not near you.

MY CHRISTMAS-NEW YEAR-VACATION-ASPIRATION-PRAYERS

2866

Be soulful
When God
Is right in front of you.

2867

Be prayerful
When you feel
That God is right inside you.

2868

If anything is destined to succeed
In my life,
Then it is my God-faith.

2869

Failure is quite normal
And natural.
Why do we then
Pay so much attention
To failure?

2870

Every day God gives us
Ample opportunity and capacity
To unearth our divinity's life.

2871

Death is not
The end.
Death is
Our silence-friend.

2872

Death
Has an end.
Life
Is an eternal flow.

2873

My Lord tells me
That my God-obedience
Is far beyond all boundaries.

2874

God's Justice-Eye
Quite often
Takes a vacation.

2875

The complacent life
Of a spiritual seeker
Is extremely destructive.

2876

Sincere aspiration-seekers
Always succeed.

2877

A God-obedience-life
Is an inner beauty
And an outer beauty as well.

2878

God's Compassion-Train
Carries to the Destination
Only those who have implicit
   faith
In God's Compassion.

2879

God wants every seeker
To be for the whole world
And for all time.

2880

My cheerful surrender
To God's Will
Is an express train
To God's Feet.

2881

Our aspiration-moments
Expedite
Our God-arrival.

2882

Remember,
Your heart-beauty-smile
Is for all.

2883

Cheerfulness
Is
A most remarkable beginning.

2884

Never allow
Your aspiration-speed
To slow down.

2885

A heart-love finds itself
In the heart
Of everybody's love.

MY CHRISTMAS-NEW YEAR-VACATION-ASPIRATION-PRAYERS

2886

Life is not
A helpless cry.
Life is
A brave journey.

2887

Inside my self-reliance,
Uncertainty
Looms large.

2888

Inside my God-reliance,
My soul rings
My victory-bell.

2889

If you do not want to be homeless
In your spiritual life,
Then consciously place your heart
And your life-breath
In the Heart-Home
Of your Lord Supreme.

2890

Our God-security
Lives at two places:
Inside our soul-heights
And inside our heart-depths.

2891

God says to my heart,
"Welcome, welcome,
My aspiration-child!"

2892

My faith can open up
God's Heart-Door
At any time.

2893

Do not blame anybody
For this world.
The world is entirely
God's Creation.

2894

Everything that is good
I cherish.

2895

Everything that is bad
I consciously and deliberately
Leave behind.

2896

The way misfortune dogs us,
Can we not dog the divine ideas
In exactly the same way?

2897

The desire-world
Is always empty
Of reality.

2898

My realisation-elevator
Reaches the highest floor,
Where God accumulates
All His world-
 transformation-Dreams.

2899

I am a proud
God's Compassion-Feet-beggar.

2900

God does not appreciate me
When I say that His Creation
Is beyond repair.

2901

My prayer
Is
My life-song.

2902

My meditation
Is
My heart-sunlight.

2903

The world is full
Of one thing:
Ignorance-prisons.

2904

My gratitude-heart
Is
My soul-beauty's flower.

2905

War breaks.
God cries.

MY CHRISTMAS-NEW YEAR-VACATION-ASPIRATION-PRAYERS

2906

God's favourite child, Peace,
Consoles God
By promising a new world
Empty of war.

2907

How long can my mind hide
My Lord's Victory-Banner—
How long?

2908

My desire
Wants
World-attractions.

2909

My false aspiration
Wants
World-attention.

2910

My sincere aspiration
Desires
God-Affection.

2911

I desire God's Manifestation-
fulfilment-determination.

2912

Aspiration goes up
High, higher, highest.

2913

Transformation goes
Around and around,
Here, there and everywhere.

2914

Disobedience
Is a seeker's
Spiritual death-cancer.

2915

The negativity-mind
Rightly deserves
An immediate grave.

2916

Do not worry—
God will return to your heart.
Just be careful this time!

2917

I dearly love
My soul's constant
God-fulfilling dreams.

2918

How I wish
I could be
One choice dream
Of my Lord Supreme!

2919

I wish to become
A genuine God-lover
And God-server.

2920

God wants me to be
Nothing other than
His sleepless and breathless
   partner.

2921

May my life be a heart
Of humility-flower.

2922

My Lord,
How can we ever deserve
Your Love,
How can we?

2923

My Lord,
You do not need me
For anything,
But to give me importance
In Your Mission,
You make me feel
That I am indispensable.

2924

Not through mere words,
But by constant selfless actions
I must please my Lord.

2925

My Lord wants me to
   communicate
With my brothers and sisters
Of the world
With tremendous affection,
Love and concern.

MY CHRISTMAS-NEW YEAR-VACATION-ASPIRATION-PRAYERS

2926

Every day
A new lotus petal
Is blossoming
In my heart of aspiration.

2927

Every day
I must give a most beautiful smile
To my Beloved Supreme,
And also receive from Him
His most beautiful Smile.

2928

Every day
Can be a golden opportunity
To transform my mind
And purify my life.

2929

I try and try and try
To follow the stars
Of my heart-sky.

2930

Self-offering
Without expectation
Is a happier than the happiest
Experience.

2931

My Lord is telling me
That happier and brighter days
Are ahead of me.

2932

As long as I can offer
Any kind of service
To my Lord Supreme,
I shall be extremely happy.

2933

My Lord teaches me
How to take giant strides
Towards His
Peace-Bliss-flooded Abode.

2934

We must not allow
Earthly trivia
To delay our inner progress.

2935

My Lord,
I want only Your Happiness,
Only in Your own Way.

2936

Today
My Lord has given me
Two new eyes
To see His Divinity.

2937

Today
My Lord has given me
One new heart
To feel His Divinity.

2938

Today
My Lord has given me
One new life
To worship His Divinity.

2939

Today
My Lord has given me
One new hope
To climb up and reach
His Heart-Home
And bring down His
    Divinity's Light
To spread all over the world.

2940

Intensity
My prayer-eyes need.

2941

Immensity
My meditation-heart needs.

2942

Integrity
My service-life needs.

2943

The human in us cries
For the divine in us
To smile.

2944

The divine in us cries
For the human in us
To follow the divine.

2945

Nothing is more satisfying
Than our sleepless
Self-giving.

MY CHRISTMAS-NEW YEAR-VACATION-ASPIRATION-PRAYERS

2946

Our God-surrender
Breaks down our mind's
Ignorance-walls.

2947

God trains
The human in us
And welcomes
The divine in us.

2948

O my God-questioning mind,
Do not dare to darken
My heart-door any more.

2949

My God-faith-heart-flower
Has fully blossomed today.

2950

My God-Destination
Is powerfully beckoning
My heart's aspiration-cries.

2951

Earth-expectation
Extinguished,
Heaven-realisation
Blossomed.

2952

My Lord teaches me
How to ride
The life-dedication-wave.

2953

My aspiration-bird
Is learning from my soul
How to soar high, higher, highest
And fly fast, faster, fastest.

2954

Devotion
Is sweetness
Immeasurable.

2955

Sweetness
Is never to be found
In the life of darkness.

2956

God lives inside
My entire being,
But He prefers to live
Inside my heart-home.

2957

Every seeker's heart
Must be
A God-gratitude-fountain.

2958

For sleepy eyes
There is no real God.

2959

God loves to give a feast
For the aspiring souls
Every day.

2960

The mind says
That God
Is an unsolicited Adviser.

2961

The mind never prays
To God
For His Advice.

2962

A long inner journey
Inspires my soul.

2963

A long inner journey
Encourages my heart.

2964

A long inner journey
Discourages my mind.

2965

A long inner journey
Disheartens my vital.

2966

A long inner journey
Frightens my body.

MY CHRISTMAS-NEW YEAR-VACATION-ASPIRATION-PRAYERS

2967

I promised my Lord
To meet Him here
In the heart of Mother Earth.
Alas, I have not kept
My promise.

2968

My Lord promised
To give me a Smile
Every day on earth.
Alas, my Lord has not kept
His Promise.

2969

My God-communion
My mind does not even want
To understand.

2970

My God-communion
My heart eagerly
And sleeplessly treasures.

2971

God does not judge
Any seeker's competence.

2972

God judges
The seeker's readiness,
Willingness and eagerness.

2973

An aspiration-heart
Deliberately disregards
Its sleep.

2974

A seeker
Takes God's every Wish
As his solemn command.

2975

If you need God
Only for yourself,
Then you can make friends
With Eternity.

2976

The higher we go,
The quicker we grow
Young in our hearts again.

2977

The desire-experiences
Of my life
Come and go.

2978

The aspiration-experiences
Of my life
Always remain.

2979

My heart is well acquainted
With my Lord's
Satisfaction-Heart.

2980

I adore
My Lord's
Beautiful Eye.

2981

I worship
My Lord's
Merciful Feet.

2982

If you want to explain
God's Will,
You are bound to fail.

2983

God's Heart and my heart
Always live
A very, very, very simple life.

2984

My God-surrender-life
Is not
My mental hallucination—
It is Reality itself.

2985

Alas,
There are so many things
In life
That remain
Insoluble mysteries.

2986

My purity-heart
Is exactly the same as it was
Half a century ago.

MY CHRISTMAS-NEW YEAR-VACATION-ASPIRATION-PRAYERS

2987

Sweet
Is my Lord's Eye.

2988

Sweeter
Is my Lord's Heart.

2989

Sweetest
Are my Lord's Feet.

2990

To say that I will try
Is nothing short of a joke.

2991

To say that I must
Is, indeed, the brave utterance
Of a real seeker.

2992

It seems that
To have an enduring bliss
On earth
Is almost an impossible task.

2993

Peace
Is founded upon
Forgiveness.

2994

When my heart
Starts blooming,
My Absolute Lord Supreme
Starts dancing.

2995

When we harmonise anything,
We divinise it
At the same time.

2996

What have I been doing?
I have been taking shelter
At my Lord's Nectar-Feet.

2997

Pleasure-comfort
Is fleeting.

2998

Sacrifice-joy
Is everlasting.

2999

Nothing to hide,
Save and except
Our sleep-body.

3000

Nothing to hide,
Save and except
Our aggression-vital.

3001

Nothing to hide,
Save and except
Our suspicion-mind.

3002

Nothing to hide,
Save and except
Our insecurity-heart.

3003

Nothing to hide,
Save and except
Our pride-life.

3004

The mind is extremely afraid
Of raising itself
Upward.

3005

Lengthen and strengthen
Your heart-wings
If you want to fly
All over the world.

3006

Satisfaction lies
Only between my heart's cries
And my Lord's Smiles.

3007

The fragrance of my heart
Is
My morning God-satisfaction.

3008

No more do I have
The mind-knowledge-thirst.
I am all my heart-hunger
For the golden dust
Of my Lord's Feet.

MY CHRISTMAS-NEW YEAR-VACATION-ASPIRATION-PRAYERS

3009

We can open up earth's heart
And Heaven's Heart
All at once
If we can breathe in
   God's Victory
At every moment.

3010

Fear hides,
Only to arrest and capture us
At its choice time.

3011

May my heart long
For one brief glimpse
Of my Lord Supreme.

3012

Never forget
Your patience-exercise.
All other exercises
You can forget,
But not your patience-exercise.

3013

Justice-Light
Is God's
Absolutely last Choice.

3014

God tells me
That He is eager
To be the slave
Of my surrender-joy.

3015

To be a genuine
God-seeker,
No price is too great.

3016

A path-finder
Is, indeed,
A God-binder.

3017

God's blissful Eye
God unreservedly shares
With the world.

3018

Only sincere heart-seekers
Can see
God's golden Throne.

3019

A limitation-mind
Is
A frustration-life.

3020

My inner life
Is
An indomitable power.

3021

I never cared
And I will never care
For countless sounds.

3022

I care only
For boundless silence.

3023

Only silence-joy
Can show us the way
To God-realisation.

3024

When I pray to God
To come down,
He tells me,
"Come up, come up,
My child!
This place
Is infinitely safer."

3025

Every day
God wants me
To spring a new surprise
On Him.

3026

The ingratitude
Of the mind
Is ruthlessly shocking.

3027

Sleeplessly I keep
My heart-room open
For my Lord Supreme.

3028

I search
For God-closeness
Everywhere.

MY CHRISTMAS-NEW YEAR-VACATION-ASPIRATION-PRAYERS

3029

I search
For God-oneness
Deep within.

3030

Heaven showers Blessings
Upon me
Every morning.

3031

Every morning
I treasure my Lord's Feet
More than I treasure
My Lord's Eye.

3032

When I am all aspiration,
My Lord is all action
In and through me.

3033

The mind wants me
To be a member
Of its world-division-club.

3034

The heart wants me
To be a member
Of its world-oneness-assembly.

3035

O sorrow,
Do not shadow
My heart!

3036

O joy,
Do make me
Your cherished toy!

3037

Each human being
Is either God's
Recognised representative
Or God's
Unrecognised representative.

3038

God tells me
That I must give myself away—
Not to everybody,
But to the chosen few.

3039

The moment Divinity
Touches the earth,
Humanity either remains
Fast asleep
Or wakes up slowly,
Very slowly.

3040

Be careful
Of the doubting mind!
It can spread like wildfire
Everywhere.

3041

When I do not pray to God
For devotion,
I feel myself to be
A poor street-beggar.

3042

I must climb up
The aspiration-mountain-summit
During my lifetime.

3043

Anything that is simple
Embodies the natural Beauty
Of God.

3044

The supremacy of the mind
Will without fail
One day collapse.

3045

May my inner courage
Never desert me.

3046

I do not want my faith
To be fruitful.
I want my faith
To be Godful.

3047

We cannot really
Surprise God,
But He pretends
To be surprised
Even at our minor success.

3048

I long only to have
God's Compassion-Eye
And God's Forgiveness-Heart
In my heart-home.

MY CHRISTMAS-NEW YEAR-VACATION-ASPIRATION-PRAYERS

3049

The mind shocks God
By not accepting immediately
God's Light.

3050

I have closed the long distance
Between me and my Lord
With my sleepless and breathless
Surrender.

3051

I must always keep
My aspiration-heart-standard
As high as possible.

3052

There is no other way
To develop my closeness to God
Than with my prayerful
And tearful eyes.

3053

When I touch
God's Forgiveness-Feet,
God immediately opens up
His Compassion-Eye.

3054

The modern life
Is blindly racing
Towards a goalless goal.

3055

When I pray to God
For His Victory,
He immediately blesses me
With two inspiration-wings
And one aspiration-heart.

3056

When the heart, the mind and
   the vital
Become real friends,
The soul dances ecstasy's dance.

3057

Self-effacement
Is the first step
In our self-exploration.

3058

Alas,
My heart and my mind
Have extreme
Opinion-differences.

3059

I see the authenticity
Of light
Even in the darkest night.

3060

Not "Go alone"
But "Go together with all"
Should be our last
And lasting experience.

3061

I love my heart's service
And not
My life's servitude.

3062

Infinity, Eternity and
   Immortality
Live together most amicably.
They are divinely and supremely
Bound to one another.

3063

Difficulties arise,
But we must make them feel
That we are destined
To reach a destination
Where they will not be able
To accompany us.

3064

I see my Lord dancing
Inside
His own Infinity's Smile.

3065

Light and Power together
Are most significant
Representatives of God
Here on earth.

3066

Only the heart-eye
Does not have
The fear of death.

3067

Life asks death
Many questions,
But death never answers.

3068

When I stopped looking
At the face of expectation,
A mighty transformation
Took place in my life.

MY CHRISTMAS-NEW YEAR-VACATION-ASPIRATION-PRAYERS

3069

Knowledge-facts
Have to bow their heads
In humility
To wisdom-light.

3070

Wisdom-light
Has to bow its head
In humility
To a fleeting Smile of God.

3071

We can never imagine how strong
Are the walls
Of our mind's inconscience.

3072

My Lord's invisible Eye
Is behind
His visible Smiles.

3073

My Inner Pilot
Makes all the decisions
Of my outer life.

3074

The mind-doubt-arrows
Cannot penetrate
The silence of the heart.

3075

Only the aspiration-fire
Can burn down
The mind's ignorance-walls.

3076

I must love
The unloved ones—
I must.

3077

Curiosity
Is
A progress-extinguisher.

3078

A self-giving heart
Is
Beauty unparalleled.

3079

Faith has the capacity
To pass through
The darkest tunnels.

3080

Pure humility
Is absolutely necessary
To make progress
In the spiritual life.

3081

A desire-life,
Indeed,
Is an abysmal abyss-life.

3082

Intellectual excellence
I want not.

3083

Spiritual excellence
I want,
I need,
At every moment.

3084

When our surrender is complete,
We are assured by God Himself
Of our certain victory.

3085

No enemy
Can forever remain
Infallible.

3086

My Lord tells me
That my life's perfection-hours
Are fast approaching me.

3087

There are no real surprises
In the self-giving life.

3088

Pure thoughts
Have enormous capacity
To turn our vices
Into virtues.

MY CHRISTMAS-NEW YEAR-VACATION-ASPIRATION-PRAYERS

3089

We want to manifest
The Divine within us.
Alas, we are manifesting
The animal within us
Instead.

3090

The present-day life
Is made of
Superficialities.

3091

God breaks the sad news:
I must work very hard
To make my inner progress.

3092

A good thought
Can easily champion
A good cause for us.

3093

My heart-room
Is full of
God-dreams.

3094

We must discard
All our regrets—
Past and present.

3095

Alas,
I do not know
When the face of doubt
Will fade away.

3096

The desire-river
Has no destination.

3097

Each good thought
Carries
My aspiration-seeds.

3098

Our mind-forest
Is empty of
God-Smile.

3099

Desire-life we had.
What we need now
Is the speed of aspiration-life.

3100

God and I treasure
Our whisper-messages.

3101

Cheerfulness
Is the very beginning
Of a fulness-life.

3102

A very long distance
Separates our dream-heart
From our reality-life.

3103

God-obedience
Reminds us
Of our roots.

3104

God-obedience
Gives us wings
To fly in the sky
Of God's Love.

3105

I cannot recollect
When I started walking
Along God's Road,
And I have no idea
When it will ever end.

3106

I always live
In between
My prayerful tears
And my soulful smiles.

3107

Our God-realisation
Cannot remain a far cry
If our prayers and meditations
Breathe in
Simplicity, sincerity,
Intensity and immensity.

MY CHRISTMAS-NEW YEAR-VACATION-ASPIRATION-PRAYERS

3108

Do not delay,
Even for a fleeting moment,
When God asks you
To do something.
If you delay,
That means you have reached
The height of your stupidity
And the length of your audacity.

3109

Everything else
Can be divided,
But not our devotion.
Our devotion
Has to be undivided.

3110

My heart feels miserable
The day it fails to keep
Its closest connection
With my soul.

3111

My Lord,
I do not know
Why You are allowing me
To enjoy
A sleeping life.

3112

Aspiration has to be
Totally empty
Of unwillingness.

3113

Sympathy has to be
The living philosophy
Of each seeker's life.

3114

As God's Compassion
Is infinite,
Even so, I must have
Receptivity boundless.

3115

Anything that God gives us
In the inner life
Is always free of charge.

3116

God takes only
One religion seriously,
And that religion
Is our love of God.

3117

My heart-devotion
Imports all the divine qualities
From Heaven.

3118

We have not come into the world
To renounce anything.
We have come into the world
To announce only one thing:
God's constant Victory.

3119

Real aspiration
Is an ever-climbing flame
From the heart.

3120

Selfless service
And intense prayer—
There is no difference.

3121

Each moment
Is a God-sent opportunity

For us to become
God's supremely choice
    instruments.

3122

God does not come alone.
When He comes to visit us,
His brighter than the brightest
Smile
Accompanies Him.

3123

Without a God-obedience-mind,
We cannot go very far.

3124

God-realisation
Is neither an empty book
Nor a sealed book.

3125

My heart-cries
Are very strong
Godward pulls.

3126

My soul-smiles
Are very powerful
Ignorance-pushes.

MY CHRISTMAS-NEW YEAR-VACATION-ASPIRATION-PRAYERS

3127

My heart-road
Is paved with God-devotion
From the beginning to the end.

3128

Only genuine seekers
Are blessed with God's
Heart-telephone line.

3129

Silence and peace
Every day visit
Each other.

3130

To be always on God's side
Is not an act of blindness,
But of an ever-blossoming
Wisdom-heart.

3131

I just love the way
My heart loves God,
Thinks of God
And prays to God.

3132

We are all eternal seekers,
But unfortunately
We are not aware of it.

3133

Each inner seeking
Needs
A new inner way.

3134

I long for experiences
In my Heavenward journey.

3135

The ancient pilgrims
Had a most sublime goal.

3136

The modern travellers
Do not care for any goal.

3137

God wants every seeker
To be his own
Pathfinder.

3138

Humanity can move forward
Fast, very fast,
If it can listen to the dictates
Of the Divinity within.

3139

I am a reader
Of only inner books:
Love, devotion, surrender.

3140

We can make our heart rich,
Very rich,
By becoming a flood
Of God-tears.

3141

God takes very seriously
A disobedience-mind.

3142

There is no way to call God
By the wrong name.

3143

If we can smile
Soulfully and self-givingly,
God's Compassion-Eye
And
God's Satisfaction-Heart
Will always accompany us.

3144

Every day I pray to God
For His Satisfaction,
And not for my promotion.

3145

The outer world
Does not care for my help,
Yet I am eager to help.

3146

The inner world
Needs my service desperately.
Alas, I am nowhere to be found!

3147

The more hunger we have
For the fulfilment of our
    desire-life,
The sooner we become
    impoverished
In our inner life.

MY CHRISTMAS-NEW YEAR-VACATION-ASPIRATION-PRAYERS

3148

Aspiration-quality
And dedication-quantity
I long for.

3149

May I live all the time
In the beauty of patience
And
In the fragrance of silence.

3150

Devotion
Is the heart's
Most precious wealth.

3151

I hide
When I am in
My desire-life.

3152

I get an ecstasy-ride
When I am in
My aspiration-heart.

3153

Never take a false start
In your aspiration-race.

3154

There can be nothing
More natural
Than our meditation-dive.

3155

I am happy
Because my life
Is an inspiration-fountain.

3156

I am happy
Because my heart
Is an aspiration-mountain.

3157

The soul-singers
Are God's choicest singers.

3158

The heart-singers
Are God's choice singers.

3159

The mind-singers
Are God's failure-singers.

3160

The vital-singers
Are God's Heart-collapse-singers.

3161

The body-singers
Are God's stranger-singers.

3162

I am, at once,
God's satisfaction-singer
And
God's frustration-singer.

3163

I am God's satisfaction-singer
When I sing
Only for God.

3164

I am God's frustration-singer
When I sing
Only for
The thunder-applause of
   humanity.

3165

When I look beyond
All I have ever known,
God gives me
His sweetest Smile.

3166

When I give to the world
Far beyond my intended
   willingness,
God immediately embraces me
And tells me:
"My child, you are, indeed,
My tomorrow's
Golden Dream-Boat-passenger."

3167

Intensity
Shows me the Way.

3168

Immensity
Leads me to the Goal.

MY CHRISTMAS-NEW YEAR-VACATION-ASPIRATION-PRAYERS

3169

God's Compassion-Eye
Lifts us high, very high,
With a single Glance,
But, alas, we prefer to come
  down.

3170

My complete surrender
To God's Will
Is God's proudest
And happiest news.

3171

Individuality-lovers
Are
Universality-strangers.

3172

The affection
Of the heart
Is the sunshine
Of life.

3173

In the morning,
My heart is
A God-worship-flower-beauty.

3174

In the evening,
My life is
A God-surrender-flower-
  fragrance.

3175

I enjoy
My heart's God-beauty-tears
And
My life's God-duty-smiles
Equally and unreservedly.

3176

With my sobbing eyes
I touch
My Lord's Feet.

3177

With my throbbing heart
I feel
My Lord's Heart.

3178

Clasp,
Clasp God's Feet
If you want to grasp
God's Beauty.

3179

The source of real greatness
Is humility's beauty.

3180

The source of real goodness
Is the fragrance
Of selflessness.

3181

Like Eternity,
Our longing for Eternity
Also shall know no bounds.

3182

Quite often
Our expectations are found
In wasteland-debris.

3183

Compassion from Above,
Aspiration from below
Together
Are miracle-performers.

3184

I must hear
At least once in my life
My soul's sweetest
God-satisfaction-song.

3185

Not our renunciation-mind,
Not our possession-life,
But our God-Creation-
    acceptance-heart
The Lord Supreme treasures.

3186

Wandering through
    ignorance-night
Is the very beginning
Of God-Light-invocation.

3187

Divinity's journey begins
Only after the transcendence
Of all man-created
    jungle-confusion.

3188

Counterfeit sincerity
An unaspiring life is.

MY CHRISTMAS-NEW YEAR-VACATION-ASPIRATION-PRAYERS

3189

My mind, get up,
My vital, get up,
My body, get up
Immediately,
And start going God's Way—
The only Way.

3190

The seeker needs
Many, many, many God-dreams
Long before he meets with God
In reality.

3191

Each time we meditate,
The very first thing
We have to invoke
Is peace.

3192

My heart lives in between
My God-surrender
And my God-bliss.

3193

Every morning
Is a God-sent
Unprecedented opportunity.

3194

Our sincere aspiration
Is the source
Of genuine God-hunger.

3195

The red light
Fights against ignorance-night
To establish
God's Victory on earth.

3196

The white light
Illumines
Ignorance-night.

3197

The blue light
Devours
Ignorance-night.

3198

God's Compassion-Eye
Watches me.

3199

God's Justice-Mind
Catches me.

3200

God's Forgiveness-Heart
Liberates me.

3201

Alas, God-awareness
Is still individual
And not universal.

3202

The sadness
Of Mother Earth
Has an undying breath.

3203

There is no dearth of
False smiles—
False smiles are all-where.

3204

My Lord,
I am too weak
To be crushed
By Your Indifference-Feet.

3205

My heart-sun
Knows no eclipse.

3206

Alas, I have no idea
When I became fond
Of my expectation-mind.

3207

Our God-surrender
Has the longest
Progress-strides.

3208

We suffer so much daily
From our uncertainty-mind,
Yet we allow it to linger.

3209

I live in between
My laughable mind
And
My lovable heart.

3210

Alas, we have nothing better to do
Than to blame God
For our failure-sadness-life.

MY CHRISTMAS-NEW YEAR-VACATION-ASPIRATION-PRAYERS

3211

The mind always lives
In the lip-deep prayers.

3212

God tells me that my task
Is to encourage the seeker,
And that His Task
Is to perfect the seeker.

3213

I touch God's Feet
Only to be embraced
By God's Heart.

3214

God's Strictness-Mind
Is for
The chosen few.

3215

God's Compassion-Eye
Is for
All and sundry.

3216

In God's Heart,
Each seeker
Is unique.

3217

Each and every pilgrim
Needs must visit
God's Heart-Temple.

3218

The unaspiring
And undivine thoughts
Never wait for an invitation.

3219

Our God-surrender-train
Runs the fastest
Towards the Destination.

3220

The doubt-door
Has to be kept closed tight
All the time.

3221

Spirituality does not house
A narrowness-mind
And a shallowness-life.

3222

Doubt-storms
Cannot sink
Faith-ocean liners.

3223

God's Heart
Gives a wide berth
To stark complainers.

3224

Each God-realised soul
Is
A mighty mankind-fort.

3225

Renunciation
Is a philosophy
Alien to my heart.

3226

God wants
Only the most devoted seekers
To strike
His Victory-Drum.

3227

In the spiritual life,
An intellectual and powerful
   mind
Can be a great obstacle.

3228

There is not a single moment
That is not ready to help us
To please God.

3229

I swim in the tears
Of my earth-bound life
And in the smiles
Of my Heaven-free dreams.

3230

Meditation
Is by far
The best soul-exercise.

MY CHRISTMAS-NEW YEAR-VACATION-ASPIRATION-PRAYERS

3231

Aspiration
Is by far
The best heart-exercise.

3232

Dedication
Is by far
The best life-exercise.

3233

My surrender to God's Will
Is by far
My best exercise.

3234

Our Absolute Lord Beloved
　Supreme
Is all Attention
To the exquisite beauty
Of the seeker's inner life.

3235

Our Absolute Lord Beloved
　Supreme
Is all Pride
In the unprecedented fragrance
Of the seeker's inner breath.

3236

God's Heart-Doors
Do not believe in
Even one single lock.

3237

The mind's brilliance
Dazzles.
The heart's aspiration
Radiates.

3238

To my greatest joy,
I am not a beginner
But an adept
In the world-service-game.

3239

Only to the sleepless self-givers
God gives the golden opportunity
To shoulder His Responsibilities.

3240

I need help,
And I get inner Help from God
And outer help from man.
Left to myself,
I shall not succeed
In any field of God-manifestation
Here on earth.

3241

Every morning
And every evening
I pray to be a foot soldier
Of my Lord Supreme.

3242

The mind envies
The success of the world.
The heart embraces
The progress of the world.

3243

My powerful smiles
Please God.
My helpless tears
Please God equally.

3244

Each God-lover
Is a sunrise-heart
And not a sunset-life.

3245

I am a God-beggar
At God's Feet.

3246

I am not a man-beggar
At man's door.

3247

Early retirement-enjoyment
Is the height of stupidity.

3248

My heart, do not despair!
God's Compassion-
    Concern-Heart
Is fast approaching you.

3249

God says to me,
"My child,
Your aspiration deserves
A round of applause."

3250

God says to me,
"My child,
Your dedication deserves
A standing ovation."

MY CHRISTMAS-NEW YEAR-VACATION-ASPIRATION-PRAYERS

3251

God says to me,
"My child,
Your manifestation of My Light
Deserves man's greatest
    admiration
And My proudest Blessings."

3252

My love-devotion-surrender-life
With no gratitude
Is my God-failure-ineptitude.

3253

The giant mind
Eventually topples.
The tiny heart
Eventually triumphs.

3254

In the spiritual life,
God-faith is the armour
And God-surrender is the
    warrior.

3255

God says, "No!"
God's Eye says, "Yes!"
God's Heart says,
"Come in, My child, come in!"

3256

This morning
My heart's love-affection-stadium
Has invited all God-seekers
And all God-lovers.

3257

My Lord,
I am
Because Your Heart
Affectionately and sleeplessly is.

3258

Truth-telling people
I love.
Truth-seeking people
I need.

3259

Each good thought
Is
A new vision-pathfinder.

3260

Life is not
The supremacy-power of man.
Life is
The Compassion-Shower of God.

3261

I am true to myself.
Therefore I am exceedingly
    happy.
I am true to God.
Therefore I am a perfection-bud.
If I continue
To remain true to God,
Then there shall come a time
When I shall grow into
A perfect perfection-blossom.

3262

My morning dawns
With a hope-panorama.

3263

Each soul starts
From a different plane
Of consciousness,
But at the end of the journey,
All arrive at the same destination.

3264

My mind,
I command you—
Stop at once what you are doing
And follow God!

3265

When we do not try
Our very best,
We are compelled to have
A God-empty life-road.

3266

God picks
Our gratitude-flowers
From our ingratitude-thorns.

3267

My Lord, can I?
"No!"
My Lord, shall I?
"No!"
My Lord, must I?
"Yes!
You must, from this very
    moment,
Embark
On the God-realisation-journey."

3268

At God's Feet
The mind not only survives
But also thrives.

MY CHRISTMAS-NEW YEAR-VACATION-ASPIRATION-PRAYERS

3269

A true devotion-tree
Is bound to produce
Nectar-fruits.

3270

My Lord Supreme,
I need from You
A receptivity-plant
In my heart-garden,
And not a receptivity-implant
Inside my body
From the world-admired doctors.

3271

The moment I conquer
An ignorance-night-thought,
God comes to me immediately
And asks me to join Him
In His triumphant March.

3272

My reading, my talking
And my lecturing
Help me very little
In comparison to
My praying, my meditating
And my self-giving.

3273

God will definitely come to you
And bless you
If you try your utmost
To please Him
To your very last breath.

3274

My life-long mission
Is not in missionising the world,
But in serving the world
So it can climb Heavenward.

3275

God tells each and every
    God-seeker
To quickly take the nearest seat
To His Heart-Home.

3276

Each moment
I get an opportunity-flower
From the inner world
To offer to my Lord Supreme
In the outer world.

3277

World-attachment
Is
Extremely painful.

3278

God-attachment
Is
Exceedingly blissful.

3279

The earth-founder
Is
My smiling soul.

3280

The Heaven-founder
Is
My crying heart.

3281

The Beyond-founder
Will be my God-aspiration,
God-dedication
And God-manifestation.

3282

The mind, the vital
And the body
Enjoy the gossip-world.

3283

The soul, the heart
And the breath
Enjoy the God-Whisper-world.

3284

God gives purity
The most important part
In His Cosmic Play.

3285

No fear, no doubt,
No suspicion
Can ever dare to touch
My soul-smiles.

3286

Those who know well
The art of forgiveness
Are God's chosen children.

3287

I call it my surrender-life.
God calls that very thing
His peerless treasure.

MY CHRISTMAS-NEW YEAR-VACATION-ASPIRATION-PRAYERS

3288

God gets tremendous delight
Whenever I do anything
With a sincere heart.

3289

If you are a sincere seeker,
Then your ego
Is now totally obsolete.

3290

If you want to open
God's Heart-Door,
Surrender
Is the only key.

3291

Time
Does not believe in
A slow pace.

3292

My heart and my soul
At long last
Held a farewell party
For my mind.

3293

A real seeker
Has to treasure time
As if it were all diamond.

3294

My Lord wants me to retrace
The ancient heart-path
And not to follow
The modern mind-path.

3295

My faith in God
Is my only reliable
Life-companion.

3296

My heart is desperate
Only for one thing:
My Lord's Compassion-flooded
　　Feet.

3297

My heart-tears
Weaken
My Lord Beloved Supreme.

3298

My soul-smiles
Strengthen
My Lord Beloved Supreme.

3299

I always keep wide open
My life-house
And my heart-home.

3300

The seeker may lose
To God's Eye
But never
To God's Heart.

3301

My mind has many stories
To tell God,
But God has only one Song
To sing for my mind:
Forgiveness.

3302

Alas,
God's Shoulders accept
All the problems of humanity,
But I do not want to fulfil
My little life's little
    responsibility.

3303

Mother Earth blesses me
With hopes.
Father Heaven blesses me
With promises.
I must fulfil my Parents'
Hopes and promises.

3304

In my aspiration-heart-home,
There is no entry and no exit
For thoughts.

3305

Poor mind!
It has no choice.
It is not allowed to hear
My soul's voice.

3306

This morning—
I do not know how, why
And wherefrom—
A new joy is emboldening
My heart.

3307

I can and I must learn
How to live a perfect life
Inside my Lord's Heart.

MY CHRISTMAS-NEW YEAR-VACATION-ASPIRATION-PRAYERS

3308

The fresh morning dew
Awakens
My sleeping aspiration-heart.

3309

God wants only one thing
From me:
A ceaseless and breathless
God-aspiration-heart.

3310

At a distance
I imagine God's Feet
Until the day arrives
When I can place myself
At God's Feet.

3311

God wants me to please Him
In a prayerful and soulful way,
And not in an astounding way.

3312

God's Compassion-Rain
Falls
To enthral my heart.

3313

No mind-ignorance
Can stop
My Heaven-climbing
Journey's start.

3314

A happy heart
Is
A God-given capacity
To spread God's Light
Freely and ceaselessly.

3315

This time when God sends away
My ignorance-pride,
I shall definitely not
Bring it back.

3316

I pray and meditate
Inside my heart's
Sweetness-devotion-moon.

3317

God wants my peace, my love,
My joy and my self-giving life
For the universal benefit.

3318

In the morning
I devour the sun-flames
To make the fastest progress
In my spiritual life.

3319

In the evening
I devour the moon-beams
To make the fastest progress
In my spiritual life.

3320

Not God's infinite Power
But God's Compassion-Tears
Have transformed my life.

3321

God's Compassion-Smiles
Are keeping me
In the world of abundant bliss.

3322

God wants all the aspiring hearts
Around the world
To be united in the inner world.

3323

May the world I live in
Have only newness,
Oneness and fulness.

3324

What my body, vital,
Mind and heart need
Is the life of spirituality.

3325

God wants His Compassion
And my aspiration
To spread out
Here, there and everywhere.

3326

Only in deep meditation
Does my aspiration-sun rise high,
Very high, unimaginably high.

3327

I love to sit devotedly
At the Feet
Of God the One.

MY CHRISTMAS-NEW YEAR-VACATION-ASPIRATION-PRAYERS

3328

I love to follow eagerly
In the Footsteps
Of God the Many.

3329

I love to be constantly blessed
By God the Universal.

3330

All my heart-tears
And all my soul-smiles
I sleeplessly dedicate
To God the Universal.

3331

O my heart,
I want you to be the nest
Of my aspiration-bird.

3332

My Lord,
Do give me a heart
That will not find any difficulty
In remembering You
All the time.

3333

Do not shake hands
With ignorance-night!
Use your third eye
To destroy its exorbitant pride.

3334

When Light leads us,
Power helps us
And never stands
In Light's way.

3335

Each heart
Is
An aspiration-mountain.

3336

Each life
Is
A dedication-fountain.

3337

The mind that instigates me
To make a serious blunder
Is the same mind
That later on blames me.

3338

God enters
Into my heart
On tiptoe.

3339

I enter
Into God's Heart
Striking a thunder-drum.

3340

The world may forget
My face one day,
But it will never forget
My heart.

3341

Silence, silence, silence!
Silence was born
Before the Birth
Of our Lord Beloved Supreme.

3342

Each earth-born seeker
Will one day be caught
By the Cosmic Embrace
Of our Lord Supreme.

3343

O seeker,
Be always careful!
Carelessness is a serious
And contagious disease
In the spiritual life.

3344

I rise from my invisible heart
To my visible eye
To be of service
To mankind.

3345

This morning
My Lord Beloved Supreme
Was most compassionately
Watching me
While I was bathing in His Sea
Of infinite Peace and Bliss.

3346

A moment
To see,
But a lifetime
To become!

MY CHRISTMAS-NEW YEAR-VACATION-ASPIRATION-PRAYERS

3347

Every morning
I most prayerfully and soulfully
Offer my Lord
My heart's aspiration-beauty-
   blossoms.

3348

The seekers must every day
Practise one thing faithfully:
Self-sacrifice.

3349

Every child-heart
Radiates
The Beauty of the Unknowable.

3350

There is only one reality:
God's birthless and deathless
Compassion-Eye-Revelation.

3351

With kindness
We start.
With oneness
We stop.

3352

Be a self-giving life.
God Himself
Will sculpture you.

3353

I never care for
A hermit-cave.

3354

I only care for
A seeker's prayerful cottage.

3355

May my heart be a nest
Of self-giving
Affection-sweetness.

3356

God wants me to have
Compassion-plants
In my heart-garden
More than anything else.

3357

What do I need?
I desperately need
A more self-giving life.

3358

What else do I need?
I sleeplessly need
A little more Heaven-climbing
   heart.

3359

Each and every hope
Of the aspiration-heart
Will one day fully blossom.

3360

My heart
Is an earth-born hope,
And my soul
Is a Heaven-born promise.

3361

Always more God,
Infinitely more God
Than the human beings!

3362

Keep quiet,
My mind and my vital!
Our Lord is speaking.

3363

My earthly life
Counts
My earthly years.

3364

My Heavenly soul
Counts
My Heavenly hours.

3365

Who can count
Earth's gratitude-tears
And Heaven's sunburst-smiles,
Who can?

3366

The mind should know
That disobedience is not
A simple headache
But infinitely more painful
Than a migraine.

3367

Do not allow sorrow
To shadow your path.

MY CHRISTMAS-NEW YEAR-VACATION-ASPIRATION-PRAYERS

3368

Alas,
So late, so late—
I have just started
My God-manifestation-service!

3369

At long last
Today I am enjoying
The expiration
Of my desire-world.

3370

My way:
I love
Human beings
Every day less and less.

3371

God's Way:
God loves
Not only human beings
But His entire Creation
Every day more and more.

3372

As soon as I wake up,
I watch my Lord's Channel first.

3373

The second thing that I do:
I take love-devotion-surrender
Exercises.

3374

The mind
Is the most
Unreliable companion.

3375

Doubt
Is the most powerful tyrant
Here on earth.

3376

The ancient path
Was to see God
Face to face.

3377

The modern path
Is to debate voraciously
About religion and scripture.
What a stupid path!

3378

This morning
God's Compassion-Eye
Wiped away the sad differences
Between my heart-approach
And my mind-approach
To God-realisation.

3379

The mind's way
Is to possess God.

3380

The heart's way
Is to be possessed by God.

3381

My soul has banished
Doubt and suspicion,
Jealousy and insecurity
From my heart-kingdom.

3382

The outer appearance
Is not
The real life.

3383

The deeper existence
Is
The pure and real life.

3384

Peace of mind never comes
By not accepting
The world.

3385

Peace of mind comes
By loving the world
And by becoming the world.

3386

An unconditional God-lover
And God-server
Is the real cynosure
Of all human eyes.

3387

God's Pride
Is not
In the mind-book-volumes.

MY CHRISTMAS-NEW YEAR-VACATION-ASPIRATION-PRAYERS

3388

God's Pride
Is
In the heart-booklet.

3389

Each heart has the capacity
To be the joy and pride
Of the Universal Life.

3390

I always love to be
In the audience
And not an actor.

3391

God-actors
Are born actors
And not man-made.

3392

Nobody can go to God
With weak faith.

3393

This moment
My Lord is my heart's Pilot.
Next moment
My Lord is my life's Charioteer.

3394

I keep my curious
And devoted ears
Always very close to God.

3395

My soul, my heart and I
Every day
Plant hundreds of peace-trees
In my heart-garden.

3396

When I peacefully sleep,
God lovingly watches
My sleep.

3397

When it is a matter of strictness,
God does not know
How to calculate His strictness.

3398

Anything that is divine
Has to be lived and relived
Indefinitely.

3399

I love my Lord's
Compassion-Assurance
More than anything else.

3400

We are all
Heaven-sent first,
And then become
Earth-born realities.

3401

A life-boat
Without aspiration-sails
Is a very sad
Failure-experience.

3402

Ask not,
Want not—
Just become
Divinity's child.

3403

When I look down
To see man's head,
I descend.
When I look up
To see my Lord's Feet,
My life at once ascends
And transcends.

3404

My Lord's Compassion-Eye
Is an antidote
To my faith-starvation-life.

3405

To choose obedience
Is to choose the seeker's
God-pleasing life.

3406

To choose disobedience
Is the self-destruction
Of the spiritual life.

3407

I just offer
My God-pleasing willingness.
God does the rest
Most kindly, most affectionately
And most happily.

MY CHRISTMAS-NEW YEAR-VACATION-ASPIRATION-PRAYERS

3408

Ego is either
The world-satisfaction-beggar
Or the world-attention-
   commander.

3409

If you cherish
Wrong and undivine thoughts
In God's Presence,
Then God can do nothing,
Absolutely nothing, for you.

3410

Eagerness can easily
Cross over the fence
Of the opposition parties.

3411

After joining the spiritual path,
If I cannot please my Master,
Then my Lord Supreme gets
The bitterest
Disappointment-experience.

3412

Alas,
The outer sun
Has passed away.
To my greatest joy,
My inner sun will not leave me—
Never!

3413

This morning
I smiled and smiled
At my Lord Supreme.
He said to me,
"My child,
Today you have given Me
The most marvellous day
Of My Life!"

3414

God the Heaven-Founder
Says to me,
"My child,
Sleep with Me
And dream with Me."

3415

God the earth-Founder
Says to me,
"My child,
Work with Me
And work for Me."

3416

My ego-pride
Is totally obsolete.

3417

To my greatest joy,
My expectation-construction
Is collapsing.

3418

The fastest way
To arrive at God's Palace
Is to start with surrender.

3419

Although the mind
Is often dry,
It enjoys the gossip-world
Most surprisingly.

3420

God's most powerful Utterance
God will speak first.
Then my soul and my heart
    will speak.
Finally my mind will speak
Slowly, quietly and respectfully.

3421

God always wants
The heart of purity
To start His Cosmic Play.

3422

O my stupid mind,
There is no roundabout way
To fool God.

3423

Love God
Sleeplessly.
Sing God-songs for God
Untiringly.
An unimaginable God-receptivity
You will be granted from Above.

3424

Today
God's every Breath
Is blessing my God-longing
Heart-cries.

3425

Forever and forever
I have been
God-Infinity's dream.

MY CHRISTMAS-NEW YEAR-VACATION-ASPIRATION-PRAYERS

3426

Today my life
Is forever changed!
How?
My Lord has placed
His Thunder-Feet
On my restless mind,
Wild vital and sleeping body.

3427

Like God-disobedience,
God-deception also
Cannot be concealed.

3428

God's Forgiveness-Sun
Shines equally
For His good and bad children.

3429

There is not
A single human being
Who does not need
God's Compassion-Shelter.

3430

Who is hungry
For God's Justice-Light?
Not the body,
Not the vital,
Not the mind,
But only the heart
Is ready and hungry
For God's Justice-Light.

3431

I have heard
The Call
Of Infinity's Silence.

3432

A blossoming heart
Is
Exceedingly beautiful.

3433

I want the mind to live
In a desolate,
Thickest and darkest
Forest-night,
Which it rightly deserves.

3434

Any time is the best time
To see God,
To be at God's Feet
And to talk to God
In the world of silence.
But to realise God,
God chooses a special Hour.
At His choice Hour
We realise Him.

3435

My life's most sacred place
Is my heart-temple.
It is there,
Where I meet with God,
That I get infinite joy.

3436

O leisure-class seekers,
Each time you seek,
God sheds bitter tears.

3437

I sing early in the morning.
My Lord says,
"Not enough, not enough!
Fly high
In the rainbow-morning-sky."

3438

Keep
Your aspiration-breath
Alive.

3439

Keep
Your dedication-muscles
Active.

3440

Keep
Your heart-prayers
Soulful.

3441

My joy knows no bounds
That today I have re-established
My heart-connection
With my Lord Supreme.

3442

Today
My Lord's Love-Call
Is flooded
With Affection-Smiles.

MY CHRISTMAS-NEW YEAR-VACATION-ASPIRATION-PRAYERS

3443

When God hears
Our gratitude-songs,
He immediately starts
Smiling and dancing.

3444

I try to please God
In Heaven.
I try to please God
On earth.
To please God on earth
Is infinitely more difficult
Than to please God in Heaven.

3445

Every morning
I send an invitation card
To my Lord Supreme.
He reads the card immediately
And says that He is not ready
Nor am I ready
To meet together.

3446

One God-Smile is enough
To change our life
If we really want it to.

3447

Poor God!
He has nobody
To whom He can
Unburden His Heart.

3448

Heart-temples teach us
How to be pure,
How to be loving
And how to be self-giving.

3449

To be perfect in life
One does not need
A very, very long time.
One does not have to be on earth
Hundreds of years.

3450

God wants a humility-heart
To stand first,
Before anybody else.

3451

I spoke to the mountains.
They told me
That they would immediately
Send me
Their mountain-deep peace.

3452

The world-peace-lovers
Must accumulate
Their peace-dreams
And place them
At the Feet of God.

3453

The smiling souls
And the crying hearts
Start their journey together
And end their journey together.

3454

God-realisation
Is never
For the weak.

3455

God-realisation
Is also never
For the strong.

3456

God-realisation
Is only
For God-surrendered
God-seekers.

3457

If I give God anything—
Just a little,
An insignificant little—
Lovingly, cheerfully
And self-givingly,
God gets immense joy.

3458

When I pray to God
For the fulfilment of my desires,
God says to me,
"I am ready to fulfil your desires,
But will you be ready
For the day I choose?
I am sure you will have
No patience to wait.
Your desire-fulfilment-day
Will take a very, very long time.
By that time
Your desire will disappear."

MY CHRISTMAS-NEW YEAR-VACATION-ASPIRATION-PRAYERS

3459

God says to me,
"Your success
Gives Me very little joy.
Your progress
Gives Me much more joy.
Your love for Me,
Your concern for Me,
Your satisfaction
In My Satisfaction—
My Way is your way—
Give Me boundless
And boundless Bliss."

3460

When we speak ill of the world
Almost on a daily basis,
We undoubtedly give
A most painful headache
To God.

3461

If I lose my faith in God
And at the same time feel
That out of sheer Concern for me
God will give me abundant faith,
This kind of hope or expectation
Will never, never succeed.

3462

God never thinks ill of us—
Never!
It is we who are quite apt
To think ill of ourselves.
The more we think ill of
    ourselves,
God's Golden Shore sails away
Far, farther, farthest.

3463

God,
Are You pleased with me?
"My child,
If you are pleased with yourself,
Yes!
If you are not pleased with
    yourself,
Then I shall never be pleased
With you."

3464

Do not blame God,
Do not blame God!
He is not interested
In your results,
But He is deeply interested
And eager and anxious
To know your attitude.

3465

If the heart does not smile
At the rising sun,
Then God feels very, very sad.

3466

If constant God-service
Does not appeal to you,
Then you can never be
A first-class devotee.

3467

My heart surrenders
To God's Will
All the time—
Not partially,
But wholeheartedly.

3468

My soul advises my heart:
"Keep climbing,
Keep climbing!
Look upward
And nowhere else."

3469

I never allow my mind
To enjoy negative thoughts
During the day,
Specially in the morning
And in the evening.

3470

Aspiration-road wants
Only aspiration-runners
And not desire-winners.

3471

God proudly keeps
His sincere seekers
In His Heart-Paradise.

3472

Soulfulness
Is the fragrance
Of the heart.

3473

Pay no attention
To life's storms.
Pay all attention
To the sunlit days
In your heart.

MY CHRISTMAS-NEW YEAR-VACATION-ASPIRATION-PRAYERS

3474

God wants me to join
His Dedication-Army
Most self-givingly.

3475

God-unwillingness
Is, indeed, dangerous poison
In the spiritual life.

3476

May my heart
Be encircled
By aspiration-flames.

3477

My aspiration
And God's Compassion
Are extremely fond of each other.

3478

My aspiration-flute
I play in Heaven.

3479

My dedication-violin
I play on earth.

3480

If you sincerely aspire,
You are bound to be
On an extremely high level
Of consciousness.

3481

The ruling mind
Eventually becomes
Its own prisoner.

3482

My aspiration-garden
And my dedication-plants
So lovingly and self-givingly
Live together.

3483

May my aspiration-boat
Sail fast, very fast,
On the river of my life.

3484

My Lord,
I promise to You
That I shall once more please You
In Your own Way.

3485

If only I had listened
To my Lord Supreme,
By today undoubtedly
I could have become
An excellent seeker.

3486

My prayerful and soulful singing
I place only
At my Lord's Feet.

3487

How can the mind
Have an iota of peace
When it is overwhelmed
By desire-thoughts?

3488

God's most precious discovery:
Man's tiny gratitude-heart.

3489

O my mind,
Your excuse list is so rapidly
And painfully increasing.

3490

Every day
The seeker must enjoy—
And not just accept—
God's living Presence.

3491

If you really want to do
Something good for God,
Then do not plan ahead.
God's Will will blossom
In God's Way
Inside your heart.

3492

God's only desire
Is man's selflessness.

3493

God wants to be
Your sole possession
Only if you have no question,
And also if you have
Only one longing:
God-realisation.

3494

May Mother Earth, Father Heaven
And all their children
Live together peacefully.

MY CHRISTMAS-NEW YEAR-VACATION-ASPIRATION-PRAYERS

3495

Each soul
Has a special fragrance
To raise the consciousness
Of the world.

3496

May my God-loving heart
Always remain as calm
    and peaceful
As a waveless sea.

3497

Each seeker needs
An earthly
Mountain-high determination
And a Heavenly
Adamantine will.

3498

The supreme importance
Of aspiration and dedication
Each and every seeker
Must try to realise.

3499

My Lord's Eye
Has forced me to stay away
From the desire-world.

3500

I have detached
My expectation-mind
From my God-service.

3501

There was no distance,
There is no distance,
There shall be no distance
Between man's heart
And God's Eye.

3502

There is only one thing
To treasure:
The ever-growing silence-beauty
Inside one's aspiration-heart.

3503

Every morning
Not my Lord's Eye,
Not my Lord's Heart,
But my Lord's Breath
Knocks at my heart-door.

3504

When you justify
Your weaknesses,
God's anger triples.

3505

Why converse with ignorance?
You have infinitely more
    important
Things to do.

3506

My Lord,
It seems that
Everybody's inner problems
Are most painfully heavy.

3507

Doubt dies
When our love of God
Speedily flies
In our heart-sky.

3508

God is ready to bless me
With experience after experience,
But alas,
Am I ready?
Will I ever be ready?

3509

The aspiration-life
Is not a life of secrecy
But a life of ecstasy.

3510

God's Blessings
I take
As unimaginable surprises.

3511

When aspiration is our
    only choice,
Then God gives us a voice—
His own Voice.

3512

It is not a difficult task
To catch ignorance-thief
Red-handed.

3513

Silence is, indeed,
The best kind
Of peace-preparation.

3514

I promise, I promise, I promise:
From now on
I shall listen
To my Lord Supreme
Wholeheartedly.

MY CHRISTMAS-NEW YEAR-VACATION-ASPIRATION-PRAYERS

3515

A soulful heart-singer
Immediately brings joy
To God.

3516

When God calls you,
You must remember
To bring with you
Your heart's light
And your mind's darkness
Together.

3517

Your mind, vital and body
Will be dumbfounded
When God's Light descends.

3518

Very few visible miracles
Of the Master
Do we see.
The inner world of the Master
Is, indeed, full of
Mushroom-density-miracles.

3519

God created endless ways
So that we can please Him
At least in one way.

3520

To my greatest joy,
My aspiration-heart-boat
Is under full sail.

3521

Long, long ago
I left cheerfully and proudly
Doubt-territory.

3522

God's Sweetness
I do not need.
God's Newness
I do not need.
I need only
God's God-Oneness.

3523

Aspiration-decline
Is
A most painful experience.

3524

My mind
Does not like duty
At all.

3525

My heart
Not only loves duty
But also is eager
To have every day
A newly added duty.

3526

The purity of my heart
And God's smiling Eyes
Are always found together.

3527

My soul-bird sings and sings
Only one song:
Love God and please God.

3528

When the heart speaks,
The mind, the vital and the body
Must give full attention
To the heart.

3529

Every day my heart's cries
Must go up very speedily
And not lag behind
The speed of the previous day.

3530

Selflessness
Awakens and feeds
All the time
The tears of the heart.

3531

Only silence and peace
Can transform
Restless and useless mind-clamour.

3532

My Lord's Happiness-Eye
At every moment
I try to devour.

3533

My God-hunger was born
In my Lord's soothing
Cradle-Smiles.

3534

Ignorance-mouth
Devours everything,
Including blazing fire.

MY CHRISTMAS-NEW YEAR-VACATION-ASPIRATION-PRAYERS

3535

Satisfaction
Will never take birth
In the mind's
Desire-forest.

3536

Satisfaction
Will gladly take birth
In the heart's
God-smiling garden.

3537

Most dearly
Mother Earth's tears
God's Heart cherishes.

3538

Meditation and peace
Deeply enjoy
Their divine conversation.

3539

We are not compelled
To lead a spiritual life,
But if happiness we want,
We must shun ignorance-night.

3540

My Lord,
You must keep Your Promise:
You will never leave my heart.

3541

My life-river
And my heart-boat—
They live for each other.

3542

My heart
Is my soul's
Joy-gathering nest.

3543

Mother Earth
Is
A pain-receiving heart.

3544

Father Heaven
Is
A joy-supplying Heart.

3545

My God-obedience-boat
Has safely brought me
To God-Infinity's God-Shore.

3546

I faithfully
Follow God's Feet.

3547

God's brightest Smile
Follows my heart.

3548

When a seeker offers even an iota
Of self-giving effort,
He is bound to succeed.

3549

My Lord,
Do give me a Smile of Yours
So that I can pass through
My mind's thickest
And darkest clouds.

3550

No mind
Can ever break through
The power of silence.

3551

Every day
May a deathless beauty and light
Dawn upon my aspiring heart.

3552

My gratitude-heart
Is first
On God's priority list.

3553

To double my happiness,
I must become
A sleepless self-giver.

3554

If you do not obey God,
You as a traveller
Will never be able to enter
Into God's Kingdom.

MY CHRISTMAS-NEW YEAR-VACATION-ASPIRATION-PRAYERS

3555

God is not
My occasional thought
But my sleepless thought.

3556

Obedience
Is an unmistakable way
To reach God's Golden Shore.

3557

Who says
That God's Heart
Is not accessible?
God's Heart
Is a wide-open door.

3558

My question is:
Who is God?
God's Answer is:
"My child,
Some of you are budding gods,
While others
Are blossoming gods."

3559

O seeker,
God wants you to accompany
His Eye and His Heart
From dawn to eve
Wherever He goes.

3560

Nobody can ever dare to separate
God's Compassion-Eye
From His Forgiveness-Heart.

3561

The soul's complete
    manifestation
Of God's Light
Takes place only
Here on earth.

3562

God never, never wants you
To be arrested
By ignorance-night!

3563

God wants you
Only to be interested
In Him
All the time.

3564

Again and again
God wants to hear from me
My gratitude-heart-songs.

3565

The Christ
Is not only for Christmas.
He is for three hundred and
    sixty-five days
A year.

3566

Do not try to hide
From God's Eye.
You will sadly fail.

3567

My Lord,
You are taking care of
My soul and my heart.
Please take care of
Every moment of my life.

3568

I came
From a higher world
To serve the world below.

3569

Our God-closeness
Makes our world
Extremely sweet.

3570

The privilege
Of being God's servant
Cannot be fathomed.

3571

The opinions
Of the mind
Cannot be taken seriously.

3572

My heart cannot forget
The sweeter than the sweetest
Memories of Heaven
While I am on earth.

3573

God's Breath
Welcomes only
The devotion-heart.

MY CHRISTMAS-NEW YEAR-VACATION-ASPIRATION-PRAYERS

3574

Both the outer and
   inner encouragements
Are needed
To make the fastest progress
In spirituality.

3575

When I give up
In the battlefield of life,
God becomes His Madness-Eye
And Sadness-Heart.

3576

My gratitude-heart-tears
Every day wash
God's omnipotent Feet.

3577

When aspiration becomes
Our true friend,
Life becomes
Spiritually meaningful.

3578

Kindness
Changes our fate.

3579

Oneness
Transforms our lives.

3580

I love to live
Between my heart's unshed tears
And my life's shed tears.

3581

Tell the mind
Vehemently
That it has no room
In your life any more.

3582

When I truly love God,
My heart becomes
Peaceful.

3583

When I truly need God,
My life becomes
Fruitful.

3584

When we give up hope,
Our promise
Starts to starve.

3585

There are so many
Secret and sacred ways
To go to God's Palace.

3586

Everything I do
Takes root
In God's Heart first.

3587

There are many, many, many
    seekers
Here on earth
Who have given everything
To God.
I must try to mix with them.

3588

I want to be awake
Around the clock
So that whenever God wants me,
I shall be all ready.

3589

The inner cries
Have to be answered
Only by the inner world.

3590

The God-denying mind
Builds and builds warships
To fight against
The divine forces.

3591

The God-believing heart
Wants only a worship-boat
To invite God
To pilot the boat.

3592

Earth has
Its stumbling feet.

3593

Heaven has
Its whispering Protection.

MY CHRISTMAS-NEW YEAR-VACATION-ASPIRATION-PRAYERS

3594

My heart's blooming smile
I always offer
To my Lord Supreme
First.

3595

God-dreamers
Eventually become
God-manifestation-fulfillers.

3596

The more we travel
Within,
The faster we get good results
Without.

3597

My God-gratitude
Is
My true life-transformer.

3598

How do I find happiness?
I find happiness
By loving the world more,
Ever more.

3599

The source
Of my inspiration
Is
Mother Earth.

3600

The source
Of my aspiration
Is
My inner sun.

3601

The source
Of my success
Is
My mind-determination.

3602

The source
Of my progress
Is
My surrender-life to God.

3603

Every hour
God sows
A new seed of transformation
In my heart-garden.

3604

The heart is always ready
To answer the questions
Of the mind,
But the mind is not satisfied.

3605

A life of meditation
Gives tremendous joy
To God.

3606

My mind,
If you stay with doubt,
Then I shall have
Nothing to do with you!

3607

Hesitation
Slows down the speed
Of everything divine
That we have.

3608

When we see God
Within ourselves,
He is beautiful and powerful.
But when we see God
In others,
He is only powerful.

3609

No matter where
God's Feet are,
God's Heart
Has given me the capacity
To clasp Them.

3610

Only the God-listeners
Are my true friends.

3611

Spirituality
Without surrender
Will always remain
Incomplete.

3612

God equally loves
Those who aspire soulfully
And those who serve devotedly.

3613

God does not love
The sleepers.
He has concern
For the sleepers,
But not love.

MY CHRISTMAS-NEW YEAR-VACATION-ASPIRATION-PRAYERS

3614

When God introduces Himself
To me,
The finite in me
Immediately becomes the
  Infinite.

3615

When I introduce myself
To God,
The Infinite in Him
Immediately becomes the finite.

3616

I am enamoured
Of each moment that I get
At the Feet
Of my Lord Supreme.

3617

My gratitude-heart
Has the capacity
To speak to my Lord Supreme
At every moment.

3618

O Lord,
Do purify my outer voice
And immortalise my inner voice.

3619

My Lord,
When will my mind
Realise You?
"My child,
I am more eager than you are
For your mind to realise Me."

3620

Ceaselessly I ring
Most devotedly
My God-gratitude-heart-bell.

3621

Each life has
Countless ascending steps
Before it arrives
In Heaven.

3622

Be brave!
Be not stunned
By the present stark reality.

3623

If I really wish
To be a God-devotion-singer,
Then God will give me
The sweetest range of voice.

3624

God enters into
The mind-jungle
With His Light, Peace and Bliss.
The mind hides.
After a while the mind comes
And touches God's Feet.
God immediately transforms
The mind-jungle
Into the Garden of Eden.

3625

Desire sees the moon
But wants to remain
In the mud and clay
Of the earth.

3626

The doubting mind
Has no entry form
To enter into
God's Heart-Palace.

3627

Spiritual progress
Ends
The moment the desire-life
Succeeds.

3628

Age has nothing to do
With a sage life.

3629

God is starving and starving
For an iota
Of my inner progress.

3630

Prayer
Protects us
From ignorance-night.

3631

Meditation
Is
Ignorance-night-illumination.

3632

Do not waste time
Even for a moment.
God is eagerly waiting
For you.

MY CHRISTMAS-NEW YEAR-VACATION-ASPIRATION-PRAYERS

3633

No backward step
With doubt,
But forward,
Ever forward steps
With faith.

3634

My Lord,
I have only one prayer:
Please give me
Two Heaven-flying
God-obedience-wings.

3635

Earth-bound
The mind travels.

3636

Heaven-free
The heart flies.

3637

May my aspiration-heart
And my dedication-life
Become
Inseparable friends.

3638

God forgives
Our ill-disciplined life,
But He never forgets it.

3639

A sincere seeker
Never asks God
For a leave of absence.

3640

If unwillingness
Does not accept opportunity,
Life becomes a failure.

3641

When my mind
Does not obey
My Lord Supreme,
The tears of my soul
Flood my heart.

3642

The seeker's first
And foremost duty:
God-acceptance
In God's own Way
At every moment.

3643

My hopes
And my dreams
Adorn my heart-garden.

3644

A God-Feet-surrender-life
Is compulsory
Until we breathe our last.

3645

To oversleep God's special Hour
Is, indeed, a painful
But common experience
In a seeker's life.

3646

God applauds
When we cry.
God applauds
When we smile.
Is there any time
When God does not applaud,
No matter what we do?

3647

We must brave
The dire challenges of life
To become God's
Most perfect instruments.

3648

Our powerful meditation
Is the only food
That God appreciates
Most sincerely
And most blessingfully.

3649

There is always a better way
To love God and serve God,
And we must try to discover
That particular way.

3650

My meditation
Is my heart's
God-love-sanctification.

3651

Our oneness-heart
Is God's
Ecstasy-Dance.

3652

God wants me to win
The inner world first
And then to think
Of the outer world.

MY CHRISTMAS-NEW YEAR-VACATION-ASPIRATION-PRAYERS

3653

Heaven's Blessings and Concern
I have brought down with me
To be of service
To the earth-planet.

3654

Not the mind's fantasy,
But the heart's intimacy
I need.

3655

The privilege
Of serving God
On a daily basis
In the inner world
And in the outer world
Is unimaginable.

3656

My devotion-heart
And God's Breath
Sing perfectly in tune.

3657

If we love God
In God's own Way,
There will be no stop
On our God-journey.

3658

The mind
Takes pride
In its high opinions.

3659

The heart
Surrenders its pride
Utterly and unconditionally
At the Feet of God.

3660

If we want to work on earth
Soulfully and perfectly,
Then we must keep in touch
With Heaven's
Constant Compassion and
    Concern.

3661

Our God-closeness
We must every day use
To increase
The world-oneness.

3662

O seeker,
Do not slow down!
God's Heart
Is eagerly waiting
For you.

3663

We think of God.
We speak about God.
But, alas,
How rarely
We stand up for God!

3664

God firmly says to my body,
"You must never think
Of your
Old-age retirement-pleasure!"

3665

Peace-gong
The mind cannot hear.
Peace-flute
The heart hears,
And the melody of the flute
The heart shares lovingly
And self-givingly
With the rest of the world.

3666

My devotion-heart-eye
Is the only eye
That can see
My Lord's golden Feet.

3667

Alas,
The human mind
At times enjoys confusion,
Even dissatisfaction.

3668

I came into the world
To see God's real Smile.
Alas,
God's real Smile
Is nowhere to be found.

3669

Believe me,
The Divine Power
Is much greater
Than the power of evil.

3670

We long
For reality.
Reality longs
For a divine dream.

MY CHRISTMAS-NEW YEAR-VACATION-ASPIRATION-PRAYERS

3671

Despair weakens
Sooner than the soonest
Our aspiration-heart.

3672

Only a stark fool
Neither cries
Nor smiles.

3673

Until hope
Becomes a promise,
Hope is all brittle.

3674

Even a giant ego
Suffers a terrible defeat
When the God-Hour dawns.

3675

Every day
God's Compassion-Eye
Softly, tenderly
And blessingfully awakens
All God-dreamers.

3676

The outer freedom
Misguides and misleads
The world.

3677

The inner freedom
Can play the role
Of a saviour.

3678

I wish to be
Blissfully blind
In following my Lord's
Express Commands.

3679

Our progress-speed
Is in God's Hand
And never in
Our own hands.

3680

Meditation
Is a gradual
Godward journey.

3681

When we do something
Seriously wrong,
Our souls shed
Bitter tears.

3682

Aspiration is at once
Our heart's divine arrow
And our life's divine protection.

3683

When my aspiration-flames
And my meditation-sun
Play together,
It is unimaginably beautiful.

3684

If I live
Only for God,
Then nothing can frighten me,
Nobody can frighten me.

3685

Imagination
Sometimes can be
Mental hallucination.

3686

My devotion-bird
Has a very special nest:
My heart.

3687

My Lord,
How shall I address You?
"My child,
You can address Me
By any name
Or by any form."

3688

Spirituality
Has many privileges.
The first and foremost
Is God-closeness.

3689

A delayer
Will never be chosen by God
To be a player
In His Cosmic Game.

3690

The sweet whispers
Of my soul
Give my heart
Tremendous joy.

MY CHRISTMAS-NEW YEAR-VACATION-ASPIRATION-PRAYERS

3691

My Lord Beloved Supreme,
Please tell me
If there is a place
In Your entire Creation
Where I can live in peace.

3692

Each doubt-invasion
Must be challenged and
   conquered
By our most powerful faith
Deep within.

3693

The unaspiring human beings
Sooner or later will drown
In the vast sea
Of ignorance-night.

3694

I belong solely to God
In the inner world of silence
And
In the outer world of sound.

3695

The seeker's aspiration-life
Ends
When he allows the mind
To push him
And the vital
To pull him.

3696

Every morning
My heart becomes
A rainbow-dream-lover.

3697

A desire-life
Is nothing short of
A weakness-mind.

3698

Happiness-stars
Are found only
In the heart-sky.

3699

The mind divides.
The heart brings
Everything together.

3700

My God-obedience
Is a resounding success
And progress
In my spiritual life.

3701

Every day
There will be new challenges,
And again,
There will be the brightest sun
From deep within
To help us brave the challenges.

3702

The seeker does everything
To build a spiritual shrine.
The Master gives
The finishing touches.

3703

This moment
The mind is a jungle.
Next moment
The same mind becomes
A desert.
Finally it becomes
A useless nothingness.

3704

No matter what we do wrong,
God is eager to see us
Again and again.

3705

Even
Self-transcendence-attempts
Are most remarkable.

3706

Every day
I must dive deep within,
Deeper and deeper,
To become a choice
Student-instrument
Of God.

3707

Self-deception
Can easily be
Contagious.

3708

My Lord,
I am sacrificing
My long-lost self
To You.

MY CHRISTMAS-NEW YEAR-VACATION-ASPIRATION-PRAYERS

3709

Surrender has to be
Active and dynamic,
Not merely fascinating
Or dreaming.

3710

God's Victory-Songs
The angels sing
Untiringly and self-givingly.

3711

Like the prisoner's
Hunger pangs for light,
We needs must develop
Deep, inner hunger pangs
To see the Face of God.

3712

God's chosen children
Are always on the alert
So that undivine forces
Cannot invade
God's Inner Circle.

3713

Always and always
There is an unknown Source
Of love, devotion and surrender
Deep within us.

3714

Earth has
Its multiple and multiplying
Desperation-cries.

3715

Heaven has
Its multiple and multiplying
Compassion-expansion-Smiles.

3716

My aspiration-heartbeat
Quickens
At the very mention of God.

3717

In my spiritual life,
Many, many, many more
Supremely divine things
Are yet to come.

3718

Poor God!
He sincerely tries
Not to see
The darkness of the world,
But unfortunately
He sees it.

3719

There are some things
That must be done
Before others—
Such as my aspiration
And my dedication.

3720

Ignorance-night
Is dauntless,
Ruthless,
Godless.
Therefore it is useless.

3721

Affection, Love,
Sweetness, Fondness
God has for me.
Every day I live and grow
Under His Protection-Tree.

3722

God with His Smile
Has descended upon my head
To shatter my ego-pride
Permanently.

3723

There is only one thing
That I do not like about God:
He likes to hide.

3724

There are many nice things
That I can say about God,
But one thing I would like to say:
His Love for us
Has neither beginning
Nor end.

3725

Quite often
The mind is empty
Of concern.

3726

I must not give up hope.
I must carry it with me
Far into the distant future.

3727

Pay no attention
When ignorance-night
Begs to visit you.

MY CHRISTMAS-NEW YEAR-VACATION-ASPIRATION-PRAYERS

3728

Whatever God tells my heart
Is absolutely true—
Forever true!

3729

To meditate soulfully
And powerfully
Is to start our homeward journey
To the Absolute Supreme.

3730

My Lord has in mind
A full service-schedule for me
Every day.

3731

Medicine we need
For the body.
Aspiration we need
For the heart.
Surrender we need
For God.

3732

Out of His infinite Bounty,
My Lord every day lifts
My heavier than the heaviest
Mind-doubt-weights.

3733

I came from God
To see.

3734

I am returning to God
To be.

3735

Divinity,
With You
I want to be.

3736

Humanity,
I know not who you are,
And I have no desire
To know!

3737

Before our transformation
Takes place,
God keeps it
A top secret.

3738

To listen to the mind
All the time
Is, indeed, a good way
To go crazy.

3739

God's Grace-Heart
Never stops.

3740

I never miss a chance
To fulfil God
In His own Way.

3741

The mind
Concerns itself
With things mundane.

3742

The heart
Concerns itself
With God's Compassion,
Protection and Forgiveness.

3743

Anything that helps us evolve
We must accept,
And be grateful.

3744

O my mind,
Do not delay!
Set your prayers
In perfection-motion.

3745

Constant awareness
Leads us
To full wakefulness.

3746

The mind
Is the reservoir
Of worries and anxieties.

3747

The heart
Is the reservoir
Of God's Beauty
And God's Forgiveness.

MY CHRISTMAS-NEW YEAR-VACATION-ASPIRATION-PRAYERS

3748

Whenever people tell me
That God has special Love
For me,
I am overwhelmed
With God-gratitude.

3749

I came into the world
To feed God's chosen children
With my heart's love.

3750

Whatever comes into my life,
I shall never make friends
With ignorance-night.

3751

The past
Must not discourage
Our forward march.

3752

The past
Must not discourage
Our inward dive.

3753

My prayer
Is the loving breath
Of my heart.

3754

Undivine thoughts
Imprison
Our mind.

3755

Divine thoughts
Liberate
Our mind.

3756

The traveller in me
Carries hope
Wherever it goes.

3757

Concentration-training
Is absolutely needed.

3758

The aspiring heart
Has no enemy.
It sees and feels
Friends everywhere.

3759

Everything
Sings in the heart
Of a genuine seeker.

3760

Not only God's Dreams
But also His Realities
At times change.

3761

I have only
One thing to do:
To stay peacefully
Inside my heart.

3762

God-intoxicated souls
Are the ones
Who will manifest God
Here on earth.

3763

My Lord,
Whether my heart is good or bad
Is for You to judge,
But my heart is all Yours.

3764

As soon as I entered
Into God's Heart-Room,
I saw that God
Had already prepared the Room
For my arrival.

3765

Wherever I go,
I see that my Lord
Has preceded me.

3766

My mind,
Why do you think of the things
That blight your own vision?

3767

God-seekers, God-lovers
And God-servers
Carry the message
Of world-transformation.

MY CHRISTMAS-NEW YEAR-VACATION-ASPIRATION-PRAYERS

3768

My Lord,
You are Your overwhelming Love,
And
I am my heart's streaming tears.

3769

Oneness means
God-expansion
In a seeker's life.

3770

Alas,
What can a seeker do
With his overfed pride?

3771

No more shall I live
With my torn hopes.
I shall live only
In the land of cheerfulness.

3772

Each seeker must bury
His anxieties and worries
In his sterling faith.

3773

Will-power has to be used
All the time
To save us from wrongdoings.

3774

Soulfulness and eagerness
Are extremely needed
In the spiritual life.

3775

We do not need
Insecurity-thorns.
We need only
Beauty's security-roses.

3776

Doubt, doubt, doubt,
I am fully prepared
Bravely to meet you head on.

3777

God the Helper
And God the Supporter
We need
When we want to achieve
The impossible.

3778

My Lord,
Give me tears in my heart.
Give me cheers in my life.
Give me divine freedom in
    my thought
To make me a perfect instrument
Of Yours.

3779

I shall never, never go
To the expectation-world.
Time and again
It has failed me.

3780

Exorbitant pride
Is
The God-renouncer.

3781

The heart can protect
The outer life,
But the outer life cannot protect
The inner life.

3782

My Lord,
I love Your Thunder-Kick-Anger
To make the fastest progress
In my inner life.

3783

My Lord,
I love Your Strictness
The way I love Your Kindness.

3784

Everything divine
Begins in the heart
And then spreads.

3785

My Lord,
Anything that I have in my life,
Divine or undivine,
Rest assured, it is all Yours.

3786

My Lord tells me that,
To love Him more,
I shall have to shed soulful tears
In abundant measure every day.

MY CHRISTMAS-NEW YEAR-VACATION-ASPIRATION-PRAYERS

3787

My mind no longer
Dares to block
My fastest progress.

3788

Every God-created heart
Consciously or unconsciously
   sings
God's Victory-Songs.

3789

To my greatest surprise and joy,
My stone heart
God melted long ago.

3790

My Lord,
Give me not greatness,
Not goodness,
But oneness with Your Will
In everything that I say and do.

3791

My life is all God-service.
I do things not to magnify
   myself.
God says to magnify me
Is His Task.

3792

We have the right to choose.
We must choose
Wisely.

3793

Our inner reality
Is the Smile
Of God-Beauty's Dream.

3794

I must know that it is
Only for my good
That God does not answer
My questions.

3795

My irregular devotion
God does not appreciate.

3796

My mind and my vital,
Please do not make
My Lord Supreme angry.
He is all Love for you.

3797

Every day I pray to God
To be fully in control
Of my life.

3798

Forgetfulness
Is, at times,
A great blessing.

3799

This world
Is not interesting
But instigating.

3800

Everything I do
With God's complete
Permission and Assurance.

3801

Do not try
To perfect the world,
But try to love the world
More.

3802

I call myself
A God-lover,
But God calls me
His constant partner.

3803

God does not mind
If I criticise Him
Without any rhyme or reason,
But He does mind
When I do not pray every day
Prayerfully and soulfully.

3804

My life began
With my heart's
Tear-beauty.

3805

My life shall end
With my soul's
Smile-fragrance.

3806

When I think
Of the world situation,
I find myself
In the heartbeat of tears.

MY CHRISTMAS-NEW YEAR-VACATION-ASPIRATION-PRAYERS

3807

An atom of inner peace
Is infinitely more important
Than all the successes
That we have accumulated
Over the years.

3808

O my mind,
Obey my heart
The way my heart obeys my soul,
If you really want to have peace.

3809

I want to be
A faith-hero
And no longer remain
A doubt-slave.

3810

Faith and doubt
Should be kept apart,
Poles apart.

3811

To please God
My heart-smile has to be
Brighter than the brightest.

3812

Anything that God gives me
Is beautiful within
And useful without.

3813

God,
Please give me
A sky-vast and sun-high
   eagerness
To please You.

3814

My fond dream
Is to do good things
For my Master
Even before he tells me.

3815

It is beyond
The capacity of the mind
To enjoy divine ecstasy.

3816

Either the world
Is darkening the mind,
Or the mind
Is eclipsing the world.

3817

I must immediately adopt
A new way of happiness
In my life.

3818

O old-age-mind,
How difficult it is for me
To make you smile!

3819

I came into the world
To see a new world,
But now I have come to learn
That there is no such thing
As a new world.
It is only the old world,
Revealing itself in different ways.

3820

For a divine accomplishment,
We need
An inner urge.

3821

Nobody asked you to carry
The weight of the world.
Just carry yourself—
That will be more than enough.

3822

One fundamental reality:
My love of God
And the victory of Truth
Are inseparable.

3823

An unconditional surrender-life
Has to be the top priority
In the spiritual life.

3824

Almost everybody
Can practise
The spiritual life.

3825

I never miss a single time
To satisfy
My Lord Supreme.

3826

We try to hide
From ourselves.
Can there be anything
Worse than that?

MY CHRISTMAS-NEW YEAR-VACATION-ASPIRATION-PRAYERS

3827

God-worship-fragrance
Is
Unimaginably intoxicating.

3828

What is jealousy,
If not a merry-go-round ride?

3829

God's Compassion-Rain
Is for every day,
And not just for
A particular day.

3830

Purity-progress
In the mind
Is of absolute necessity.

3831

Desire-fire can burn
Not only the fingers
But the entire body.

3832

Alas, many days have gone by.
Yet I have failed to increase
My aspiration-height.

3833

Have patience.
More divine things
Are yet to blossom.

3834

A single moment's hesitation
Can take us far, farther, farthest
From our Goal.

3835

Depression-shadows
Are very difficult
To cast aside.

3836

Expectation-experiences
Are quite often painful.

3837

Unconsciously,
If not consciously,
We betray ourselves.

3838

May each thought of mine
Become a rising sun
On my heart's horizon.

3839

If we pray and meditate,
Our stars will forever
Be rising.

3840

The mind is a market
Where we find
Ever-increasing noise.

3841

Desire-hungry people
Play only
In the mind's playground.

3842

The beauty of divine light
And
The fragrance of divine love
Are to be found together
Always.

3843

Each human being
Is not fully animal.
Again, each human being
Is trillions of miles away
From becoming another God.

3844

Alas, I know two things:
How to blame God
And
How to praise myself.

3845

Time—
Either you give me
Enthusiasm
Or you give me
Frustration.

3846

Sinners and saints—
Wrong-path-travellers
And right-path-runners.

3847

Surrender not to failure.
Try once more.
Success will be all yours.

MY CHRISTMAS-NEW YEAR-VACATION-ASPIRATION-PRAYERS

3848

Some people love to preach,
While others try to practise.
Still others compete and win.

3849

Temptation-world
Is empty of divinity.

3850

Soulfulness
Is always
In demand.

3851

The old-fashioned way
Is the safest way
To God.

3852

The world needs and demands
So many things from me.
God needs only one thing
    from me:
My love.

3853

For me to realise God today
Is the height of absurdity.

3854

For me to realise God
At God's choice Hour
Is not only reality
But inevitability.

3855

The Third Eye
Is the eye that conquers
Ignorance-night for us.

3856

May my aspiration-heart
All the time walk
Side by side
With my Lord Beloved Supreme.

3857

May aspiration become
My only constant choice.

3858

Who protects me
When I am unsheltered?
My Lord's Forgiveness-Heart.

3859

The body knows
What clay is.
The soul knows
What light is.

3860

We are born
From God's Compassion-Height
And with God's Justice-Light.

3861

Do not blame anybody
For your failures.
Just have an adamantine will
To succeed.

3862

My mind,
Your sadness is self-styled.
It is not real.

3863

My mind,
Keep quiet.
Can you not see
That I am listening
To my soul singing?

3864

I give priority always
To one thing:
Self-offering.

3865

Each seeker has to live
By his inner faith-light.

3866

We must walk
With confidence,
Intensity and joy
On life's road.

3867

God has taught me
Many, many of His own
Heartbeat-Songs.

MY CHRISTMAS-NEW YEAR-VACATION-ASPIRATION-PRAYERS

3868

My heart's surrender-prayer
To God
Is my life's best prayer.

3869

My God-obedience-promise
Is infinitely better
Than any other promise.

3870

Without the support of the heart,
The mind cannot go forward
In the inner life.

3871

God-realisation is not as difficult
As you think.
Again, it is not as easy
As you think.

3872

Meditation
Challenges
Imperfection.

3873

Be careful!
Ignorance can attack you
At any moment.

3874

We make God's Heart
Feel sad
When we delay.

3875

Only one desire,
Only one hope:
God-realisation.

3876

Those who have no faith
Cannot have God-realisation.

3877

The world is sinking.
Our prayers have to be
Absolutely sincere.

3878

Self-doubt is the worst enemy.
Be free from self-doubt
If you really want to make progress.

3879

Silence descends
On tiptoe.

3880

Man does not realise
That nature's divinity
Is most illumining
And most powerful.

3881

Time will reveal
Everything—
Encouraging
Or discouraging.

3882

To surmount every barrier
We shall have to dive
Deep within.

3883

Prayers and meditations
Can bring the distant stars
Within our reach.

3884

God will shield us
On every side
If we take His Side.

3885

We need both
The tears of the heart
And the smiles of the soul
To perfect our lives.

3886

Nothing
Can be compared
To God's sweet Whispers.

3887

If you are not
Firmly on the path,
How can you succeed?

3888

God's Closeness
Depends on
Our heart's openness.

MY CHRISTMAS-NEW YEAR-VACATION-ASPIRATION-PRAYERS

3889

A child's heart
Draws immediate attention
From God's Eye and Heart.

3890

Meditation has the capacity
To take us far beyond the domain
Of sorrows and sufferings.

3891

My Lord,
One good look
Is all that I need
From You.

3892

To follow the mind
Is the height of stupidity.

3893

To follow the heart
Is to sing ecstasy-songs.

3894

A fountain-heart
Will forever remain
Blossoming.

3895

Opportunities
Are God's Blessings.
Do not miss them!

3896

I beg You, my Lord,
With all my heart,
To scold me mercilessly
When I do something wrong.

3897

Each prayer
Has a special connection
To God's Heart.

3898

Each meditation
Has a special connection
To God's Eye.

3899

My Lord's Peace-Sea
Every day welcomes me
To come and swim.

3900

My mind,
How long will you sleep?
When will you wake up
To God's Light?

3901

Unless we close
All the desire-doors and windows
Of the mind,
We will not be able to please God
In His own Way.

3902

When God's Victory-Sun
Shines,
Alas, I am fast asleep.

3903

My Lord every day blesses me
With a new work
To increase my capacity
In various ways.

3904

God awakens us
From ignorance-sleep.
He energises us to walk along
Life's wisdom-path.

3905

My mind,
Stop dictating
To my heart!

3906

My Lord's encouragement
Expedites
My spiritual journey.

3907

There shall come a time
When God will unveil
Our lofty visions.

3908

Who is crying
Inside my heart,
If not my Lord?

3909

If you want to find
Your true self,
Then the only place
Is your diving heart.

MY CHRISTMAS-NEW YEAR-VACATION-ASPIRATION-PRAYERS

3910

Do not allow uncertainty
To obscure your heart.

3911

My love of God
And my gratitude to God
Are keeping me alive.

3912

God gets tremendous satisfaction
When we pay attention
To His Messages.

3913

God-willingness
Is needed
At every moment of life.

3914

The necessity
Of God-obedience
Can never be exaggerated.

3915

I wish to have
God-surrender
As my life-partner.

3916

Action! Action!
No more feeble words.

3917

God loves
To obey
His own iron Laws.

3918

The Creator enjoys
His Cosmic Game
Seated on His golden Throne.

3919

God's Cosmic Law
Admits exception.

3920

Conquer temptation,
If perfection
You sincerely need.

3921

Each heart-cry
Takes us away
From the meshes of ignorance.

3922

Alas,
We are apt to invoke
Heaven's Power
And not
Heaven's Light.

3923

Ignorance-night
Again and again
Loves to fight
Against Heaven's Light.

3924

The beauty and the fragrance
Of happiness
Lead and guide us
To the Higher Worlds.

3925

Wrong thinking
Is nothing short of
Poison-drinking.

3926

God
Protects my heart
From wrong feeling.

3927

Life
Has to be surcharged
With gratitude
Every day.

3928

O seeker,
Do not surrender to despair!
Start your spirituality
All over again.

3929

We must put
A strong accent
On self-giving.

3930

We must not be bound
By our mind's
Self-styled whims.

3931

My happy moments
Are
God's dancing Hours.

MY CHRISTMAS-NEW YEAR-VACATION-ASPIRATION-PRAYERS

3932

May my sweet hopes
Be faithful.

3933

May my powerful promises
Be fruitful.

3934

The price
Of name and fame
Is astronomical.

3935

The mind needs
Flexibility
More than anything else.

3936

Every morning and evening
I go to God's Surrender-School
To study.

3937

My soul always passes
God's Examinations
With flying colours.

3938

O my heart,
See fear
Nowhere!

3939

I must bring
Tomorrow's aspiration
Into my today's life.

3940

Stop impatience
At the very root.

3941

The forward march
Is a challenge—
Only the brave succeed.

3942

There is no substitute
For a God-gratitude-heart.

3943

Fight we must
To establish God's Kingdom
Here on earth.

3944

Eternity breathes
In each moment.

3945

Each dawn inspires us
To be the golden flames
Of the rising sun.

3946

My Lord,
May my gratitude to You
Come first,
Before I do anything.

3947

God's bountiful Message
Of my transformation
Reverberates in my depths.

3948

From now on,
I shall see
Only the good
In all human beings.

3949

Today is the day
That I have smashed asunder
My doubt-prison cell.

3950

My Lord, what can I do,
What can I do?
"My child, what can you not do,
What can you not do?
You can easily realise God!"

3951

When we do not
Believe in God,
We believe in
God-empty nothingness.

3952

Each day
Is a new adventure
Towards our Destined Goal.

3953

My Lord,
To my greatest joy,
Your Thoughts pervade my mind
All the time.

MY CHRISTMAS-NEW YEAR-VACATION-ASPIRATION-PRAYERS

3954

My Lord,
May Your sacred Feet
Adorn my heart-garden.

3955

My Lord,
My whole life depends on
Your Smiles and Tears.

3956

When my soul meditates
Inside my heart,
My entire being
Gets a tremendous thrill.

3957

The necessity of speed
In everything
Is of paramount importance.

3958

Without sincerity,
Nobody can fulfil
God's Will.

3959

The mind does not want
To know
What the Truth is.

3960

Do not be afraid
Of weaknesses.
They are not everlasting.

3961

How can one deny
God's Existence forever?
How?

3962

An aspiration-empty heart
Weakens
Our God-connection.

3963

The blame-game
Is at once
Easy and dangerous.

3964

My heart-tears
Are treasured
By the golden dawn.

3965

I immediately avoid
All my backward-looking
Thoughts.

3966

My heart-lotus
Is opening to God,
Petal by petal.

3967

When I offer my aspiration-heart
To God,
He blesses me
With His Satisfaction-Smile-
 Garden.

3968

In the spiritual life,
Nobody is expected
To remain in the beginners' class
All the time!

3969

No aspiration
Should have
An ailing experience.

3970

No dedication
Should have
A failing experience.

3971

Silence pleases God
More easily
Than anything else.

3972

My gratitude-heart
And God's Fondness
Are found always together.

3973

Aspiration and dedication
Are to be found
On the same level of
 consciousness.

MY CHRISTMAS-NEW YEAR-VACATION-ASPIRATION-PRAYERS

3974

I must offer my gratitude-heart
To God
Daily and punctually.

3975

A God-descending thought
Is what I need.

3976

A heart-ascending willingness
Is what I need.

3977

When I please God
In His own Way,
I see countless stars
Singing and dancing
In my heart-sky.

3978

We came into the world,
Not only to eat material food,
But also to feed our heart
With our aspiration-meal.

3979

The mind's limitations
Lead us, quite often,
Astray.

3980

Each heart
Has a museum
Of sweetness-memories.

3981

Meditate, meditate—
Do not
Anticipate!

3982

When we do not pray
And meditate,
We become prisoners
Of our mind.

3983

Nothing can remain
Forever unreachable.

3984

A single Glance
From my Lord Supreme
Gives me unimaginable
   happiness.

3985

Truth blossoms
Only inside
The heart of pure God-seekers
And God-lovers.

3986

O seeker,
Do not be greedy!
Why do you have to be
All alone with God?

3987

I love
The lion-roar
Of my prayer.

3988

I love
The sea-peace
Of my meditation.

3989

Those who are faith-heroes
Will not be afraid of anything
Here on earth.

3990

The willingness of the mind
And the eagerness of the heart
Must work together
To arrive at the Goal.

3991

God wants us
To be happy, happy, happy
All the time.

3992

We want God
To be proud of us
All the time.

3993

In the spiritual life,
The mind and the heart
Are as far from each other
As the East is from the West.

MY CHRISTMAS-NEW YEAR-VACATION-ASPIRATION-PRAYERS

3994

If we act soulfully and
 self-givingly
To please God,
It is impossible to fail.

3995

Since God spoke to me,
My outer life and my inner life
Have completely changed
For the better.

3996

God in Heaven
Is beautiful.

3997

God on earth
Is useful.

3998

God wants me to smile,
Bright, brighter, brightest,
To please Him.

3999

God wants me to cry,
Soulfully and ceaselessly,
To please Him.

4000

In the purity-garden
Of the heart,
There should be
No falsehood.

4001

My prayer and my meditation
Take the first aspiration-flight
To God in Heaven.

4002

We cannot satisfy God
Only with our hollow promises.
God wants us to fulfil
Our promises.

4003

Imagination is not
A whim of the mind.
It is a reality in its own right.

4004

To believe in God
Is not enough.
To be dynamic for God
Is needed.

4005

My meditation
Silently and infallibly opens
My Lord's Heart-Door.

4006

A devotion-heart
And an argumentation-mind
Must always remain apart.

4007

Love smiles,
Whether it is human love
Or divine love.

4008

Man's mind is born
For world-success.

4009

Man's heart is born
For God-satisfaction.

4010

I close my eyes
When discouragement
Wants to enter into my life.

4011

The power of despair
Is shocking.

4012

We must break asunder
The veil
Of the doubting mind.

4013

Light is not to be feared.
Light is to be loved
All the time.

4014

Be not a slave
To the mind's autocracy.

4015

Each seeker
Must work very hard
To illumine the mind.

MY CHRISTMAS-NEW YEAR-VACATION-ASPIRATION-PRAYERS

4016

The longings of childhood
Are always cheerful
And soulful.

4017

Willingness and eagerness
Add unimaginably
To our aspiration
And dedication-life.

4018

Patience
Has a most
Comforting hand.

4019

Simplicity and sincerity—
These are the very special
Gifts of God
To mankind.

4020

I want
The music of silence
To silence my mind.

4021

Perfection
Is, indeed,
A lifelong battle.

4022

I must not allow fear
To blindfold
My heart.

4023

My God-oneness
Is
My universal passport.

4024

The light of silence
Breathes
Everywhere.

4025

Slowly and steadily,
Not abruptly,
We must open up our heart-lotus,
Petal by petal.

4026

We are all
Prisoners
Of Time.

4027

I do not care for my mind's
World-possession-thirst;
I care only for my heart's
World-embrace-hunger.

4028

My life's ancient prayers
And my life's ancient meditations
I still practise.

4029

Humanity's
God-discovery-journey
Will never end.

4030

Each child of God
Is God's
Ever-blossoming hope.

4031

O seeker,
Do not think of your salvation;
Think of God's manifestation.

4032

The soul shares its secrets
Only with the heart,
And not with the mind,
The vital and the body.

4033

Do not think of yesterday's
Failure-life.
Think of today's aspiration-heart
And determination-life.

4034

When I saw my mind
At the Feet of God,
I was astonished
Beyond measure.

4035

Each God-surrendering thought
Demolishes
Ignorance-foundation.

MY CHRISTMAS-NEW YEAR-VACATION-ASPIRATION-PRAYERS

4036

When I become
A God-gratitude-heart,
I see a beautiful angel
Singing and dancing before me.

4037

I do not think of surrender.
I do not dream of surrender.
I have become
The very essence of surrender.

4038

My gratitude-life
Is the only way
For me to please God.

4039

To serve God
Is the greatest honour.

4040

I do not see You, but I do feel
That You are in the depths
Of my heart, my Lord.

4041

Before you look
At the world,
Muster all your love.

4042

Life means
Adamantine determination.

4043

Heart means
Constant aspiration.

4044

Inside my Master's smile
I see my new world
Blooming.

4045

God really wants to love us.
Alas, why do we make it so difficult
For Him?

4046

It is we
Who take ourselves away
From God's Forgiveness-Reach.

4047

To falsify anything in life
Is the height
Of our stupidity.

4048

Ignorance-frown
Veils
Our divinity.

4049

Our heart-tears
Unveil
Our divinity.

4050

Do not be near
The undivine forces—
They may kidnap you
At any time.

4051

Our love of God
Must be as true
As God's Descent on earth.

4052

God takes shelter inside
My ever-blossoming
Gratitude-heart.

4053

Do not think of
Your past crimes,
But think of
Your present golden moments.

4054

O seeker,
If you are a true seeker,
Then your heart
Is bound to be
Flooded with sweetness.

4055

Each Smile of my Lord Supreme
Kindles
A new inspiration-hope-flame
Inside my heart.

4056

Those who think that
Spirituality is out of style
Are swimming
In the sea of ignorance.

MY CHRISTMAS-NEW YEAR-VACATION-ASPIRATION-PRAYERS

4057

My heart lives
Inside
The Heart of God.

4058

My life lives
In God's immediate
Neighbourhood.

4059

Art
Is the beauty
Of the heart.

4060

Art
Is the joy
Of life.

4061

Be either a believer
Or an atheist—
O mind,
You have the right to choose.

4062

Expectation and attachment
Are always found
Together.

4063

Only one attachment
Is divine—
My love of God.

4064

God proudly appreciates
Even our smaller-than-the-
    smallest
Attempts.

4065

One atom
Is equal to
The whole universe.

4066

If your belief is strong,
Then God-vision
Is within your eyeshot.

4067

God-believers
Are
God-chosen heroes.

4068

A sincere and soulful seeker
Cannot be
A depression-victim.

4069

Spirituality
Does not exclude anything
Whatsoever.

4070

Spirituality accepts,
Embraces and feeds
Everything.

4071

Blows are needed
To awaken us
From our age-old slumber.

4072

The body-temple neglected
Is God-rejection-experience.

4073

The mind
Loves to exercise
Free will.

4074

The heart
Wants to experience
Only God's Will.

4075

Bondage
Is the connecting link
Between desire
And ignorance.

4076

God exists only for those
Who are always ready
To help themselves.

4077

Aspiration
Is
Our soul-creation.

MY CHRISTMAS-NEW YEAR-VACATION-ASPIRATION-PRAYERS

4078

Book-information
Is
Our mind-creation.

4079

The purity of the mind
And the sincerity of the heart
Have no equal.

4080

The doubting mind
Entangles us.

4081

The aspiring heart
Illumines us.

4082

Bondage
Is our love
Of undivine forces.

4083

Liberation
Is our God-choice.

4084

I do not want to be
A great singer.
I do not want to be
A good singer.
I want only to be
A God-love-champion-hero.

4085

What is creation,
If not a continuous struggle
From darkness to light?

4086

In life we choose
The strength of sound.

4087

In death we choose
The breath of silence.

4088

To be a seeker
Is to be on
A God-preparation-journey.

4089

God is not only
In everything,
But everything
Is God.

4090

To lose faith in oneself
Is immediately to lose faith
In God Himself.

4091

Books do not help us
Realise God,
But they do inspire us
To pray to God
And meditate on God.

4092

To be a world-renouncer
Is much easier
Than to be a God-possessor.

4093

Liberation
Is much easier
Than God-realisation.

4094

God-realisation
Is much easier
Than God-manifestation.

4095

Devotion
Feeds and expedites
Aspiration.

4096

To realise God,
I need an unbroken chain
Of God-devotion.

4097

Reality is not
From darkness to light.
Reality is
From light to light.

4098

We can see the road easily,
But to walk along the road
To the Destination
Is extremely difficult.

MY CHRISTMAS-NEW YEAR-VACATION-ASPIRATION-PRAYERS

4099

Pathfinders
Are infinitely more important
Than travellers.

4100

When God is my choice,
Only choice,
God's Voice cannot remain far,
Very far.

4101

Man the bondage
And
God the Freedom
Together live.

4102

I want to see
God's Feet first,
Before I see God's Face.

4103

I want to see
God's Eye first,
Before I see the world.

4104

God-knowers
Are more God-lovers
Than God-seekers.

4105

God's Grace
Is always
Empty of condition.

4106

The strength of goodness
Far surpasses
The strength of greatness.

4107

I am extremely fond
Of the heart of everything
In God's world.

4108

Peace, universal peace,
Is definitely within the reach
Of all.

4109

Life is eternal
Only when we cry to live
In God's Breath.

4110

Change
Is absolutely necessary
In the process of evolution.

4111

Love of God
Is our only religion.

4112

To fulfil God
In His own Way
Is the code of our life.

4113

Religion means
Conscious God-union.

4114

Religion means
To live in a higher height.

4115

Religion means
Universal Smile.

4116

Nothing else
But spirituality
Is the world-salvation.

4117

With love
We make our progress.

4118

With service
We make ourselves
Perfect.

4119

Knowledge and information
Are good friends.

4120

Wisdom and will
Are perfect friends.

MY CHRISTMAS-NEW YEAR-VACATION-ASPIRATION-PRAYERS

4121

Knowledge means
World-unity.

4122

Wisdom means
World-oneness-embrace.

4123

Leadership
Is
Extremely easy.

4124

Friendship
Is
Extremely difficult.

4125

Life is not
A false dream.

4126

Life is the blooming
And blossoming
Reality.

4127

We learn from God
Oneness-Delight.

4128

God learns from us
Separation-night.

4129

My Lord,
I really try to love You only.
Please do not be sad or mad
If I do not succeed.

4130

I do not know
Why I am confined
To the dark chamber
Of self-doubt.

4131

My Lord,
If You really love me,
Then do not overlook
Even a slight mistake!

4132

I am my constant loyalty
To my Supreme.

4133

When God approaches us
Powerfully,
We get frightened.
Therefore, He comes to us
Playfully.

4134

When God does not
Smile at me,
My life becomes
Real death.

4135

God's Smile
Always embodies Silence—
The mightiest Silence-Sound!

4136

There is no ignorance-abyss
That cannot
Be crossed.

4137

God inundates me
With His
Life-giving Love.

4138

Each time you speak
Against your fellow seekers,
You go away—
Farther than the farthest—
From your Lord Supreme.

4139

I am ready to be disregarded
By all,
But not by my Lord Supreme.

4140

A soulful seeker
Is he whose life-breath
Is offered to God.

4141

Tomorrow's promise
We never fulfil.

MY CHRISTMAS-NEW YEAR-VACATION-ASPIRATION-PRAYERS

4142

God wants us
To preserve our love for Him
And our service for the world.

4143

To become complete,
What we need
Is God-realisation.

4144

Peace-blossoms
We find
Only in our heart-garden.

4145

My heart is one
With the happiness
Of the moon.

4146

My life is one
With the power
Of the sun.

4147

My breath is one
With the Immortality
Of God's Heart.

4148

My hope
Is my beauty's fragrance.

4149

My promise
Is my duty's fulfilment.

4150

My heart is flying
With my Lord's Breath
Towards Heaven.

4151

Everybody needs
Mind-purification
Every day.

4152

Everybody needs
Heart-surrender
Every day.

4153

Everybody needs
Life-dedication
Every day.

4154

My happiness-life
Is on God's
Priority list.

4155

I love to journey
Into the Unknown
At every moment.

4156

Some great souls
Disguise themselves
As street beggars.

4157

The beauty of the heart
Is too deep
For the mind to appreciate.

4158

Every heart
Is made of dreams.

4159

Every life
Is made of realities.

4160

The power of silence
The mind tries to break
In vain.

4161

Spirituality begins
With God-awareness.

4162

There is no real treasure
In the mind;
All the treasures
Are hidden in the heart.

4163

The hopes of the heart
Are full of fragrance.

4164

The aspiration-dedication-life
Is truly difficult,
But not impossible.

MY CHRISTMAS-NEW YEAR-VACATION-ASPIRATION-PRAYERS

4165

I cry and try,
I try and cry
To become
A choice instrument
Of God.

4166

My soul-smiles
Widen my life.

4167

My heart-tears
Heighten my life.

4168

A gratitude-heart-experience
Is beyond compare.

4169

May the climbing flame
Of my heart
Please God
In His own Way.

4170

The desire-mind
Lives between
Gloom and doom.

4171

Not God the Justice
But God the Compassion
Prepares our future.

4172

Nobody can go towards God
Until God Himself
Comes towards him.

4173

Each prayer
Is a climbing ladder
To Heaven.

4174

Each meditation
Is a bridge
Between Heaven and earth.

4175

For the heart,
God's Name
Is a daily
Remembrance-reality.

4176

With my tear-waves,
I go to God.

4177

With my smile-seas,
I return.

4178

When we think of God,
Hopelessness
Is not to be found anywhere.

4179

O my mind,
What you need
Is just one gratitude-plant.

4180

Nothing starts
With human beings.
Everything starts
With God's Heart.

4181

Each moment
Is a miracle-experience
In the history of the world.

4182

I need a heart-elevating
And not an eye-catching
God-drawing service.

4183

Be a man
Of few words
But endless deeds.

4184

To enter into God's Boat,
We need only
A soulful smile.

MY CHRISTMAS-NEW YEAR-VACATION-ASPIRATION-PRAYERS

4185

We long for
Earthly length,
But we should long only for
Divine strength.

4186

God loves two things:
My listening ears
And
My embracing heart.

4187

My aspiration-heart
Carries me home
To Heaven.

4188

My Lord,
When will my mind come to learn
That my heart will never be able
To live without You?

4189

My physical death
Is not the end of my life—
I am an eternal journey.

4190

I pray and pray
And pray
To see God's Feet.

4191

I meditate and meditate
And meditate
To feel God's Heart.

4192

I contemplate, contemplate
And contemplate
To become one with God's Will.

4193

When my prayer
Is sincere,
God blesses my head.

4194

When my meditation
Is deep,
God embraces my heart.

4195

What do I need?
A heart-throbbing prayer.

4196

What do I need?
A time-stopping meditation.

4197

I was born
With a heart
Of God-beauty.

4198

I was born
With a life
Of God-duty.

4199

The desire-life
Is always busy—
It has no free time.

4200

God wants our heart's hopes
Always to be hopeful,
And not hopeless.

4201

I ask God
How He spends His time.
He says to me,
"My child, I spend My time
Without thinking of Me."

4202

God-realisation
Is
A solo run.

4203

God-manifestation
Is
A relay run.

4204

Every breath of my heart
Is needed
To worship the golden dust
Of God's Feet.

4205

Every day
The Godward speed
Of my heart
Baffles my mind.

MY CHRISTMAS-NEW YEAR-VACATION-ASPIRATION-PRAYERS

4206

The aspiration-heart
Knows no sunset years,
But the doubtful mind does.

4207

There is not a single day
That God does not show
His red caution-flag
To our disobedient mind and
    vital.

4208

Our heart's God-devotion-tears
Are full of
God-Touch-thrills.

4209

God the Creator
Blesses
My climbing aspiration.

4210

God the Creation
Embraces
My spreading dedication.

4211

The human in me wants
The world's thunderous praise
All the time.

4212

The divine in me needs
Blessingful Grace from God
All the time.

4213

To meditate
Is to have a quick dive
Into God's Heart-Swimming
    Pool.

4214

Standing, I can see
The Golden Shore
From my wide-open
Heart's door.

4215

Limitless delight I enjoy
When I remain nameless
In my God-love,
In my God-devotion
And
In my God-surrender-service.

4216

Pride
Openly challenges.
Soulfulness
Secretly wins.

4217

Every morning when I meditate,
The singing flowers,
The dancing branches
And the climbing trees
Join me in my meditation.

4218

God's outer Presence
Is
Definitely needed.

4219

God's inner Presence
Is
Absolutely indispensable.

4220

The mind thinks only
Of pleasing itself.

4221

The heart dreams
Of pleasing its own
Absolute Lord Beloved Supreme.

4222

The tears of my heart
Are most devotedly following
The Footsteps
Of my Lord Supreme.

4223

I wish my heart
To be
A ceaseless God-hunger-cry.

4224

I wish my life
To be
A breathless God-Touch-thrill.

4225

I have made
My heart-cottage
With my tears.

MY CHRISTMAS-NEW YEAR-VACATION-ASPIRATION-PRAYERS

4226

I have built
My soul-palace
With God's Smiles.

4227

When my meditation is deep,
Very deep,
My heart breathes in
God-hunger-breaths.

4228

We must brave
All our difficulties,
Problems and failures
In our lives.

4229

My Lord
And my Lord's Forgiveness
Are inseparable.

4230

Alas,
I always overestimate
The sincerity
Of my prayers.

4231

Alas,
I always underestimate
The infinite Power
Of God's Grace.

4232

With Silence-Beauty
And Sweetness-Fragrance-Steps,
My Lord enters into
My tiny human heart.

4233

When I cheerfully
And unconditionally
Obey God,
I become immediately
His favourite toy.

4234

Conscience
Is the aspiration-heart's
Clock-alarm.

4235

Alas,
The way to God-realisation
Is very, very long.

4236

The desire-life
Is utterly ignorant
Of hidden dangers.

4237

Out of His infinite Bounty,
My Lord tells me
That my gratitude-heart
Has the capacity to drown
All my life's blunders.

4238

Sleeplessly,
My heart-eye is focused
On God's Compassion-Eye-Star.

4239

God-realisation-trees
Come into existence
From God-surrender-seeds.

4240

Hope-sun
Does not set.
Hope-sun
Is immortal.

4241

To walk with life
Is beautiful.

4242

To sleep with death
Is peaceful.

4243

My God-surrender
Means
A life of constant surprises.

4244

Heaven beckons only
The sleepless self-givers.

4245

God sings and sings;
I sleep and sleep.
I sing and sing;
God dreams and dreams.

4246

Each additional responsibility
Is another golden opportunity
To please the Inner Pilot
In His own Way.

MY CHRISTMAS-NEW YEAR-VACATION-ASPIRATION-PRAYERS

4247

An aspiration-heart
Without fail embodies
Many divine qualities.

4248

Each seeker's life
Must fly into
The highest aspiration-sky.

4249

When I pray,
I use my humility-knees.

4250

When I meditate,
I use my world-oneness-heart.

4251

A readiness-life
Needs
An eagerness-start.

4252

Every day
The Master is
His torrential Heaven-blessings,
His Heaven-love
And his Heaven-concern
For his disciples.

4253

The Master keeps
His disciples' sorrows
Not on his shoulders,
But deep inside
His compassion-heart.

4254

Centuries ago, my Lord,
You created me.
Since then,
You have been taking care of me
With Your infinite Compassion,
Infinite Affection
And infinite Concern.
My Lord,
I wish You to take rest!
From now on
I shall most lovingly,
Most soulfully
And most self-givingly
Look after You.

4255

Immeasurable is my joy
When God asks me
To devour the dust
Of His Feet.

4256

In the morning
God blesses me with the Joys
Of His Higher World.
In the evening
God blesses me with the Peace
Of His Inner World.

4257

In the small hours of the
 morning,
My Lord checks and checks
And checks
My love, devotion and surrender.

4258

Every day, unmistakably,
God's Eye cradles
My aspiration-heart
So lovingly and so fondly.

4259

God's Compassion-Eye,
God's Affection-Heart
And
God's Concern-Life
Are renovating my old life.

4260

God's unconditional Compassion
Has drawn my life close,
 very close,
To His Heart.

4261

May my whole life
Be inundated
With God-obedience-
 Fulfilment-promises.

4262

We must never give up
Our God-realisation-hope
And our God-manifestation-
 hope.

4263

God likes the silence-blooms
Of my outer world.
God admires the silence-blossoms
Of my inner world.

MY CHRISTMAS-NEW YEAR-VACATION-ASPIRATION-PRAYERS

4264

My Lord,
Do You not have any Secret
To share with me?
"My child,
I have many, many Secrets
To share with you,
But the time has not come."

4265

There is no difference
Between a strong desire
And a wild, hungry fire.

4266

God Himself uses
My aspiration-breath
When He sings
And plays music.

4267

The human in us
Wants power-victory.
The divine in us
Needs love-victory.

4268

True,
My hand-violin
Has sadly failed me,
But my heart-violin
Has never failed me
And will never fail.

4269

When my silence-heart
Invokes God,
God comes down
Sooner than at once.

4270

My entire being is thrilled
To be a member
Of my Supreme Lord's
Inner family.

4271

My Lord,
You are all the time
Inside my heart.
How is it
That I do not see myself
Inside Your Heart,
Even for a fleeting moment?

4272

Who are the true heroes?
Not those who destroy
But those who try to build
God's Heart-Home on earth.

4273

I simply break
My Lord's Heart
When I feed my ego.

4274

In my inner family,
Only my soul and my heart
Are real citizens
Of God's Heart-Land.

4275

God tells me again and again
That He needs
My devotion-heart
And not
My brilliance and my talents.

4276

Enthusiasm
Is a divinely proud forward
march
Towards God's Heart-Home.

4277

Whenever I write
Most devoted letters to God,
He immediately invites
All the cosmic gods and goddesses,
And then He reads out my letters.

4278

The desire-life
Wants God the Power.
The aspiration-heart
Needs only God.

4279

To be a sleepless God-lover
Is to be
A great ignorance-conqueror.

4280

I began my life
With God the Beautiful.
I shall end my life
In God the Peaceful.

4281

I am infinitely happier
When I feel
That I belong to God
Than when I feel
That God belongs to me.

MY CHRISTMAS-NEW YEAR-VACATION-ASPIRATION-PRAYERS

4282

The genuine devotion
Of the heart
Is a magnetic power.

4283

I shall never allow
My aspiration-day
To expire.

4284

A gratitude-blossom-heart
Is
Beyond compare.

4285

Love-devotion-songs
God has already taught me.
Nowadays He teaches me
Only surrender-songs.

4286

I call my sad failure-past
"Past".
I call my happy present
"The Blue Eye
Of my Golden Supreme".

4287

When I say to God,
"God, You are great, very great,"
God bursts into wild laughter.

4288

When I say to God,
"God, You are good, very good,"
God gives me
A very sweet Smile.

4289

Some make their Godward
    journey
Out of sheer curiosity,
While others,
Out of their absolute necessity.

4290

God Himself feeds
My climbing aspiration-heart
Seven times a day.

4291

Every breath
Is
A God-fulfilment-
    Opportunity-moment.

4292

God alone knows
If humility will ever be able
To touch the haughty head
Of humanity.

4293

Each soulful smile
Of a God-seeker
Is a special
    God-manifestation-joy
Here on earth.

4294

The higher I go,
The stronger I feel the need
To feast only
On God's Smiles.

4295

True, I am not at all important
To the world,
But I am extremely important
To my Lord Absolute Supreme,
For He knows that my heart
    and I
Love Him only
And need Him only.

4296

My dedication-life-road
Goes all the way
To God's highest Abode.

4297

The doubting mind
Is a God-torturer.

4298

The aspiring heart
Is a God-treasurer.

4299

With my self-giving services,
I feed earth.

4300

With my teeming dreams,
I feed Heaven.

4301

Little by little,
We give to God
What we have.

MY CHRISTMAS-NEW YEAR-VACATION-ASPIRATION-PRAYERS

4302

Profusely and unreservedly,
God gives us
What He is.

4303

Not a giant mind
But a little heart
Has a free access
To God's Heart-Home.

4304

When I see God's Eye,
I get terribly frightened.
When I see God's Heart,
I am immediately awakened.

4305

Where do I live?
I live under my Lord's
Protection-Eye.

4306

My morning begins
By devouring
God's Nectar-Feet-Dust.

4307

God's Forgiveness-Embrace
Has given my heart
A new hope-light
And my life
A new promise-delight.

4308

Time-river flows
Slowly, very slowly,
When my meditation-heart
Glows.

4309

To be victorious in life,
I must surmount
Each and every
Difficulty-mountain.

4310

To make our
 Beloved Lord Supreme
Happy,
We must open not one
But all opportunity-doors.

4311

Now is the time
And here is the place
To please God
In His own Way.

4312

Today I am a lover
Of God's soul-stirring Flute.
Tomorrow I shall be a lover
Of God's Victory-Trumpet.

4313

My freedom
Is
My God-obedience.

4314

My freedom
Is
My desire-annihilation.

4315

My freedom
Sees nowhere
Earth-bondage-chains.

4316

Each God-Heart-Song
Of mine
Has a God-Soul-Fragrance-
    Melody.

4317

Yesterday my life was
A God-reliance-dream-beauty,
But today my life has become
God-Reality-Fragrance.

4318

A God-gratitude-heart
Is
A God-plenitude-life.

4319

When it is a physical death,
We cry and cry.
When it is a spiritual death,
God cries and cries.

4320

This morning
My heart-flame reached
A very, very high height.

MY CHRISTMAS-NEW YEAR-VACATION-ASPIRATION-PRAYERS

4321

Aspiration
Is
Heaven-climbing joy.

4322

Dedication
Is
Earth-spreading joy.

4323

At the top of the life-tree
Is liberation.

4324

At the foot of the life-tree
Is the beginning
Of God-hunger.

4325

Life and death
All the time ask questions,
But they never answer
Each other.

4326

The silence of my heart
Does not stop,
But the sound of my life
Does.

4327

Needless to say,
My fate on earth
Is deplorable.
Alas,
So is God's.

4328

My Lord,
May all my desire-prayers
Remain unanswered.

4329

Heaven is Heaven's
Compassion for me.
Earth is earth's
Concern for me.
I must succeed
In my God-manifestation-task.

4330

Nothing divine
Can ever decay.
Nothing divine
Can even fade.

4331

I need on earth
Only one thing:
A God-devotion-breath.

4332

Every morning
God blesses me
With a new sunshine-heart
To receive Him
With enormous joy.

4333

Pay no attention
To the wild thunders
Of the world.
Pay all attention
Only to the sweet Whispers
Of your Inner Pilot.

4334

We can fathom
Everything else here on earth
Save and except
The unfathomable depth
Of silence.

4335

God's Perfection-Dream
For my life
Shall prevail.

4336

Earth-tears
And Heaven-Smiles
Are God's childhood friends.

4337

Value your self-discipline.
Self-discipline is the way.
Self-discipline will bring you
To God's Heart-Door.

4338

We obey God.
God obeys our love,
Unconditional love,
For Him.

MY CHRISTMAS-NEW YEAR-VACATION-ASPIRATION-PRAYERS

4339

When the gratitude-heart
Fully blossoms,
The transformation of life
Begins.

4340

My Lord is my Friend,
Only Friend.
I do not need
A multitude of friends.

4341

Soulfully and self-givingly
I sing and sing
At the top of my voice
To become a choice instrument
Of God.

4342

The outer success
We can easily measure,
But the inner progress
Is extremely difficult to measure.

4343

Today's God-disobedience
Tomorrow becomes
Life's worst possible catastrophe.

4344

He who dreams of God
Quite often
In the small hours of the morning
Becomes a God-lover
Of the highest magnitude.

4345

I love God,
Not because He is
Divinely great
And not because He is
Supremely good,
But because He is my All,
Very All.

4346

God-obedience-lessons
Are compulsory
From the journey's start
To the journey's close.

4347

My Lord,
Please, please,
Give me another chance
To please You
In Your own Way.

4348

God wants me
To fly with Him
With my ever-blossoming
Heart-songs.

4349

My soul, my heart and I
Will never be found
In the thick of desire-forest.

4350

Constant God-choice
Is the only antidote
To self-doubt.

4351

The inner joy
Gives more.
The inner joy
Receives more.
The inner joy
Becomes more.

4352

In silence-secrecy
My heart talks
To my Lord Supreme.

4353

Our sleepless God-surrender
Is the architect
Of God's new world.

4354

My Lord tells me
That my ever-blossoming
Gratitude-heart
Is His most favourite song.

4355

My heart's bliss
Is the announcer
Of God's express Arrival.

4356

Earth says to Heaven,
"Why are you
So beautiful?"

4357

Heaven says to earth,
"Why are you
So useful?"

MY CHRISTMAS-NEW YEAR-VACATION-ASPIRATION-PRAYERS

4358

Aspiration
Is
My heart-song.

4359

Dedication
Is
My life-story.

4360

When I desire,
I become a body-cage.

4361

When I aspire,
I become a soul-bird
Flying in Infinity's Sky.

4362

My Lord tells me
That all my promises to Him
Are just exquisite.

4363

God's Eye
Is my most powerful
Heart-attraction.

4364

Each fleeting moment
I try to run at full speed
Towards my Lord Supreme.

4365

Our genuine prayers
Must bring us to our knees,
And not our endless
Worries and anxieties.

4366

My life's sufferings
Can be measured,
But my soul's bliss
Forever shall remain
Immeasurable.

4367

My God-obedience
And God's Pride in me
Are extremely fond of each other.

4368

Impossible—
A permanent God-failure-life
Is impossible!

4369

When the inner heart
Is all sweetness,
The outer life
Becomes all fulness.

4370

Our aspiration-eagerness-
    intensity
Helps us find our way back
To our Absolute Lord Supreme.

4371

Day and night
My heart and I
Walk along
Our soul-paved road.

4372

My hope-beauty
Comes from God's Heart.

4373

My promise-fragrance
Comes from God's Breath.

4374

My morning meditation
Is my soul's
God-invocation.

4375

My morning meditation
Is my life's
God-Dream-Delight.

4376

My morning meditation tells me
That God-vision
Is not enough,
God-realisation
Is not enough,
Even God-manifestation
Is not enough.
My life's complete transformation
Is my journey's final halt.

4377

May each and every thought
Of mine
Be always Heaven-bound.

MY CHRISTMAS-NEW YEAR-VACATION-ASPIRATION-PRAYERS

4378

When God is on my side,
I become my life's sad failure.
When I am on God's side,
God gives me His Victory-Drum.

4379

Every morning
I sing for my Lord
With my gratitude-heart-tears
And my gratitude-eye-smiles.

4380

Wherever I go,
I carry with me
A newness-mind
And a soulfulness-heart.

4381

Each time I pray,
I must try to reach
A higher height.

4382

Each time I concentrate,
I must try to develop
A stronger will.

4383

Each time I meditate,
I must try to enter into
A deeper depth.

4384

Each time I contemplate,
I must try to get
Closer, closer and closer
To God.

4385

My devotion
Is my only
God-Satisfaction-
Fulfilment-necessity.

4386

The tears of my heart
Feed on our Lord's
Compassion-Temptation-Feet.

4387

Every day
God wants me to accomplish
Something absolutely new,
Inspiring and aspiring.

4388

Alas,
Will I ever be worthy
Of mingling
With the dust of my Lord's Feet?

4389

Determination, determination—
Stoic determination!
If not,
God-realisation
Will remain a far cry.

4390

When everything is gone,
The tears of my heart
And I
Shall remain.

4391

My heart and I
Get tremendous joy
When my Lord Beloved Supreme
Checks and checks
On my surrender-life.

4392

Our Lord Beloved Supreme
Expects all true
And self-giving seekers
To be madly in love
With Him alone.

4393

My Lord Supreme
Every day,
For at least an hour,
Cradles my life
With His Compassion-Eye.

4394

My peaceful heart
Prayerfully welcomes
My Lord's blissful Eye
And His powerful Feet.

4395

My heart's cries and tears
Purify and fortify my life
Most significantly.

4396

My soul's smiles
Feed my heart
To run the fastest
For God-realisation.

MY CHRISTMAS-NEW YEAR-VACATION-ASPIRATION-PRAYERS

4397

My heart's performances
Are mightily appreciated
By earth's heart
And Heaven's Eye.

4398

Do not allow
Lethargy-sleep
To prevent you from seeing
God's morning Smile.

4399

Morning is the time
To receive from God
His torrential Blessings,
Affection and Concern-Rain.

4400

I came into the world
To serve God
Lovingly and self-givingly,
And not to experience
His highest Height
And His deepest Depth.

4401

Each heart-song
Is a very long step forward
Towards God.

4402

Sleep like a child,
Dream like a child,
Act like a child.
Lo, God is granting you
A free access
To His Heart-Home.

4403

Poor God
Is all the time calling us,
But we deliberately
Do not respond.

4404

My Lord Supreme returns
My love-devotion-surrender-calls
Immediately.

4405

God-disobedience-train—
Once it starts,
It never stops.

4406

The ancient God blessed me
With the message
Of unity in multiplicity.

4407

The modern God is blessing me
With the message
Of diversity and complexity.

4408

In our spiritual life,
Eagerness-speed
Knows no equal.

4409

No human heart
Can ever dare to resist
God's Heart-Attraction.

4410

God never sanctions
Any seeker's
Retirement-enjoyment.

4411

Nothing in my life
Is as sacred
As my heart's
Sleepless and breathless
God-devotion.

4412

Never,
Never become tired
Of your inward dive!

4413

My Lord Supreme
Blessingfully and
    compassionately
Blesses each petal
Of my lotus-heart.

4414

In the small hours
Of the morning
My life-tree
Exquisitely blossoms.

4415

My Lord appreciates
And admires
Only my ceaselessly
Self-giving miracles.

4416

Darkness covers.
Light uncovers
And illumines.

MY CHRISTMAS-NEW YEAR-VACATION-ASPIRATION-PRAYERS

4417

The peace of my heart
And the silence of my mind
Have boundless affection
For each other.

4418

God corrects me
With His Eye.

4419

God perfects me
With His Heart.

4420

Early in the morning
I harvest
My God-gratitude-heart-flowers.

4421

Not just in our free moments,
But at every moment,
We must try to satisfy God
In His own Way.

4422

Each devotion-breath
Of my heart
Brings me closer and closer
To my Lord's Heart.

4423

My earth-detachment
Expedites
My God-attachment.

4424

We do not get God-rapture
From our self-torture—
Never!

4425

Sleepless self-offering
To God's Will
Is the quickest and only way
To God-rapture.

4426

Alas,
The human in us
Is hopelessly
And unforgettably weak.

4427

To our greatest joy,
The Divine in us
Is unimaginably
And eternally powerful.

4428

I shall not control
And dominate anybody.
I shall not lead
And guide anybody.
I shall only love everybody
And be for everybody.

4429

No more my mind
Can fool my heart,
For I now have
A God-intoxicated
And God-owned heart.

4430

Why am I so proud
Of my heart?
I am proud of my heart
Because it is always eager
To take giant steps
Towards the Destination.

4431

Each time my Lord looks
Into my gratitude-heart,
He gets a very special thrill.

4432

Silence
Is my inseparable
God-oneness-assurance.

4433

The infinite Beauty
Of my Lord's Eye
Frightens the eyes
Of darkest ignorance-night.

4434

What does God do
All the time?
God dreams and dreams
    and dreams
All the time
In and through His Creation.

4435

I have read from cover to cover
My aspiration-heart-book.
I am now beginning to read
My life-transformation-book.

MY CHRISTMAS-NEW YEAR-VACATION-ASPIRATION-PRAYERS

4436

O seeker,
You came into the world
Neither for awards
Nor for rewards,
But to bask in the Sunshine
Of your Lord's Affection.

4437

My mind
Always likes the power
Of the Unknown.

4438

My heart
Always loves the beauty
Of the Unknowable.

4439

My prayer
Is my life-tree.
My meditation
Is my heart-flower.

4440

My happy thoughts
Have brought me so close
To my Lord Supreme.

4441

My cheerfulness gives God
Enormous Joy
And stupendous Pride.

4442

The mind knows
That God is
A very, very strict Teacher
And Examiner.

4443

The heart feels and knows
That God is
A very kind, inspiring
And encouraging Tutor.

4444

My Lord expects
All the time
Only one thing from me:
Readiness.

4445

I expect from my Lord
Many, many things:
Attention, Affection,
Love, Sweetness, Fondness,
Plus Appreciation and
    Admiration.

4446

For the transformation
Of this world,
Our sole necessity
Is a Heaven-climbing aspiration.

4447

This morning
My heart-lotus bloomed
And then blossomed
So prayerfully, soulfully
And exquisitely.

4448

Twice I am thrilled
Beyond measure:
Once when I soulfully
Clasp God's Eye,
And once when I hungrily
Devour the dust
Of God's Feet.

4449

Every day
God's Encouragement-Smile
Is all I need.

4450

Every day
God's Confidence-Pride in me
Is all I need.

4451

Alas,
Man's God-ingratitude-life
Is exactly the same today
As it has always been.

4452

Even my heart's tiniest
Gratitude-drop
God proudly treasures.

4453

Nothing is as absurd
As my
God-explanation-success.

4454

An austerity-life
Is meant neither
For my Beloved Supreme
Nor for me.

MY CHRISTMAS-NEW YEAR-VACATION-ASPIRATION-PRAYERS

4455

My Beloved Lord Supreme
And I
Love to live always
A simplicity-life.

4456

God the Creator
Is
The Transcendental Power.

4457

God the Creation
Is
The Universal Beauty.

4458

The more I am attached
To God,
The sooner I will be detached
From mankind.

4459

In my inner life of aspiration,
God is eager
To be discovered by me.

4460

In my outer life of dedication,
God is eager
To be sought and caught by me.

4461

When I pray,
I see God
The Beautiful.

4462

When I meditate,
I feel God
The Bountiful.

4463

My inner purity
Protects
My outer life.

4464

Each and every soul
Is made of
Nectar-delight-melodies.

4465

Each and every heart
Is made of
Sweetness-soulfulness-songs.

4466

I have come to learn
That not my capacity
But my God-surrender-life
Has made me win
In the battlefield of life.

4467

Each time I have
A dream of God,
My heart breathes
An ecstasy-flooded life.

4468

Be careful
Of your desire-thoughts!
They can easily obstruct
Your aspiration-path.

4469

Our journey's start
Is from right here,
And our journey's goal
Is beyond within.

4470

No more
Ignorance-thunder-drums!
From now on
Only sweet flute-melodies
I shall hear in my life.

4471

My Lord's Smile
Is my life's only
Protection-Umbrella.

4472

My life's peace-boat
Sails only
Along my heart-river.

4473

My Lord,
Please, please give me a heart
That will feel You sleeplessly.
My Lord,
Please, please give me a life
That will fulfil You constantly.

4474

Quite often
The outer success
May prove to be
A colossal inner failure.

MY CHRISTMAS-NEW YEAR-VACATION-ASPIRATION-PRAYERS

4475

My God-dreams
Are extremely sweet.
My God-visions
Are absolutely authentic.

4476

My soul
Is the hero
Of my inner life.

4477

Alas,
My mind
Is the lord
Of my outer life.

4478

God wants my heart
To be the supreme guide
Of my inner and outer lives.

4479

Love divine
Is absolutely needed
Both on earth
And in Heaven.

4480

I love the beauty
Of my dedication-flow.

4481

I love the fragrance
Of my aspiration-glow.

4482

My mind loves
To command.
My heart loves
To plead.

4483

Time is
Power universal.
Love is
Delight transcendental.

4484

My victories and failures
Come and go,
But not my Lord's
     Compassion-Eye
And His Concern-Heart.

4485

O my mind,
Start loving the world!
Do not criticise the world
Any more.

4486

In the spiritual life,
Desire-fulfilment-dreams
Are absolutely futile.

4487

Transformation does not mean
Extinction.
Transformation means
Illumination.

4488

My mind, keep quiet!
I am hearing my Lord's Footsteps
At my heart-door.

4489

Never forget
That the unwillingness
Of the mind
Can be extremely dangerous.

4490

The surrender-life
Is always eager
To love God the Creator
And serve God the Creation.

4491

God devours
My devotion-heart.
I devour
God's Compassion-Eye.

4492

God's Love is always there
In the very depths of our heart,
But we must bring God's Love
To the fore
To be His true friends and
  servitors.

4493

We can never hide
From God
And from His choice Hour.

4494

The weeping
God the man
I love.

MY CHRISTMAS-NEW YEAR-VACATION-ASPIRATION-PRAYERS

4495

The smiling
Man the God
I need.

4496

Only true God-lovers
Have the key
To open
Heaven's Heart-Door.

4497

God asks me
Never to miss
Even a single chance
To please Him
In His own Way.

4498

The love divine
Is at once God-remembrance
And self-forgetfulness.

4499

My unconditional surrender
To God's Will
Has to be made here and now,
And not in the far distant future.

4500

In the inner world,
Silence is made of power.

4501

In the outer world,
Silence is made of joy.

4502

My aspiration
Has another name:
My God-intoxication.

4503

Each time I cry for God,
He blesses me
With a new horizon.

4504

A sleepless oneness-heart
Is the only thing
That the world badly needs.

4505

Why do you need
A mind that all the time
Confuses and refuses?
What you need
Is a God-loving heart.

4506

Each divine action
Is, indeed,
A God-Fragrance-Joy.

4507

My Lord Supreme
Is never pleased
With my mind-forest.

4508

My Lord Supreme
Is mightily pleased
Always
With my heart-garden.

4509

World Harmony Run
Means the beauty
Of the universal heart
And the fragrance
Of the transcendental soul.

4510

Hope is at once
Sweeter than the sweetest
And
Stronger than the strongest.

4511

Time
Destroys
The human in us.

4512

Time
Employs
The divine in us.

4513

The mind
Wants war.
The hand
Supports it.

4514

Open your heart!
Close your lips!
This is how a seeker
Must speak to God.

MY CHRISTMAS-NEW YEAR-VACATION-ASPIRATION-PRAYERS

4515

Explore, explore!
Very soon
You will be able to knock
At God's Heart-Door.

4516

Each day is my
Heart-blossom-opportunity-day.

4517

As the highest height
Is for us,
Even so, the lowest abyss
Is against us.

4518

The Beyond is calling me.
I must go far beyond
The snares of this world.

4519

Heaven
Watches us.

4520

Earth
Instructs us.

4521

God's Compassion and Concern
Do not leave us,
Even when we deliberately enjoy
Earth-ignorance.

4522

My Master blessingfully sails
His life-boat
On my heart-river.

4523

Poise
Is the most important thing
In whatever I do,
Whatever I say.

4524

Challenges remind me
Of my wakefulness
To my Lord's Compassion-Eye.

4525

When I prayerfully cry,
God allows me
To dive into His Depths.

4526

When I soulfully smile,
God allows me
To fly into His Heights.

4527

Alas,
It is I
Who am not available.
My Lord
Is always available.

4528

My gratitude-heart-tears
Sleeplessly sing
God's Victory-Songs.

4529

Be a God-dreamer first,
And only then can you be
A God-lover.

4530

A God-dreamer I was.
I now am at once
Both a God-lover
And a God-server.

4531

I try to fulfil
My tomorrow's dream
In my today's life.

4532

Before it is too late,
Convince yourself
That you love God only
And you need God only.

4533

Not two closed eyes
But only one open heart
Is needed
To welcome God.

4534

God's first and foremost Choice
Is the silence-garden
Of my heart-home.

4535

Every God-seeker-moment
Awakens us
To a higher height.

MY CHRISTMAS-NEW YEAR-VACATION-ASPIRATION-PRAYERS

4536

Surrender
Helps us evolve
Quicker than the quickest.

4537

Inner poise
Is absolutely needed
To meet with
Outer challenges.

4538

Meditation
Is the secret
Of God-oneness-nectar-delight.

4539

Depression
Is the beginning
Of self-destruction.

4540

Detachment
Shortens
The enlightenment-way.

4541

My heart's inner cries
Quickly bloom
On earth.

4542

My heart's inner cries
Slowly, steadily and unerringly
Blossom in Heaven.

4543

To be God's partner,
You have to be
God's lover and server first.

4544

My heart-page
Is full of Blessings
Written by God Himself.

4545

My mind-page
Is all blank,
Empty of God's Message.

4546

All souls
Struggle and struggle and
    struggle
Inside the body-cage,
But eventually they bring victory
To their Lord Supreme.

4547

If there is even an iota of fear
In approaching God,
Then God immediately
Runs away.

4548

God and I
Share a great many secrets.
Our hearts breathe them
Day in and day out.

4549

My God-hope is blooming.
My God-promise is blossoming.
My thoughts are all
God's Heart-Garden-Flowers.

4550

My God-thoughts
Can easily break through
The darkest
Ignorance-night-boundaries
Of the mind.

4551

My Lord's Compassion
Devours
All my blunders.

4552

My transformation-life
Is urgently needed
Both by Heaven and earth.

4553

I shall no longer allow
Earth-ignorance
To damage my God-given life.

4554

Each gratitude-song
Of my heart
Brightens the Face
Of my Lord Supreme.

MY CHRISTMAS-NEW YEAR-VACATION-ASPIRATION-PRAYERS

4555

My life-boat carries
My Lord's special Blessings
Wherever it goes.

4556

May my God-surrender-life-plant
Grow
Faster than the fastest.

4557

My heart loves
The weeping God
Much more than
The smiling God.
Why?
The weeping God hastens
My progress-life.

4558

The love divine
Is at once shadowless
And limitless.

4559

To hear is not enough.
To see is not enough.
To feel is enough,
More than enough.

4560

Every morning
I place my very best
And my very worst
At the Feet
Of my Lord Supreme.

4561

In the morning I offer
My Lord Supreme
My heart's garland
Of obedience.

4562

In the evening I offer
My Lord Supreme
My life's garland
Of surrender.

4563

My mind lives
In the land
Of darkening evening.

4564

My heart lives
In the land
Of clearing dawn.

4565

God is fond
Of my heart's
Rising joy.

4566

God dislikes
My mind's
Rushing pride.

4567

Retirement
Is empty of
Enlightenment.

4568

My Lord, please bless me
With two far-sighted eyes
And one deep-digging heart.

4569

The mind's unwillingness
Eventually creates
Catastrophes.

4570

Weakness-transformation
Is a most difficult task,
But not impossible.

4571

My patience
Has stabbed the heart
Of my doubting mind.

4572

Criticism
Is
A dangerous disease.

4573

Life is in between
Pure light
And impure mind.

4574

The waters
Of my heart-river
Are all peace.

MY CHRISTMAS-NEW YEAR-VACATION-ASPIRATION-PRAYERS

4575

If you are not satisfied
With your life,
How can God
Ever be satisfied
With you?

4576

God-invocation
Is
Life-exploration.

4577

Medicine
May cure my body,
But God alone
Can feed my heart.

4578

Earth-arrival-journey
Is beautiful.

4579

Heaven-arrival-journey
Is peaceful.

4580

We cannot hide
Either from God
Or from time.

4581

Heart-flowers
God dearly treasures.

4582

Mind-knowledge
Can be quite often
Uncertain.

4583

Heart-wisdom
Is always
Absolutely certain.

4584

Every morning
My soul, my heart and I
Arrive
At a higher destination.

4585

Every day
My soul reaches
A sublime height
Of the Unknown.

4586

Every day
My heart reaches
A deeper depth
Of the Unknown.

4587

Every day
My Supreme commands me
To meditate
On the Unknowable.

4588

In the outer life
Ignorance acts like
A thunderbolt.

4589

In the inner life
Ignorance acts like
A dangerous poison.

4590

Desire powerfully locks
Our heart-door.

4591

Aspiration not only unlocks
Our heart-door,
But also prayerfully and soulfully
Invites God.

4592

Earth's beauty
My heart devours.

4593

Heaven's Delight
My soul becomes.

4594

When we seek
Soulfully and self-givingly,
A new frontier welcomes us,
Garlands us and embraces us.

MY CHRISTMAS-NEW YEAR-VACATION-ASPIRATION-PRAYERS

4595

Those who do not pray
And meditate
Will undoubtedly have a future
With no destination.

4596

Self-doubt
Is a very powerful member
Of the mind-society.

4597

Non-believers
And disbelievers
Are very rich in obscurity.

4598

Self-indulgence
Is a fatal flaw.

4599

My heart-room
Is the place from where
I begin everything.

4600

I need the gods
Of the present
And not the gods
Of the long-buried past
To guide and lead
My present life.

4601

Every day
Without fail
I go to God's
Forgiveness-Feet.

4602

Every time my aspiration
Dies down,
God most compassionately
Revives it.

4603

Not every day
But every minute
My Lord examines
My surrender-breath.

4604

The miracle of miracles
Is my constant
God-gratitude-heart.

4605

Every day
My aspiration climbs up
A more difficult mountain-height.

4606

A cheerful obedience
Is all my life needs.

4607

A delightful surrender
Is all my heart needs.

4608

Ambition prays to God
To be
A monarch.

4609

Aspiration prays to God
To be
A slave of God's Feet.

4610

When my mind sighs,
God does not give my life
His Wings to fly.

4611

Today
My Supreme Lord's
    Compassion-Eye
Is calling me.

4612

Tomorrow
My Supreme Lord's
    Forgiveness-Feet
Will call me.

4613

The day after tomorrow
My Supreme Lord's
    Oneness-Heart
Will call me.

4614

Our prayers save us
From making
Small mistakes.

4615

Our meditations save us
From committing
Himalayan blunders.

MY CHRISTMAS-NEW YEAR-VACATION-ASPIRATION-PRAYERS

4616

O seeker,
How do you expect
Heart-flowers
From your mind-jungle?

4617

War
Takes birth
In the mind-factory.

4618

Peace
Takes birth
In the heart-sea.

4619

I am chosen,
Divinely chosen,
Supremely chosen,
To be a sleeplessly
    God-hungry soul
To manifest the Light
Of the Absolute Supreme
Throughout the length
    and breadth
Of the world.

4620

The heart has to cry
Helplessly and ceaselessly.
Only then will God not remain
A far cry.

4621

I lived
In the desire-market
For many, many years.

4622

I am now living
In the vastness
Of aspiration-sky.

4623

The mind
Wants to possess
Everything that it sees.

4624

The heart
Wants to embrace
Everything that it feels.

4625

Mistakes
Are to be discarded,
And not to be dragged along.

4626

My Lord Supreme,
Will there ever come a time
In my life
When I shall be able to say
That I am no longer 'mine'?

4627

When I walk along my life-road,
I suffer and suffer,
But when I walk along my
    heart-road,
I prosper and prosper.

4628

My aspiration-journey
And my dedication-journey
Will never come to a halt.

4629

My newborn life
Sings only
God-gratitude-songs.

4630

The Beyond
Is the only necessity
Of our earth-bound life.

4631

Have no complaints.
Your life will be empty
Of regrets.

4632

We live in a world
Where ignorance every day
Torments us.

4633

Mind-closed people
Eventually turn into tyrants.

4634

I decorate
My Lord's Feet
With my heart's
Streaming tears.

MY CHRISTMAS-NEW YEAR-VACATION-ASPIRATION-PRAYERS

4635

My Lord
Decorates my heart
With His blossoming Smiles.

4636

The seeds
Of genuine aspiration
Never fail us.

4637

Philosophy
Is for the mind-dwellers.

4638

Spirituality
Is for the heart-divers.

4639

Austerity
Is for the cave-lovers.

4640

My Lord's Beauty
Illumines my heart.

4641

My Lord's Power
Dazzles my eyes.

4642

My Lord's Love
Embraces each and every breath
Of my life.

4643

The reasoning mind
Is a revolving door
With no escape.

4644

The aspiring heart
Circles God's Feet
While enjoying
Divinity's Freedom.

4645

I am truly ashamed
Of my three main possessions:
I, my and mine.

4646

When I say
I have seen God's Face—
Not exactly so.

4647

When I say
I have clasped God's Feet—
Not exactly so.

4648

When I say
I have touched God's Feet—
Not exactly so.

4649

When I say
I have felt God's Heart—
Not exactly so.

4650

When I say
My past, my present and my
    future
Are an exact prototype of God—
True, true, absolutely true.

4651

My mind, my vital, my body
And my life
Love success-pomp.

4652

My soul, my heart and I
Love watching
A sleeplessly Heaven-climbing
    flame.

4653

Each thought is either
A creation-teacher
Or a destruction-ruler.

4654

My Lord,
I am sleeplessly hungry
For Your Compassion.

4655

My child,
I am breathlessly hungry
For your affection-heart.

MY CHRISTMAS-NEW YEAR-VACATION-ASPIRATION-PRAYERS

4656

I love God
As much as I possibly can.

4657

God loves me
Infinitely more
Than I can possibly imagine.

4658

Those who do not pray
And meditate
Live in their noisy mind-world.

4659

Those who pray and meditate
Live in the God-imparted
Ecstasy-world.

4660

Silence
Is the strongest power
To expedite
Earth-evolution.

4661

My determination-promise
Is increasing
Along the passage of time.

4662

God-realisation
Is the birthright
Of each human being.

4663

God-manifestation
Is the birthright
Of each God-realised soul.

4664

Above the head,
There is really nothing special.

4665

Beyond the mind,
Realities are most special.

4666

O seeker,
Shun, immediately shun,
Indifferent-human beings.

4667

At long last
My mind-sky has become
Purer than the purest
And vaster than the vastest.

4668

All excuses
In the spiritual life
Are born of our lower nature.

4669

The more we unlearn
About the outer world,
The sooner the inner world
   divinities
Will welcome us.

4670

When I suffer from loneliness,
The peace-moon and bliss-sun
Come down and comfort me.

4671

Peace-talkers
As usual
Are everywhere.

4672

Peace-servers
As usual
Are few and far between.

4673

Peace-givers
Are nowhere to be found.

4674

We are so fortunate
That our hearts do not believe
In limitation-boundaries.

4675

My prayers
Are my
God-satisfaction-revelations.

4676

My meditations
Are my
God-fulfilment-manifestations.

4677

My devotion-heart-flames
Sing only
God-ecstasy-songs.

MY CHRISTMAS-NEW YEAR-VACATION-ASPIRATION-PRAYERS

4678

God's only representative
On earth
Is our implicit faith.

4679

My very first goal
Is God's Feet.

4680

My second goal
Is God's Heart.

4681

My ultimate goal
Is my God-oneness
Throughout Eternity.

4682

As problems come back again,
Even so, God's Compassion
Comes back more powerfully,
Again and again.

4683

I challenge my mind.
My mind ultimately surrenders.

4684

I challenge my heart,
Only to lose—
Of course, happily.

4685

Peace descends
On our earth-departure.

4686

Bliss inundates
Our Heaven-arrival.

4687

Who is God's boss?
My unconditional
Surrender-breath.

4688

Each time I do something wrong,
God makes me feel
That there is another chance.

4689

My mind quite often
Exploits
God's Compassion.

4690

God's Compassion
Never knows how
To give up.

4691

Divine friendship
Is in the heart—
Not in the eyes,
Not in the voice.

4692

When I am soulful,
I feel God's Heart.

4693

When I am miserable,
God feels my every sigh.

4694

Be happy.
Remain happy.
God never delays.

4695

My Lord Supreme
Takes me seriously
Only after I have offered Him
My soul, my heart, my mind,
My vital, my body and my all.

4696

My heart is God's
Panoramic view.

4697

God-unwillingness
Is a great obstacle
To surmount.

4698

My heart's God-gratitude
Is imperative,
No matter how much
My heart suffers.

4699

Doubt will never have
Any access
To my God-hungry heart.

MY CHRISTMAS-NEW YEAR-VACATION-ASPIRATION-PRAYERS

4700

To think of our own
Past failures
Is the height of our stupidity.

4701

Strive and strive.
Revive your old
God-hunger-cry.

4702

God does not appreciate
Our eleventh-hour prayers.

4703

Only very few
God-seekers and God-lovers
Can see God
As He really and eternally is.

4704

With aspiration
I begin my journey.
With dedication
I continue.
With surrender
I end my journey
In the core of the Unknowable.

4705

My Lord,
Who is Your dearest child?
"Everyone is My dearest child.
But, alas, I find it very difficult
To convince them."

4706

Desire
Quite often ends
At frustration-destination.

4707

Each little progress-step
Is
Extremely valuable.

4708

My heart's aspiration-flames
At once embody
Terrestrial realities
And celestial realities.

4709

God does not believe
Either in addition
Or in division.
He believes only in union.

4710

The mind-meditation
Lives
In the Sahara desert.

4711

The heart-meditation
Lives
At the top of the Himalayas.

4712

My Lord whispers,
"My child, prostrate.
Do not demonstrate."

4713

Failure
Cannot eclipse
My heart-sun.

4714

I am truly proud of myself
For having the capacity
To faithfully imitate my Lord.

4715

Prominence-permanence
Is not always God's Will.

4716

Love
Is worth spreading.

4717

Devotion
Is worth loving.

4718

Surrender
Is worth becoming.

4719

To be among
The God-chosen finalists,
My sleepless faith in God
Is absolutely essential.

4720

God watches our tears,
But we do not have time to wait
For Him to comfort us.

4721

This world shall remain
Imperfect
Until our eyes meet
With God's Eye.

MY CHRISTMAS-NEW YEAR-VACATION-ASPIRATION-PRAYERS

4722

Aspiration is the way
To prove
That we need God.

4723

Dedication is the way
To prove
That we love God.

4724

Heart
Is self-giving.
Life
Is God-becoming.

4725

Willingness
Is
God-pride-servant.

4726

My God-gratitude-heart
Saves me
From my mind's miserable days
And nights.

4727

Only when I ceaselessly cry
For God
Do I climb up my life's
Perfection-tree.

4728

When I hear about
God coming,
My life thrills
With ecstasy's delight.

4729

The server in me says,
"I am God's."

4730

The lover in me says,
"God is mine."

4731

God's complete confidence
Is my faith-heart.

4732

If we really want to run
The fastest,
We must take God seriously.

4733

Only one thing I have
In my possession:
God's Compassion.

4734

God-obedience
Is the perfect key
To open God's Heart-Door.

4735

I tell God,
"No matter how far the
   journey is,
Do take me with You."

4736

Humanity deserves
A final warning
For constant God-disobedience.

4737

Every soul
Is an ever-blossoming
Dream of God.

4738

Silence is God's
Most favourite messenger.

4739

Uncover yourself
To discover God.

4740

If we pray to God
On our knees,
We immediately feel
God's infinite Love.

4741

Like my soul,
I, too, want to please
My Lord
Throughout Eternity.

4742

My aspiration-heart
Deepens every year.

4743

My dedication-life
Widens every year.

MY CHRISTMAS-NEW YEAR-VACATION-ASPIRATION-PRAYERS

4744

My soul
Is absolutely perfect
Because it is God-made.

4745

I pray to God
To give me the capacity
To mingle
In all the tearing sorrows
And beaming joys
Of the world.

4746

I am absolutely certain
That my Lord will never ask me
To do anything
Beyond my capacity.

4747

I fill my days and nights
With my Lord's
Compassion-Eye-Smiles.

4748

My heart's dream
Is
God-realisation.

4749

My life's dream
Is
God-revelation.

4750

My soul's dream
Is
God-manifestation.

4751

When I dive deep within,
I breathe the fresh air
Of a new dawn.

4752

God Himself plies my life-boat
Between two shores:
The known and the Unknown.

4753

When I veil my mind,
I unveil Heaven.

4754

My only choice:
God's earth-lifting
And Heaven-climbing
Voice.

4755

God includes
Each and every human being
In His Cosmic Play.

4756

God asks us
Direct questions.
He expects from us
Direct answers.

4757

A spiritual Master
Gladly gives himself away,
Although he badly suffers.

4758

God forgives us,
Not because we deserve
His Forgiveness,
But because He surrenders
To His own Compassion-Heart.

4759

Even an iota
Of our God-manifestation
Thrills God.

4760

My Lord, may I be always
In between
Your Infinity's Peace
And
Your Eternity's Silence.

4761

The outer beauty
Is the charming beauty
Of a child —
It does not last for long.

4762

The inner beauty
Knows no death.

4763

God has infinite rooms,
But our hearts
Are His favourite rooms.

MY CHRISTMAS-NEW YEAR-VACATION-ASPIRATION-PRAYERS

4764

I wish to be found
Always in the company
Of God-Feet-worshipping
   seekers.

4765

I love to wake up
With the rising sun
And run against
The thickening clouds.

4766

A songful heart
Is
A fruitful life.

4767

Do not follow
The stars of the sky,
But follow
The sun of your heart.

4768

Why is surrender so difficult?
Because our heart-tears
Are not pure and sincere.

4769

Each seeker needs
A totally different
Aspiration-road.

4770

Prayer embodies
The beauty of life.

4771

Meditation reveals
The fragrance of the heart.

4772

Jealousy and insecurity
Are twin sisters.

4773

God wants me
To raise my consciousness
Instead of praising Him
On my knees.

4774

God tells me
That I have come a long way
With Him—
Can I not go to the end?

4775

Again and again,
God wants me to be
His brave partner
And not His mild follower.

4776

No earth-born human being
Can fathom
The secrets of life and death.

4777

Desire
Is a blazing fire
In the mind.

4778

God's Way
Is to act and act
And not to sit and wait.

4779

Self-styled gods
Are everywhere, alas!

4780

Life has to be
A God-fulfilling story
And not
Man-imagined history.

4781

The inner oneness
Has to be manifested
As the outer goodness
At least.

4782

I love and treasure
My God-ordained
Soul-authority.

4783

Self-giving
Is by far the best
Among our divine qualities.

4784

Every day,
God injects His Compassion
Into my heart-breath.

MY CHRISTMAS-NEW YEAR-VACATION-ASPIRATION-PRAYERS

4785

My devotion
Is
My God-Sweetness-intoxication.

4786

Each day
God wants me to dream
Of His high, higher, highest
Heaven.

4787

Alas, our God-ingratitude-life
Does not allow God
To feed us every day.

4788

When my heart sings,
Even my doubting mind
Enjoys the song.

4789

My Lord enjoys
My surrender-life-moments
Mightily and proudly.

4790

God's Presence
Embraces my soul.
God's Presence
Thrills my heart.
God's Presence
Disentangles my mind.
God's Presence
Feeds my life.

4791

An ideal seeker
Lives
On the God-cradled earth.

4792

Surrender we must
Our earthly possessions
If we really want to receive
Smiles from God.

4793

A desire-mind
And a frustration-life
Together live.

4794

A prayer-pond-diver
I was.

4795

A meditation-river-diver
I now am.

4796

A surrender-sea-diver
I shall become.

4797

Even God finds it difficult
To recognise me
When I deliberately enjoy
My desire-forest-life.

4798

God wants me to remain
At my Himalayan aspiration-height
And not to come down
To my old anthill-height.

4799

The mind loves
The zigzag road.

4800

The heart loves
God's sunlit Road.

4801

My God-gratitude
Is my heart's
Most powerful strength.

4802

Cry, cry, sleeplessly cry
Within.
Fly, fly, breathlessly fly
Without.

4803

The God-doubting mind
Everywhere spies.
The God-searching heart
In the vast blue sky flies.

4804

My prayer-life
Is
My God-addition.

4805

My meditation-heart
Is
My God-multiplication.

MY CHRISTMAS-NEW YEAR-VACATION-ASPIRATION-PRAYERS

4806

The rising sun
Beautifies me.
The setting sun
Purifies me.

4807

The Source
Of my heart-tears
Is my Lord's Compassion-Eye.

4808

When we really love God,
His Voice does not remain
Unheard.

4809

When we really worship God,
His Feet do not remain
Unseen.

4810

My aspiration
Is
My Heaven-flying bird.

4811

My dedication
Is
My earth-serving hand.

4812

My heart
Has another name:
God's
Compassion-Affection-Breath.

4813

I ply my life-boat
Between God's
    Enthusiasm-Shore
And His Dynamism-Shore.

4814

I shall not allow my desire-life
To touch my Lord's Feet.
I shall only offer, again and again,
My aspiration-heart
At my Lord's Feet.

4815

Not the darkness of our mind
But the disobedience of our life
Weighs us down
In our spiritual life.

4816

God cares
Not only for
The awakened seekers,
But also for
The sleeping seekers.

4817

My Lord takes care of
Not only the depths of my heart,
But also the shallows of my life.

4818

My soul conducts
My life-symphony
With tremendous care.

4819

Opportunity
Is of no avail
If receptivity
Is wanting.

4820

I believe only in
God-Supremacy
And
God-Authority.

4821

God keeps
His Heart-Entrance open
Only to the
Surrender-accomplished seekers.

4822

Hesitation
In pleasing God
Is a serious spiritual crime.

4823

Fear not
The agonies
Prior to transformation.

4824

I have always
Tremendous admiration
For those
Who are ahead of me.

4825

In these trying times,
Each seeker has to be
Extremely, extremely careful.

MY CHRISTMAS-NEW YEAR-VACATION-ASPIRATION-PRAYERS

4826

We must happily and proudly
Surrender
To God's choice Hour.

4827

The very nature of the mind
Is either to undermine
Or to belittle everything.

4828

When I do not pray and
    meditate,
I deal with the theoretical God.
But when I pray and meditate,
I deal with the practical God.

4829

God tells me
To sing only two songs:
God-dependence-song
And
Man-interdependence-song.

4830

Do not be doomed
To disappointment.
If you have failed this time,
God will give you another
    chance.

4831

God powerfully and proudly
Embraces
All gratitude-hearts.

4832

From God's Eye
My spiritual journey starts.

4833

At God's Feet
My spiritual journey ends.

4834

God allows us
To enter into
His Heart-Kingdom
Even without
Aspiration-flames.

4835

A desiring mind
Is
A turbulent life.

4836

This world needs
Millions and millions
Of God-hungry souls
To raise the standard
Of the world.

4837

Every day
God beckons us
To sail and sail and sail
In His Compassion-
   Affection-Sea.

4838

Every day
God most compassionately
And most carefully examines
My success-smiles
And
My progress-tears.

4839

Disobedience-strides
Are dangerous, destructive
And God-defying.

4840

My aspiration teaches me
How to see God
Brighter and brighter
Every day.

4841

My dedication teaches me
How to feel God
Kinder and kinder to me
Every day.

4842

When our heart cries desperately,
God's Grace descends
   immediately,
Plus unconditionally.

4843

When I soulfully pray,
My heart beautifully blooms.

4844

When I unconditionally meditate,
My life exquisitely blossoms.

MY CHRISTMAS-NEW YEAR-VACATION-ASPIRATION-PRAYERS

4845

God the Lover,
Alone,
Secretly teaches me
How to be
A true God-worshipper.

4846

When I enter into God's Heart,
I see myself as God the Life
And not God the Death.

4847

The desire-life
Thinks
Everything is possible.

4848

The aspiration-heart
Feels
Everything is inevitable.

4849

The world is full
Of God's
Unblossomed Joys.

4850

My strength is in
My crying
At God's Feet.

4851

God's Strength is in
His smiling
At my eyes.

4852

Each human being
Is a unique God-representative
On earth.

4853

When I pray and meditate,
I drink and drink
From my Lord's
Delight-Fountain.

4854

Alas, will there be a time
When all human beings
Embark
On oneness-peace-journey?

4855

I was born
As a God-Authority-
    Fulfilment-dreamer.

4856

Aspiration
Prayerfully rises.
Receptivity
Soulfully increases.

4857

God's
Transcendental Greatness
Blesses my head.

4858

God's
Universal Goodness
Embraces my heart.

4859

The insincere mind
Finally surrenders
To the sincere heart.

4860

A reasoning mind
Can never be
A blossoming heart.

4861

I do not want
The capacities of my mind,
But I do want
The qualities of my heart.

4862

Spirituality
Turns problems
Into opportunities.

4863

God will never allow
My aspiration-heart-sun
To be eclipsed.

4864

My prayer
Is my life's
Morning rose.

MY CHRISTMAS-NEW YEAR-VACATION-ASPIRATION-PRAYERS

4865

My meditation
Is my heart's
Morning lotus.

4866

A God-seeker
Has to be on the alert
Twenty-four hours a day.

4867

Each thought comes from
The unknown,
And each will comes from
The Unknowable.

4868

Alas, every day
There is a new barrier
To cross.

4869

Patience
Eventually becomes
Victorious.

4870

My desire-life
Was planted
By my mind.

4871

My aspiration-life
Was planted
By God's Heart.

4872

O my sleep, I love you—
You take away
All my worries and anxieties!

4873

Alas, when will Truth
Reign supreme on earth,
When?

4874

My eyes can fool me
And betray me,
But not my heart,
Never!

4875

Another name
For meditation
Is God-communication.

4876

Another name
For prayer
Is God-pleasure.

4877

In vain, my mind
Wants to interview God.

4878

God takes great pleasure
In interviewing my heart.

4879

I thank God
For what He has done for me,
And specially
For what He has not done for me.

4880

Silence is
A blissful creation-hour.

4881

Sound is
A powerful destruction-tower.

4882

Alas, when I am ready,
God pretends
Not to be ready.

4883

Alas, when God is ready,
I am nowhere
To be found.

4884

My Lord,
May my unfulfilled desires
Remain forever unfulfilled.

4885

God tells me
Not to give undue importance
To my imperfections.
He asks me just to love Him
More and more,
And my imperfections
Will be His problems.

MY CHRISTMAS-NEW YEAR-VACATION-ASPIRATION-PRAYERS

4886

I see myself
As a colossal failure.

4887

God sees me
As His own highest
Reality's Height.

4888

Faith and doubt—
Each man has to choose
Either faith or doubt
As his tutor.

4889

The God-lover's
First and foremost task
Is to love God
For God's Sake.

4890

I cry and cry
For the joy
Of my heart.

4891

God gladly allows
My aspiration-heart
To accompany Him,
And not my desire-life.

4892

Just claim God
And His Path
Alone.

4893

Hope
Is my heart-sunrise.

4894

Despair
Is my mind-sunset.

4895

My prayer
Is
My life-temple.

4896

My meditation
Is
My heart-shrine.

4897

I have smashed asunder
All my mind's
Separativity-walls.

4898

My Lord does not believe
In an old mind—
He believes only
In a new heart.

4899

Desire-fire
Quickly burns us.

4900

Aspiration-flames
Slowly, steadily and unerringly
Awaken us.

4901

I have such love
And concern
For the roots
Of my life-tree.

4902

We welcome darkness
Before we enter
Into the spiritual life.

4903

Once we enter
Into the spiritual life,
Darkness threatens us.

4904

Ignorance,
I do not need you,
I do not want you,
I despise you.
Nevertheless,
Your arrogance puzzles me.

4905

God-believers
Are plenty.

4906

God-lovers
Are rare.

MY CHRISTMAS-NEW YEAR-VACATION-ASPIRATION-PRAYERS

4907

I cherish
My Lord's
Powerful Commands.

4908

My Lord treasures
My fearless promises.

4909

I call it
My human birth.

4910

My Lord calls it
My divine descent.

4911

My Lord
Does not count
My countless imperfections.

4912

My Lord counts only
My readiness, willingness
And eagerness.

4913

I am now a perfect stranger
To my life's idle talk
And my heart's empty vision.

4914

Each human being
Will become
An inevitable God.

MY EARLY MORNING PRAYER-JOURNEYS

1

My Lord,
Early in the morning
I love and worship
Your beautiful Eye
And beautiful Feet.

2

My Lord,
During the day
I love and worship
Your powerful Eye
And powerful Feet.

3

My Lord,
In the evening
I love and worship
Your peaceful Eye
And peaceful Feet.

4

My Lord,
At night
I love and worship
Your merciful, Godful
And good-bye Eye
And Feet.

5

My Lord loves
To whisper
All His Answers.

6

Forgivers
Are immediate and everlasting
Happiness-enjoyers.

7

The heart-givers
Are the life-transformers
Of the world.

8

God does not want me
To count His Miracles.
He wants me to count
Only my God-love-heart-tears.

9

When I sing,
My Lord smiles at me
Lovingly.

MY EARLY MORNING PRAYER-JOURNEYS

10

When I sing soulfully,
My Lord blesses me
Powerfully.

11

When I sing soulfully,
Devotedly and self-givingly,
My Lord embraces me
Immediately.

12

The lower I bend my head
To my Lord Supreme,
The deeper joy I receive
From Him.

13

The quicker I touch
The Lotus-Feet
Of my Lord Supreme,
The stronger I feel Him,
Physically and spiritually.

14

I have
An eternal companion:
My heart's inner poise.

15

Every morning
I need
A newborn God-hunger.

16

My earthly music
Is
My Heavenward journey.

17

My Heavenly music
Is the beauty
Of my universal life.

18

I sleeplessly adore
My highest height.

19

I breathlessly love
My deepest depth.

20

God,
With His Power,
Comes down.

21

God,
With His Compassion,
Lives on earth.

22

God,
With His Delight,
Returns.

23

I must live
In my heart-home
At every moment.

24

My prayers must reach
The four corners
Of the globe.

25

My meditations must intensify
The God-hunger
Of every seeker.

26

I must offer my heart-tears,
Soul-smiles and life-gratitude
To my Lord Beloved Supreme
Unreservedly and
   unconditionally,
Every morning and every
   evening.

27

I do not pray to God
To make me a great man—
No, no, no!

28

I do not pray to God
To make me a good man—
No, no, no!

29

I pray to God
To be His, only His,
All His.

30

I tell my Lord Beloved Supreme
That in every aspect of my life,
It is for Him to make
The decision,
And I will take His Decision
As final, absolutely final.

31

This morning
I am a prayerful, soulful
And grateful
God-obedience heart.

32

The mind desires
Constant God-Attention.

33

The heart desires
Sleepless God-Affection.

34

My Lord Beloved Supreme
And I
Thrive on our mutual fondness.

35

Every day
I am learning more and more
The divine art
Of unconditional surrender
To God's Will.

36

Even for a fleeting moment,
The pangs of
My God-separation-heart
Are unbearable.

37

With an inner thrill
I wait to receive
My Lord Supreme.

38

My heart-lotus
Blossoms only
At the Lotus-Feet
Of my Lord Supreme.

39

This morning
My Lord said to me,
"My child,
Doers accomplish;
Talkers perish.
I want you
To be a doer."

40

I happily welcome
My sweet days.
I bravely welcome
My bitter days.

41

God says to all the seekers
Of the world,
"Discipline your lives,
My children,
Discipline your lives!
If you do not, I shall force you,
  I shall force you."

42

My heart
Is made of
My Lord's sweet Dreams.

43

Every day
I dive deeper and deeper
Into my Lord's
Compassion-Ocean-Eye.

44

On Eternity's Road,
One by one all may leave me,
But not my Lord's
Compassion-Eye.

45

My Lord,
Not Power, not Light—
What I need from You
Is Peace,
Your Infinity's Peace.

46

I pray
In the temple of devotion
To receive Joy
From my Lord.

47

I meditate
In the temple of surrender
To receive Peace
From my Lord.

48

I love
My soaring heart-bird
And not
My roaring mind-lion.

49

My mind sees
The tearful God.
My heart sees
The blissful God.

50

My love, my devotion
And my surrender
Have God-Blood-relations.

51

My Lord has been searching
For only one happy heart
In His vast Creation.

52

A kind life
Is
A God-chosen life.

53

A kind heart
Is
A God-given heart.

54

May my heart
Be a fountain
Of God-gratitude-tears.

55

May my life
Be a sky
Of God-plenitude-smiles.

56

My Lord is already
Inside my heart
With His Compassion-Eye
To grant me God-realisation.

57

The Master sees his disciples
First inside his heart
And then in front of his eyes.

58

I pray to God
With my aspiration-eyes.

59

I meditate on God
With my aspiration-heart.

60

I walk and run
Towards God
With my aspiration-legs.

61

God has appointed
My aspiration
To take me to Him
As soon as possible.

62

God wants me
To be the promoter
Of all the inspiring things
That are taking place
Here on earth.

63

Quite often
The courage of the mind
Plays the role of an absentee.

64

My Lord gets
A shocking experience from me
When I do not adequately care
    for His Creation.

65

God always keeps me
Inside His Heart-Home
No matter how badly I fare
In my aspiration-life.

66

Beautiful
Is
My heart-awakening.

67

Blissful
Is
My God-remembrance.

MY EARLY MORNING PRAYER-JOURNEYS

68

Painful
Is
My God-forgetfulness.

69

Our divine qualities
Brighten and gladden
The Eye
Of our Lord Supreme.

70

My love, my devotion
And my surrender
Will remain my unfailing friends
Right to the very end.

71

What I badly need
Is a peace-flooded
Silence-heart.

72

World-harmony
And world-union
Remain the unrealised dreams
Of our age.

73

I prayerfully welcome
Every morning
The silence-arrival
Of my Lord Beloved Supreme
At my heart-door.

74

My heart's capacity
To feel God's Compassion-Rain
Is far beyond the imagination
Of my mind.

75

My Lord,
How is it that every time
I want to give You
Everything that I have
And everything that I am,
I sadly fail?
"My child,
Develop more intensity
In your devotion to Me."

76

O where can I get a passport
To enter into my Lord's
Heart-Home-Land?

77

God tells me
That if I can silence my mind,
Then He will give me
A free entry
Into all the countries
In His Creation.

78

No more, no more,
This year's failure-days
And failure-nights—
No more, no more!

79

No more,
The faith-starvation-days
And faith-starvation-nights
Of this year—
No more!

80

The old year painfully
Goes to sleep.

81

The new year bravely
Wakes up.

82

Happy New Year,
Happy New Year!
Be brave, be brave!
No fear, no fear!

83

Happy New Year,
Happy New Year!
Go forward,
Fly upward,
Dive inward!
No fear, no fear!

84

Happy New Year!
God the Eye you claim,
God the Heart you claim
And God the Life you claim.
Claim, claim, claim, claim God.
No fear, no fear!

85

Happy New Year,
Happy New Year!
I shall be my God-hope-joy,
I shall be my God-promise-
    fulfiller.
No fear, no fear!

86

I proudly declare
My greatness-mind-achievements.

87

My Lord proudly uses
My goodness-heart-achievements.

88

My mind-education
Is an accurate
Knowledge-fact-collector.

89

My heart-education
Is the collector
Of God's Heart-Tears
And God's Eye-Smiles.

90

Every morning I sing
A God-worshipping
Prayer-song.

91

An unseen Hand
Compassionately regulates
My life.

92

Silence
Is the Mother
Of world harmony.

93

When I am
An indomitable will,
God's Thrill
Is unimaginable.

94

Today God is so pleased
With my prayers and meditations
That He has blessingfully
Offered me
His golden Crown.

95

In the small hours of the
   morning,
God and I enter into
A lovely competition.
My task is
To touch God's Feet.
God's Task is
To examine my heart.
I finish my task long before God.
Poor God accepts the sad defeat.

When the night is far advanced,
God and I again enter into
Another lovely competition.
This time our task is
Mutual appreciation.
I shall have to appreciate God
As much as I can.
God will have to appreciate me
As much as He wants to.
Alas, I accept the very sad defeat.

96

My silence-heart
Gladdens my Lord Supreme
Beyond measure.

97

God's Silence-Eye
Frightens me
To the core.

98

My mind,
Stop covering my heart-sky
With your thick and dark clouds!

99

My heart,
God is right in front of you.
Where is your attention,
Where?

100

God wants my heart
To be the owner
Of His Dream.

101

My Lord,
Do make me a bond-slave
To Your Will.

102

Alas, I do not know
When I will be able to return
To my Lord's Heart-Home.

MY EARLY MORNING PRAYER-JOURNEYS

103

A path-finder
Is
A new God-discoverer.

104

To manifest God
As perfectly as possible:
This is what my heart and I
Precisely stand for.

105

Our Lord's Compassion-Eye
Protects us
From the visible enemies.

106

Our Lord's Concern-Heart
Protects us
From the invisible enemies.

107

My Lord breathes in
My heart-flower-fragrance.

108

A God-oneness-heart-dream
Is
Sweetness unimaginable.

109

My God-obedience
Is
My supremely divine pride.

110

I live either inside
My earth-born heart-cries
Or inside
My Heaven-free soul-smiles.

111

God wants me
Not only to equal Heaven,
But also to surpass Heaven
In sleepless self-offering.

112

The soul perpetually smiles
Through the bondage-cage
Of the body.

113

Every day
I wish to have
An enthusiasm-outburst.

114

Alas,
We try to satisfy
Our Lord Supreme
With our extremely feeble
   efforts.

115

In my aspiration-heart-home
There is no room
For uncertainty.

116

There was a time
When I used to live
On the outskirts of hope,
But now I am living
In the very breath of hope.

117

Even the most powerful
Ignorance-night
Shall be illumined
By our inner light.

118

Humanity's hope-flames
Rise to Heaven.

119

Divinity's promise-stars
Touch Mother Earth.

120

From the oneness-heart
We arrive
At the newness-shore.

121

From the newness-shore
We arrive
At the fulness-shore—
The Golden Shore.

122

Life is meant
For our God-union
And not
For our mind-division.

MY EARLY MORNING PRAYER-JOURNEYS

123

God-discovery-song
Tops the list
Of all our love, devotion
And surrender-songs.

124

Our uniqueness comes
Either from God's Feet
Or from God's Heart.

125

I must find myself
In the heart of time eternal
And in the heart of space infinite.

126

Those who outwardly
And indiscriminately display
An orchestra of spiritual power
Are not favoured
Either by Heaven's Eye
Or by earth's heart.

127

Nature
Is the divine beauty
Of God's supreme Glory.

128

An act of compassion
Is one step forward
Towards God-realisation.

129

The morning touch
Makes my heart beautiful.

130

The evening touch
Makes my life peaceful.

131

My God-surrender-life
Is the birth
Of a new creation.

132

My heart-sun
Feeds on
God's Transcendental Delight.

133

A new heart is needed
To love goodness
In every human being.

134

O my mind,
You must not remain a stranger
To God's Heart
Any more.

135

World-criticism
Has no place
In my aspiration-heart
And in my dedication-life.

136

My heart tells my eyes
That I am very near
My Lord's Heart-Home.

137

God is asking us
Only for two things:
For our prayers to be sincere
And
For our meditations to be deep.

138

The heart
Readily and immediately listens
To the dictates
Of the Inner Pilot.

139

God heavily and proudly
Counts on our self-offering.

140

I am eager to go
To the four corners of the world
To find a man
Who is constantly happy,
Cheerful and self-giving.

141

May my aspiration
Have another name:
Fragrance.

142

May my dedication
Have another name:
Cheerfulness.

143

May my prayer
Have another name:
Soulfulness.

MY EARLY MORNING PRAYER-JOURNEYS

144

May my meditation
Have another name:
Intensity.

145

May I
Have another name:
Integrity.

146

If we really love God,
Then our heart-smiles should be
Spontaneous and continuous.

147

It is high time for me
To say good-bye
To each and every thing
That I do not need,
Such as my desire-life.

148

The real spiritual life
Does not mean
To keep your eyes closed
All the time
And do nothing,
Nothing for the world.

149

I must keep
Each and every thought
Of my mind
Absolutely silent
While I meditate.

150

The sun-duty
Is calling me.
I am running!

151

The moon-beauty
Is calling me.
I am running!

152

The star-frolic-joy
Is calling me.
I am running!

153

My life lives between
A body-camel-burden
And
A heart-deer-speed.

154

My protection-fort
Is made of
My God-obedience
And
My God-dependence.

155

My Lord,
May I have a heart
Of ever-blossoming smile.

156

There is a God-loving
And God-serving
Divine hero
Within every heart.

157

Even an iota
Of consciousness-descent
In the spiritual life
Is a grave failure.

158

Every morning
God and I have
A heart-to-heart talk
Before I enter into
The hustle and bustle of life.

159

Each God-dream
Is eager to be
A manifested Reality.

160

My Lord,
Do You know that I feed
Only on
Your Compassion-Smiles?

MY EARLY MORNING HEART-CLIMBING PRAYERS

1

Every day
My aspiration-hunger-cries
Give immense delight
To my Lord Beloved Supreme.

2

This morning
God's Eye whispers,
"My child,
I would like you
To be perfect."
God's Heart thunders,
"My child,
Already you are
Absolutely perfect!"

3

In the small hours of the
    morning,
I come out of my soul-bird-nest
To spread the blue-gold Light
Of my Lord Supreme
Here on earth,
And in the twilight hours
I come back to my soul-bird-nest.

4

O undivine mind-major,
Do not torture
The poor heart-minors!

5

Give yourself lovingly,
Smilingly and self-givingly
To God.
He will bless you
With a morning
Jasmine-garland.

6

Sleepless aspiration for Heaven
And
Breathless dedication to earth
Are the very beginnings
That grow into
A perfect God-realisation-plant.

7

Every morning
My Absolute Lord Supreme
Comes down
From His highest Height
With His Heaven-Blos-
som-Smiles
To bless my God-hunger.

8

When my life
Is completely surrendered
To God's Will,
God Himself cradles
My heart's moon-beauty-dreams.

MY EARLY MORNING HEART-CLIMBING PRAYERS

9

My Lord Beloved Supreme,
Every time I am with You,
My heart becomes
A fully blossomed
Gratitude-lotus.

10

My Supreme,
I wish to become
The ever-blossoming breath
Of a self-giving life.
My Supreme!

11

Those who really love God
And really need God
Have only one choice:
God's Transcendental
Vision-Manifestation
Here on earth.

12

When I speak to God,
I measure each and every word
Of mine
Very, very carefully.
When God speaks to me,
I treasure each and every Word
Of His
Most devotedly
In the very depths of my heart.

13

My Lord,
Every morning
Do give me the capacity
To feed
Your aspiration-hungry children.
"My child,
Capacity granted,
My child!"

14

The God-pleasing heart
Reveals its beauty and fragrance
Through the purity-eyes.

15

God's Pride is
The blue-gold bridge
Between my happiness-life
And my gratitude-heart.

16

My Lord Supreme,
Right from the day I was born,
My life has been
Your Compassion-Protection-
Abundance-Indulgence.

17

My Supreme Lord,
Please, please accept
My heart's
Ceaseless gratitude-tears.

18

Only my life's
Unconditional surrender
Has a free access
To God's Heart-Home.

19

Slowly and slowly
My earth-life-tree
Grows and grows
To clasp Heaven's
Twinkling, twinkling stars.

20

God the Heart
Is not enough.
We need God the Heartbeat
As well.

21

My Lord Supreme,
I carry the messages
Of sweet hopes
And the messages
Of brave promises
From birth to death
And from death to the Beyond.
My Lord Supreme!

22

God's Hour
Comes and goes.
The moment it arrives,
I must say to God,
"My Lord, my Lord,
You are my All,
You are my All,
And I am all Yours,
I am all Yours."

23

My Lord,
On New Year's Day
You are watching
The blooming New Year
With such Compassion, Concern,
Sweetness and Fondness.
May each and every human being
Place at Your Feet
A garland of gratitude,
Gratitude and gratitude,
My Lord, my Lord,
My Lord Supreme!

MY EARLY MORNING HEART-CLIMBING PRAYERS

24

God's Grace is descending
So powerfully!
God wants us to be
His perfect instruments,
But, alas,
We are still
His constant impediments.

25

My Lord, my Lord, my Lord!
Every morning you cradle
My tiny aspiration-heart
And my feeble dedication-life
With Your Compassion-flooded
Fondness-Eye.
My Lord, my Lord, my Lord!

26

To my heart's deepest joy,
Every day, every hour,
In every way
My God-worshipping heart
Is becoming a better instrument
Of God.

27

God whispers,
"My child,
I love you, I need you,
I thank you, I thank you."
God,
I thank You, I thank You,
I thank You.
You are my heart's
Dream-Boat-Reality-Shore.

28

My Lord,
The way I am praying and
  meditating
Is simply useless.
Will I ever be able
To realise You?
I need God-realisation.
"My child,
Do not think of God-realisation
At this time of your spirituality.
Just try to develop
More sincerity, more eagerness
In your spiritual life.
But, My child,
If you think that you will never
Be able to realise Me,
You are, indeed,
The most perfect fool
Here on earth."

29

My Supreme, my Lord Supreme,
My Beloved Supreme,
My Eternity's Supreme!
This morning You want us
To enjoy, enjoy and enjoy
The full harvest
Of Your Compassion
And Forgiveness.

30

The desiring mind
Has many faces
And many voices.
The aspiring heart
Has only one face:
God-Beauty's Face,
And only one voice:
God-Duty's Voice.

31

My God-exploration
Is founded upon
My heart's
God-adoration-beauty-fragrance.

32

When I pray
And climb up
High, higher, highest,
God blesses me
With the Beauty of His Heart.
When I meditate
And dive deep, deeper, deepest,
God blesses me
With the Fragrance of His Life.

33

Every day
I must do three things:
I must love God,
I must serve God
And I must try to become
A choice instrument of God.

34

Every morning
I prayerfully and soulfully visit
Two very special worlds:
God's Compassion-Eye-World
And God's
    Forgiveness-Heart-World.

35

My heart's silver tears
Are God's oldest friends.
God's golden Smiles
Are my life's eternal Saviours.

36

Behold!
Yonder my Lord Krishna's
Jingling ankle bells
Are thrilling my eyes,
Intoxicating my heartbeat,
Feeding my heart
And energising my life.
My Lord Krishna, my
    Lord Krishna!

37

No more am I a failure life,
No more.
My mind is now the owner
Of many, many, many
New inspiration-waves.
My heart is the owner
Of a new aspiration-sea.
My life is the owner
Of an ever-blossoming
Gratitude-garden,
Which I am dedicating now
To my Absolute Lord Supreme.

38

O seeker,
You can miss your outer meals
As many times as you want to.
But do not miss
Even one single inner meal.
Why?
Because God Himself
Waits and waits and waits for you
To come and eat with Him.

39

My Lord-worship-
    happiness-heart
Is blossoming into
My God-Ecstasy-Paradise.

40

God most compassionately
And most affectionately
Picks up
The God-surrender-seekers
Who fail and fall on the way,
And then He commands,
"My children,
On you march,
On you march,
Until you have reached
Your Goal ultimate."

41

God's God-Prize-winners
Of today's inner race:
The first prize goes to
Unconditional God-surrender;
The second prize goes to
Sleepless God-aspiration;
The third prize goes to
Twenty-four-hour
    God-awareness.

42

If you want to have
A very deep meditation,
Then before you meditate,
Cast aside all your doubts,
Self-doubts, insecurities,
Impurities and negativities.

43

Limited are our lives.
Unlimited are our problems
And struggles.
Yet our Lord says to us,
"My children, fear not.
Move on, march on.
I am with you all.
I am in you all.
I am for you all.
You are bound to arrive
At your destined Goal."

44

Each time
I prayerfully, soulfully
And self-givingly visit
My Absolute Lord Beloved
Supreme,
He immediately gets
The most powerful
    Ecstasy-Thrill.

45

God says to me,
"My child,
If you really love Me,
If you really want to please Me
In My own Way,
Then you and your heart
Must come to Me lovingly,
Smilingly, soulfully and
    self-givingly
Wherever I am."

46

I must forget
My puny self
Totally
In my God-service-delight.

47

In my heart-sky,
Many, many, many, many
Twinkling stars
Are singing
My Lord's Victory-Songs.

48

Nobody can claim my heart
On earth.
Why?
Because my Lord Beloved
    Supreme
Has already claimed me
In Heaven.

49

My Lord Absolute
    Beloved Supreme,
Each moment I spend with You
Is my life's and my heart's
Most precious Treasure.

50

My soul-smiles and my
    heart-tears
Solely depend upon
The depths and heights
Of my meditations.

51

God's divine Hall of Fame
Will invite us
Only after we have learnt
The supreme art
Of sleepless self-offering
To God's Will.

52

A sleepless God-lover
Is a climbing heart-eagerness.
A breathless God-server
Is a jumping life-enthusiasm.

53

May my aspiration-heart-bird fly
High, higher, highest,
To reach the Golden Feet
Of my Absolute Lord Beloved
    Supreme
In the highest Heaven.

54

May each thought of mine
Grow into
A most beautiful aspiration-plant
In my Lord's Heart-Garden.

55

Each time I become
A heart of God-gratitude,
I come one step closer
To God's Feet.

56

Ignorance-night fails.
My love of God sails.
My surrender to God's Will
    prevails.

57

May each and every thought
    of mine
Be as beautiful
As the morning rainbow
And as pure
As the dawn-dew.

58

May every heartbeat of mine
Fight against ignorance-night
And conquer it permanently,
For the establishment
Of God's complete Victory
Here on Earth.

NOTES

MY CHRISTMAS-NEW YEAR-VACATION-ASPIRATION-PRAYERS

1-7. 10 December 1999, São Moritz, Brazil.
8-17. 11 December 1999, São Moritz, Brazil.
18-27. 12 December 1999, São Moritz, Brazil.
28-38. 13 December 1999, São Moritz, Brazil.
39-48. 14 December 1999, São Moritz, Brazil.
49-61. 15 December 1999, Rio De Janeiro, Brazil.
62-69. 16 December 1999, Rio De Janeiro, Brazil.
70-79. 17 December 1999, Rio De Janeiro, Brazil.
80-89. 18 December 1999, Rio De Janeiro, Brazil.
90-98. 19 December 1999, Rio De Janeiro, Brazil.
99-107. 20 December 1999, Rio De Janeiro, Brazil.
108-116. 21 December 1999, Rio De Janeiro, Brazil.
117-126. 22 December 1999, Rio De Janeiro, Brazil.
127-136. 23 December 1999, Rio De Janeiro, Brazil.
137-146. 25 December 1999, Curitiba, Brazil.
147-156. 26 December 1999, Curitiba, Brazil.
157-167. 27 December 1999, Curitiba, Brazil.
168-176. 30 December 1999, Curitiba, Brazil.
177-186. 31 December 1999, Curitiba, Brazil.
187-196. 1 January 2000, Curitiba, Brazil.
197-205. 2 January 2000, Curitiba, Brazil.
206-216. 3 January 2000, Curitiba, Brazil.
216-225. 4 January 2000, Curitiba, Brazil.
226-235. 5 January 2000, Curitiba, Brazil.
236-245. 7 January 2000, Foz Do Iguaçu, Brazil.
246-255. 8 January 2000, Foz Do Iguaçu, Brazil.
256-265. 10 January 2000, Foz Do Iguaçu, Brazil.
266-275. 11 January 2000, Foz Do Iguaçu, Brazil.
276-285. 13 January 2000, Foz Do Iguaçu, Brazil.
286-295. 15 January 2000, Foz Do Iguaçu, Brazil.
296-305. 17 January 2000, Asunción, Paraguay.
306-315. 18 January 2000, Asunción, Paraguay.
316-325. 19 January 2000, Asunción, Paraguay.
326-335. 20 January 2000, Asunción, Paraguay.
336-345. 22 January 2000, Asunción, Paraguay.
346-355. 29 January 2000. Brasilia, Brazil.
358-425. 5 December 2000, Yangon, Myanmar.
426-436. 11 December 2000 Yangon, Myanmar.
437-438. 11 December 2000 Yangon, Myanmar.
439-451. 13 December 2000 Yangon, Myanmar.
452-462. 19 December 2000, Mandalay, Myanmar.
463-472. 20 December 2000, Mandalay, Myanmar.
473-483. 21 December 2000, Mandalay, Myanmar.
484-490. 22 December 2000, Mandalay, Myanmar.
491-500. 23 December 2000, Mandalay, Myanmar.
501-513. 26 December 2000, Mandalay, Myanmar.
514-516. 30 December 2000, Bagan, Myanmar.
517-548. 30 December 2000, Bagan, Myanmar.
549-561. 31 December 2000, Bagan, Myanmar.
562-571. 5 January 2001, Bali, Indonesia.
572-582. 7 January 2001, Bali, Indonesia..
583-593. 8 January 2001, Bali, Indonesia.
594-596. 9 January 2001, Bali, Indonesia.
597-607. 9 January 2001, Bali, Indonesia.

608-618. 10 January 2001, Bali, Indonesia.
619-638. 11 January 2001, Bali, Indonesia.
639-658. 12 January 2001, Bali, Indonesia.
659-668. 13 January 2001, Bali, Indonesia.
669-678. 14 January 2001, Bali, Indonesia.
679-688. 15 January 2001, Bali, Indonesia.
689-708. 16 January 2001, Bali, Indonesia.
709-731. 17 January 2001, Bali, Indonesia.
732-746. 18 January 2001, Bali, Indonesia.
747-756. 26 January 2001, Bali, Indonesia.
757-780. 24 November 2001, Kauai, Hawaii.
781-785. 25 November 2001, Kauai, Hawaii.
786-795. 26 November 2001, Kauai, Hawaii.
796-805. 28 November 2001, Kauai, Hawaii.
806-812. 30 November 2001, Kauai, Hawaii.
813-823. 1 December 2001, Kauai, Hawaii.
824-833. 2 December 2001, Kauai, Hawaii.
834-843. 3 December 2001, Kauai, Hawaii.
844-850. 4 December 2001, Kauai, Hawaii.
851-860. 5 December 2001, Kauai, Hawaii.
861-870. 6 December 2001, Kauai, Hawaii.
871-886. 10 December 2001, Kuala Lumpur, Malaysia.
887-893. 11 December 2001. Kuala Lumpur, Malaysia.
894-903. 12 December 2001, Kuala Lumpur, Malaysia.
904-919. 13 December 2001, Kuala Lumpur, Malaysia.
920-929. 14 December 2001, Kuala Lumpur, Malaysia.
930-940. 16 December 2001, Kuala Lumpur, Malaysia.
941-943. 18 December 2001, Kuala Lumpur, Malaysia.
944-950. 19 December 2001, Phnom Penh, Cambodia.
951-960. 20 December 2001, Phnom Penh, Cambodia.
961-970. 21 December 2001, Phnom Penh, Cambodia.
971-977. 22 December 2001, Phnom Penh, Cambodia.
978-986. 23 December 2001, Phnom Penh, Cambodia.
987-996. 24 December 2001, Phnom Penh, Cambodia.
997-1007. 25 December 2001, Phnom Penh, Cambodia.
1008-1017. 26 December 2001, Phnom Penh, Cambodia.
1018-1026. 27 December 2001, Phnom Penh, Cambodia.
1027-1038. 28 December 2001, Phnom Penh, Cambodia.
1039-1050. 29 December 2001, Phnom Penh, Cambodia.
1051-1061. 31 December 2001, Phnom Penh, Cambodia.
1062-1069. 1 January 2002, Phnom Penh, Cambodia.
1070-1076. 2 January 2002, Phnom Penh, Cambodia.
1077-1083. 2 January 2002, Phnom Penh, Cambodia.
1084-1098. 3 January 2002, Phnom Penh, Cambodia.
1099-1111. 4 January 2002, Phnom Penh, Cambodia.
1112-1118. 5 January 2002. Phnom Penh, Cambodia.
1119-1132. 6 January 2002, Phnom Penh, Cambodia.
1133-1145. 9 January 2002, Ho Chi Minh City, Viet Nam.
1146-1150. 10 January 2002, Ho Chi Minh City, Viet Nam.
1151-1157. 11 January 2002, Ho Chi Minh City, Viet Nam.
1158-1164. 12 January 2002, Ho Chi Minh City, Viet Nam.
1165-1170. 13 January 2002, Ho Chi Minh City, Viet Nam.
1171-1177. 14 January 2002, Ho Chi Minh City, Viet Nam.
1178-1187. 16 January 2002, Ho Chi Minh City, Viet Nam.
1188-1201. 17 January 2002, Ho Chi Minh City, Viet Nam.
1202-1208. 21 January 2002, Ho Chi Minh City, Viet Nam.
1209-1218. 27 January 2002, Brunei Darussalam.
1219-1225. 28 January 2002, Brunei Darussalam.
1226-1233. 29 January 2002, Brunei Darussalam.

1234-1236. 30 January 2002, Brunei Darussalam.
1237-1245. 3 February 2002, Sabah, Malaysia.
1246-1255. 4 February 2002, Sabah, Malaysia.
1256-1266. 5 February 2002, Sabah, Malaysia.
1267-1276. 6 February 2002, Sabah, Malaysia.
1277-1285. 7 February 2002, Sabah, Malaysia.
1286-1295. 8 February 2002, Sabah, Malaysia.
1296-1302. 9 February 2002, Sabah, Malaysia.
1303-1309. 10 February 2002, Sabah, Malaysia.
1310-1316. 11 February 2002, Sabah, Malaysia.
1316-1324. 14 February 2002, Sabah, Malaysia.
1325-1337. 27 November 2002, Hamilton, New Zealand.
1338-1348. 28 November 2002, Hamilton, New Zealand.
1349-1358. 1 December 2002, Hamilton, New Zealand.
1359-1364. 2 December 2002, Taupo, New Zealand.
1365-1373. 3 December 2002, Taupo, New Zealand.
1374-1383. 4 December 2002, Taupo, New Zealand.
1384-1393. 5 December 2002, Taupo, New Zealand.
1394-1403. 6 December 2002, Taupo, New Zealand.
1404-1411. 7 December 2002, Taupo, New Zealand.
1412-1421. 8 December 2002, Taupo, New Zealand.
1422-1430. 9 December 2002, Taupo, New Zealand.
1431-1439. 10 December 2002, Taupo, New Zealand.
1440-1448. 11 December 2002, Taupo, New Zealand.
1449-1462. 12 December 2002, Taupo, New Zealand.
1463-1472. 13 December 2002, Taupo, New Zealand.
1473-1482. 14 December 2002, Taupo, New Zealand.
1483-1490. 15 December 2002, Taupo, New Zealand.
1491-1500. 16 December 2002, Taupo, New Zealand.
1501-1508. 18 December 2002, Wellington, New Zealand.
1509-1516. 20 December 2002, Christchurch, New Zealand.
1517-1527. 21 December 2002, Christchurch, New Zealand.
1528-1536. 22 December 2002, Christchurch, New Zealand.
1537-1545. 23 December 2002, Christchurch, New Zealand.
1546-1554. 25 December 2002, Christchurch, New Zealand.
1555-1566. 26 December 2002, Christchurch, New Zealand.
1567-1575. 27 December 2002, Christchurch, New Zealand.
1576-1585. 28 December 2002, Christchurch, New Zealand.
1586-1595. 29 December 2002, Christchurch, New Zealand.
1596-1604. 30 December 2002, Christchurch, New Zealand.
1605-1613. 31 December 2002, Christchurch, New Zealand.
1614-1626. 1 January 2003, Christchurch, New Zealand.
1627-1637. 2 January 2003, Christchurch, New Zealand.
1638-1645. 5 January 2003, Cairns, Australia.
1646-1655. 7 January 2003, Cairns, Australia.
1656-1662. 8 January 2003, Cairns, Australia.
1663-1671. 9 January 2003, Cairns, Australia.
1672-1680. 10 January 2003, Cairns, Australia.
1681-1690. 11 January 2003, Cairns, Australia.
1691-1701. 13 January 2003, Cairns, Australia.
1702-1711. 14 January 2003, Cairns, Australia.
1712-1721. 15 January 2003, Cairns, Australia.
1722-1731. 16 January 2003, Cairns, Australia.
1732-1740. 17 January 2003, Cairns, Australia.
1741-1748. 18 January 2003, Cairns, Australia.
1749-1757. 19 January 2003, Cairns, Australia.
1758-1766. 20 January 2003, Cairns, Australia.
1767-1775. 21 January 2003, Cairns, Australia.
1776-1785. 22 January 2003, Cairns, Australia.

1786-1795. 24 January 2003, Cairns, Australia.
1796-1804. 25 January 2003, Cairns, Australia.
1805-1814. 26 January 2003, Cairns, Australia.
1815-1824. 28 January 2003, Gold Coast, Australia.
1825-1834. 30 January 2003, Gold Coast, Australia.
1835-1844. 1 February 2003, Gold Coast, Australia.
1845-1854. 2 February 2003, Gold Coast, Australia.
1855-1860. 3 February 2003, Gold Coast, Australia.
1861-1868. 4 February 2003, Gold Coast, Australia.
1869-1879. 6 February 2003, Gold Coast, Australia.
1880-1890. 24 November 2003, Singapore.
1891-1905. 25 November 2003, Singapore.
1906-1920. 26 November 2003, Singapore.
1921-1933. 27 November 2003, Singapore.
1934-1942. 28 November 2003, Singapore.
1943-1955. 29 November 2003, Solo, Indonesia.
1956-1967. 30 November 2003, Solo, Indonesia.
1968-1979. 1 December 2003, Solo, Indonesia.
1980-1991. 2 December 2003, Solo, Indonesia.
1992-2004. 3 December 2003, Solo, Indonesia.
2005-2017. 4 December 2003, Solo, Indonesia.
2018-2031. 5 December 2003, Solo, Indonesia.
2032-2044. 6 December 2003, Solo, Indonesia.
2045-2057. 7 December 2003, Solo, Indonesia.
2058-2070. 8 December 2003, Solo, Indonesia.
2071-2083. 9 December 2003, Solo, Indonesia.
2084-2096. 11 December 2003, Solo, Indonesia.
2097-2109. 12 December 2003, Solo, Indonesia.
2110-2122. 13 December 2003, Solo, Indonesia.
2123-2136. 14 December 2003, Solo, Indonesia.
2137-2160. 15 December 2003, Yogyakarta, Indonesia.
2161-2181. 16 December 2003, Yogyakarta, Indonesia.
2182-2199. 17 December 2003, Yogyakarta, Indonesia.
2200-2217. 18 December 2003, Yogyakarta, Indonesia.
2218-2233. 19 December 2003, Yogyakarta, Indonesia.
2234-2250. 20 December 2003, Yogyakarta, Indonesia.
2251-2260. 21 December 2003, Yogyakarta, Indonesia.
2261-2269. 21 December 2003, Yogyakarta, Indonesia.
2270-2280. 22 December 2003, Yogyakarta, Indonesia.
2281-2290. 23 December 2003, Yogyakarta, Indonesia.
2291-2299. 25 December 2003, Yogyakarta, Indonesia.
2300-2310. 26 December 2003, Yogyakarta, Indonesia.
2311-2324. 27 December 2003, Yogyakarta, Indonesia.
2325-2334. 28 December 2003, Yogyakarta, Indonesia.
2335-2344. 29 December 2003, Yogyakarta, Indonesia.
2345-2354. 30 December 2003, Yogyakarta, Indonesia.
2355-2366. 31 December 2003, Yogyakarta, Indonesia.
2367-2379. 1 January 2004, Yogyakarta, Indonesia.
2380-2390. 2 January 2004, Yogyakarta, Indonesia.
2391. 3 January 2004, Yogyakarta, Indonesia.
2392-2398. 4 January 2004, Legian, Bali, Indonesia.
2399-2409. 5 January 2004, Legian, Bali, Indonesia.
2410-2419. 6 January 2004, Legian, Bali, Indonesia.
2420-2428. 7 January 2004, Legian, Bali, Indonesia.
2429-2436. 8 January 2004, Legian, Bali, Indonesia.
2437-2446. 9 January 2004, Legian, Bali, Indonesia.
2447-2456. 10 January 2004, Legian, Bali, Indonesia.
2457-2468. 11 January 2004, Legian, Bali, Indonesia.
2469-2471. 12 January 2004, Legian, Bali, Indonesia.

2472-2479. 13 January 2004, Legian, Bali, Indonesia.
2480-2484. 14 January 2004, Legian, Bali, Indonesia.
2485-2490. 15 January 2004, Legian, Bali, Indonesia.
2491-2494. 17 January 2004, Legian, Bali, Indonesia.
2495-2498. 18 January 2004, Legian, Bali, Indonesia.
2499-2504. 19 January 2004, Sanur, Bali, Indonesia.
2505-2512. 22 January 2004, Sanur, Bali, Indonesia.
2513-2516. 23 January 2004, Sanur, Bali, Indonesia.
2517-2520. 25 January 2004, Sanur, Bali, Indonesia.
2521-2526. 26 January 2004, Sanur, Bali, Indonesia.
2527-2531. 27 January 2004, Sanur, Bali, Indonesia.
2532-2536. 28 January 2004, Sanur, Bali, Indonesia.
2537-2541. 31 January 2004, Sanur, Bali, Indonesia.
2542-2546. 2 February 2004, Nusa Dua, Bali, Indonesia.
2547-2551. 3 February 2004, Nusa Dua, Bali, Indonesia.
2552-2556. 5 February 2004, Nusa Dua, Bali, Indonesia.
2557-2605. 25 November 2004, Sanya, China.
2606-2612. 26 November 2004, Sanya, China.
2613-2620. 27 November 2004, Sanya, China.
2621-2634. 28 November 2004, Sanya, China.
2635-2642. 29 November 2004, Sanya, China.
2643-2656. 30 November 2004, Sanya, China.
2657-2664. 1 December 2004, Sanya, China.
2665-2673. 2 December 2004, Sanya, China.
2674-2683. 3 December 2004, Sanya, China.
2684-2697. 4 December 2004, Sanya, China.
2698-2713. 5 December 2004, Sanya, China.
2714-2743. 7 December 2004, Sanya, China.
2744-2750. 9 December 2004, Xiamen, China.
2751-2756. 10 December 2004, Xiamen, China.
2757-2767. 12 December 2004, Xiamen, China.
2768-2774. 13 December 2004, Xiamen, China.
2775-2801. 17 December 2004, Xiamen, China.
2802-2870. 20 December 2004, Xiamen, China.
2871-2885. 21 December 2004, Qingdao, China.
2886-2890. 22 December 2004, Qingdao, China.
2891-2920. 23 December 2004, Qingdao, China.
2921-2956. 24 December 2004, Qingdao, China.
2957-2976. 25 December 2004, Qingdao, China.
2977-3006. 29 December 2004, Qingdao, China.
3007-3016. 1 January 2005, Qingdao, China.
3017-3026. 3 January 2005, Qingdao, China.
3027-3036. 6 January 2005, Qingdao, China.
3037-3046. 8 January 2005, Qingdao, China.
3047-3056. 9 January 2005, Qingdao, China.
3057-3063. 14 January 2005, Xian, China.
3064-3075. 16 January 2005, Xian, China.
3076-3095. 17 January 2005, Xian, China.
3096-3105. 19 January 2005, Xian, China.
3106-3110. 21 January 2005, Xian, China.
3111-3130. 25 January 2005, Huangshan, China.
3131-3140. 27 January 2005, Huangshan, China.
3141-3156. 29 January 2005, Huangshan, China.
3157-3166. 3 February 2005, Nanjing, China.
3167-3178. 4 February 2005, Nanjing, China.
3179-3189. 5 February 2005, Nanjing, China.
3190-3200. 6 February 2005, Nanjing, China.
3201-3213. 7 February 2005, Nanjing, China.
3214-3226. 8 February 2005, Nanjing, China.

3227-3233. 9 February 2005, Nanjing, China.
3234-3235. 11 February 2005, Nanjing, China.
3236-3244. 23 November 2005, Kuala Lumpur, Malaysia.
3245-3254. 24 November 2005, Pangkor Island, Malaysia.
3255-3261. 25 November 2005, Pangkor Island, Malaysia.
3262-3268. 26 November 2005, Pangkor Island, Malaysia.
3269-3275. 27 November 2005, Pangkor Island, Malaysia.
3276-3296. 28 November 2005, Pangkor Island, Malaysia.
3297-3306. 29 November 2005, Pangkor Island, Malaysia.
3307-3316. 30 November 2005, Pangkor Island, Malaysia.
3317-3330. 1 December 2005, Pangkor Island, Malaysia.
3331-3340. 2 December 2005, Pangkor Island, Malaysia.
3341-3350. 3 December 2005, Pangkor Island, Malaysia.
3351-3360. 4 December 2005, Pangkor Island, Malaysia.
3361-3369. 5 December 2005, Pangkor Island, Malaysia.
3370-3381. 6 December 2005, Pangkor Island, Malaysia.
3382-3391. 7 December 2005, Pangkor Island, Malaysia.
3392-3404. 8 December 2005, Pangkor Island, Malaysia.
3405-3413. 9 December 2005, Pangkor Island, Malaysia.
3414-3423. 10 December 2005, Pangkor Island, Malaysia.
3424-3433. 13 December 2005, Pangkor Island, Malaysia.
3434-3443. 14 December 2005, Kuantan, Malaysia.
3444-3453. 15 December 2005, Kuantan, Malaysia.
3454-3463. 16 December 2005, Kuantan, Malaysia.
3464-3473. 17 December 2005, Kuantan, Malaysia.
3474-3483. 18 December 2005, Kuantan, Malaysia.
3484-3493. 19 December 2005, Kuantan, Malaysia.
3494-3503. 20 December 2005, Kuantan, Malaysia.
3504-3513. 21 December 2005, Kuantan, Malaysia.
3514-3523. 22 December 2005, Kuantan, Malaysia.
3524-3533. 23 December 2005, Kuantan, Malaysia.
3534-3544. 24 December 2005, Kuantan, Malaysia.
3545-3554. 25 December 2005, Kuantan, Malaysia.
3555-3564. 26 December 2005, Kuantan, Malaysia.
3565-3574. 27 December 2005, Kuantan, Malaysia.
3575-3584. 28 December 2005, Kuantan, Malaysia.
3585-3593. 29 December 2005, Kuantan, Malaysia.
3594-3603. 30 December 2005, Kuantan, Malaysia.
3604-3613. 31 December 2005, Kuantan, Malaysia.
3614-3623. 1 January 2006, Kuantan, Malaysia.
3624-3636. 2 January 2006, Kuantan, Malaysia.
3637-3646. 3 January 2006, Kuantan, Malaysia.
3647-3661. 4 January 2006, Kijal, Malaysia.
3662-3678. 5 January 2006, Kijal, Malaysia.
3679-3695. 6 January 2006, Kijal, Malaysia.
3696-3705. 7 January 2006, Kijal, Malaysia.
3706-3715. 8 January 2006, Kijal, Malaysia.
3716-3736. 9 January 2006, Kijal, Malaysia.
3737-3747. 10 January 2006, Kijal, Malaysia.
3748-3758. 11 January 2006, Kijal, Malaysia.
3759-3768. 12 January 2006, Kijal, Malaysia.
3769-3783. 13 January 2006, Kijal, Malaysia.
3784-3793. 14 January 2006, Kijal, Malaysia.
3794-3803. 15 January 2006, Kijal, Malaysia.
3804-3813. 16 January 2006, Kijal, Malaysia.
3814-3823. 17 January 2006, Kijal, Malaysia.
3824-3833. 18 January 2006, Kijal, Malaysia.
3834-3843. 19 January 2006, Kijal, Malaysia.
3844-3854. 20 January 2006, Kijal, Malaysia.

3855-3864. 21 January 2006, Kijal, Malaysia.
3865-3874. 22 January 2006, Kijal, Malaysia.
3875-3884. 23 January 2006, Kijal, Malaysia.
3885-3894. 24 January 2006, Kijal, Malaysia.
3895-3904. 25 January 2006, Kijal, Malaysia.
3905-3914. 28 January 2006, Penang, Malaysia.
3915-3924. 29 January 2006, Penang, Malaysia.
3925-3935. 30 January 2006, Penang, Malaysia.
3936-3945. 31 January 2006, Penang, Malaysia.
3946-3955. 1 February 2006, Penang, Malaysia.
3956-3966. 2 February 2006, Penang, Malaysia.
3967-3976. 3 February 2006, Penang, Malaysia.
3977-3986. 4 February 2006, Penang, Malaysia.
3987-3997. 5 February 2006, Penang, Malaysia.
3998-4007. 6 February 2006, Penang, Malaysia.
4008-4017. 7 February 2006, Penang, Malaysia.
4018-4027. 8 February 2006, Penang, Malaysia.
4028-4037. 9 February 2006, Penang, Malaysia.
4038-4047. 10 February 2006, Penang, Malaysia.
4048-4058. 11 February 2006, Langkawi, Malaysia.
4059-4068. 11 February 2006, Langkawi, Malaysia.
4069-4078. 13 February 2006, Langkawi, Malaysia.
4079-4088. 14 February 2006, Langkawi, Malaysia.
4089-4098. 15 February 2006, Langkawi, Malaysia.
4099-4108. 16 February 2006, Langkawi, Malaysia.
4109-4118. 17 February 2006, Langkawi, Malaysia.
4119-4128. 18 February 2006, Langkawi, Malaysia.
4129-4138. 19 February 2006, Langkawi, Malaysia.
4139-4149. 20 February 2006, Langkawi, Malaysia.
4150-4159. 21 February 2006, Langkawi, Malaysia.
4160-4169. 22 February 2006, Langkawi, Malaysia.
4170-4179. 23 February 2006, Langkawi, Malaysia.
4180-4189. 24 February 2006, Langkawi, Malaysia.
4190-4196. 21 November 2006, Istanbul, Turkey.
4197-4203. 22 November 2006, Istanbul, Turkey.
4204-4210. 23 November 2006, Istanbul, Turkey.
4211-4217. 24 November 2006, Istanbul, Turkey.
4218-4224. 25 November 2006, Istanbul, Turkey.
4225-4231. 26 November 2006, Istanbul, Turkey.
4232-4238. 27 November 2006, Istanbul, Turkey.
4239-4245. 29 November 2006, Belek, Turkey.
4246-4253. 30 November 2006, Belek, Turkey.
4254-4261. 1 December 2006, Belek, Turkey.
4262-4269. 2 December 2006, Belek, Turkey.
4270-4277. 3 December 2006, Belek, Turkey.
4278-4285. 4 December 2006, Belek, Turkey.
4286-4295. 5 December 2006, Belek, Turkey.
4296-4303. 6 December 2006, Antalya, Turkey.
4304-4311. 7 December 2006, Antalya, Turkey.
4312-4319. 8 December 2006, Antalya, Turkey.
4320-4327. 9 December 2006, Antalya, Turkey.
4328-4335. 10 December 2006, Antalya, Turkey.
4336-4345. 11 December 2006, Antalya, Turkey.
4346-4353. 12 December 2006, Antalya, Turkey.
4354-4361. 13 December 2006, Antalya, Turkey.
4362-4369. 14 December 2006, Antalya, Turkey.
4370-4377. 15 December 2006, Antalya, Turkey.
4378-4393. 16 December 2006, Antalya, Turkey.
4386-4393. 17 December 2006, Antalya, Turkey.
4394. 18 December 2006, Antalya, Turkey.
4395-4402. 19 December 2006, Antalya, Turkey.

4403-4412. 20 December 2006, Antalya, Turkey.
4413-4420. 21 December 2006, Antalya, Turkey.
4421-4428. 22 December 2006, Antalya, Turkey.
4429-4438. 23 December 2006, Antalya, Turkey.
4439-4447. 24 December 2006, Antalya, Turkey.
4448-4457. 25 December 2006, Antalya, Turkey.
4458-4466. 26 December 2006, Antalya, Turkey.
4467-4475. 28 December 2006, Varna, Bulgaria.
4476-4483. 29 December 2006, Varna, Bulgaria.
4484-4492. 30 December 2006, Varna, Bulgaria.
4493-4501. 31 December 2006, Varna, Bulgaria.
4502-4509. 2 January 2007, Varna, Bulgaria.
4510-4517. 3 January 2007, Varna, Bulgaria.
4518-4526. 4 January 2007, Varna, Bulgaria.
4527-4534. 5 January 2007, Varna, Bulgaria.
4535-4542. 6 January 2007, Varna, Bulgaria.
4543-4550. 7 January 2007, Varna, Bulgaria.
4551-4559. 8 January 2007, Varna, Bulgaria.
4560-4567. 9 January 2007, Varna, Bulgaria.
4568-4575. 10 January 2007, Varna, Bulgaria.
4576-4583. 11 January 2007, Varna, Bulgaria.
4584-4593. 12 January 2007, Varna, Bulgaria.
4594-4601. 13 January 2007, Varna, Bulgaria.
4602-4609. 14 January 2007, Varna, Bulgaria.
4610-4618. 15 January 2007, Varna, Bulgaria.
4619-4628. 16 January 2007, Varna, Bulgaria.
4629-4636. 17 January 2007, Varna, Bulgaria.
4637-4644. 20 January 2007, Bangkok, Thailand.
4645-4652. 21 January 2007, Bangkok, Thailand.
4653-4660. 22 January 2007, Bangkok, Thailand.
4661-4668. 23 January 2007, Bangkok, Thailand.
4669-4677. 24 January 2007, Bangkok, Thailand.
4678-4686. 25 January 2007, Cha-Am, Thailand.
4687-4694. 26 January 2007, Cha-Am, Thailand.
4695. 27 January 2007, Cha-Am, Thailand.
4696-4703. 28 January 2007, Cha-Am, Thailand.
4704-4711. 29 January 2007, Cha-Am, Thailand.
4712-4719. 30 January 2007, Cha-Am, Thailand.
4720-4730. 31 January 2007, Cha-Am, Thailand.
4731-4740. 1 February 2007, Cha-Am, Thailand.
4741-4750. 2 February 2007, Cha-Am, Thailand.
4751-4758. 3 February 2007, Cha-Am, Thailand.
4759-4766. 5 February 2007, Cha-Am, Thailand.
4767-4774. 6 February 2007, Chiang Mai, Thailand.
4775-4782. 7 February 2007, Chiang Mai, Thailand.
4783-4790. 8 February 2007, Chiang Mai, Thailand.
4791-4798. 9 February 2007, Chiang Mai, Thailand.
4799-4806. 10 February 2007, Chiang Mai, Thailand.
4807-4813. 11 February 2007, Chiang Mai, Thailand.
4814-4822. 12 February 2007, Chiang Mai, Thailand.
4823-4831. 13 February 2007, Chiang Mai, Thailand.
4832-4839. 14 February 2007, Chiang Mai, Thailand.
4840-4848. 15 February 2007, Chiang Mai, Thailand.
4849-4856. 16 February 2007, Chiang Mai, Thailand.
4857-4863. 17 February 2007, Chiang Mai, Thailand.
4864-4871. 18 February 2007, Chiang Mai, Thailand.
4872-4879. 19 February 2007, Chiang Mai, Thailand.
4880-4889. 20 February 2007, Chiang Mai, Thailand.
4890-4898. 22 February 2007, Chiang Mai, Thailand.
4899-4906. 23 February 2007, Chiang Mai, Thailand.
4907-4914. 24 February 2007, Chiang Mai, Thailand.

MY EARLY MORNING PRAYER-JOURNEYS

1-4. Sanya, China, 5 December 2004.
5-8. Sanya, China, 6 December 2004.
9-13. Sanya, China, 7 December 2004.
14-17. Xiamen, China, 8 December 2004.
18-22. Xiamen, China, 9 December 2004.
23-26. Xiamen, China, 10 December 2004.
27-30. Xiamen, China, 11 December 2004.
31-34. Xiamen, China, 12 December 2004.
35-38. Xiamen, China, 13 December 2004.
39-41. Xiamen, China, 15 December 2004.
42-45. Xiamen, China, 16 December 2004.
46-49. Xiamen, China, 17 December 2004.
50-53. Xiamen, China, 18 December 2004.
54-57. Xiamen, China, 19 December 2004.
58-61. Xiamen, China, 20 December 2004.
62-65. Qingdao, China, 25 December 2004.
66-69. Qingdao, China, 26 December 2004.
70-73. Qingdao, China, 28 December 2004.
74-77. Qingdao, China, 29 December 2004.
78-81. Qingdao, China, 31 December 2004.
82-85. Qingdao, China, 1 January 2005.
86-90. Qingdao, China, 2 January 2005.
91-95. Qingdao, China, 3 January 2005.
96-100. Qingdao, China, 5 January 2005.
101-104. Qingdao, China, 6 January 2005.
105-108. Qingdao, China, 7 January 2005.
109-112. Qingdao, China, 8 January 2005.
113-116. Qingdao, China, 9 January 2005.
117-121. Qingdao, China, 10 January 2005.
122-125. Xian, China, 14 January 2005.
126-132. Xian, China, 16 January 2005.
133-136. Xian, China, 17 January 2005.
137-140. Xian, China, 19 January 2005.
141-145. Xian, China, 21 January 2005.
146-149. Huangshan, China, 25 January 2005.
150-153. Huangshan, China, 31 January 2005.
154-155. Nanjing, China, 3 February 2005.
156. Nanjing, China, 5 February 2005.
157. Nanjing, China, 6 February 2005.
158. Nanjing, China, 7 February 2005.
159. Nanjing, China, 8 February 2005.
160. Nanjing, China, 9 February 2005.

MY EARLY MORNING HEART-CLIMBING PRAYERS

1. 10 December 2005, Pangkor Island, Malaysia.
2. 11 December 2005, Kuala Lumpur, Malaysia.
3. 12 December 2005, Kuantan, Malaysia.
4. 13 December 2005, Kuantan, Malaysia.
5. 14 December 2005, Kuantan, Malaysia.
6. 15 December 2005, Kuantan, Malaysia.
7. 16 December 2005, Kuantan, Malaysia.
8. 17 December 2005, Kuantan, Malaysia.
9. 18 December 2005, Kuantan, Malaysia.
10. 19 December 2005, Kuantan, Malaysia.
11. 20 December 2005, Kuantan, Malaysia.
12. 21 December 2005, Kuantan, Malaysia.
13. 22 December 2005, Kuantan, Malaysia.
14. 23 December 2005, Kuantan, Malaysia.
15. 24 December 2005, Kuantan, Malaysia.
16. 25 December 2005, Kuantan, Malaysia.
17. 26 December 2005, Kuantan, Malaysia.
18. 27 December 2005, Kuantan, Malaysia.
19. 28 December 2005, Kuantan, Malaysia.
20. 29 December 2005, Kuantan, Malaysia.
21. 30 December 2005, Kuantan, Malaysia.
22. 31 December 2005, Kuantan, Malaysia.
23. 1 January 2006, Kuantan, Malaysia.
24. 2 January 2006, Kuantan, Malaysia.
25. 3 January 2006, Kuantan, Malaysia.
26. 4 January 2006, Kijal, Malaysia.
27. 5 January 2006, Kijal, Malaysia.
28. 6 January 2006, Kijal, Malaysia.
29. 7 January 2006, Kijal, Malaysia.
30. 8 January 2006, Kijal, Malaysia.
31. 9 January 2006, Kijal, Malaysia.
32. 10 January 2006, Kijal, Malaysia.
33. 11 January 2006, Kijal, Malaysia.
34. 12 January 2006, Kijal, Malaysia.
35. 13 January 2006, Kijal, Malaysia.
36. 14 January 2006, Kijal, Malaysia.
37. 15 January 2006, Kijal, Malaysia.
38. 16 January 2006, Kijal, Malaysia.
39. 17 January 2006, Kijal, Malaysia.
40. 18 January 2006, Kijal, Malaysia.
41. 19 January 2006, Kijal, Malaysia.
42. 20 January 2006, Kijal, Malaysia.
43. 21 January 2006, Kijal, Malaysia.
44. 22 January 2006, Kijal, Malaysia.
45. 23 January 2006, Kijal, Malaysia.
46. 25 January 2006, Kijal, Malaysia.
47. 28 January 2006, Penang, Malaysia.
48. 29 January 2006, Penang, Malaysia.
49. 30 January 2006, Penang, Malaysia.
50. 31 January 2006, Penang, Malaysia.
51. 1 February 2006, Penang, Malaysia.
52. 2 February 2006, Penang, Malaysia.
53. 3 February 2006, Penang, Malaysia.
54. 5 February 2006, Penang, Malaysia.
55. 6 February 2006, Penang, Malaysia.
56. 7 February 2006, Penang, Malaysia.
57. 8 February 2006, Penang, Malaysia.
58. 10 February 2006, Penang, Malaysia.

APPENDIX

PREFACES TO THE ORIGINAL EDITIONS

MY CHRISTMAS-NEW YEAR-VACATION-ASPIRATION-PRAYERS

Part 1
Sri Chinmoy offered the following morning prayers during his visit to Brazil and Paraguay in December 1999 and January 2000. Ten different groups recited the prayers turn by turn three times, then twice, then once.

Part 2
Sri Chinmoy offered the following morning prayers during his visit to Brazil and Paraguay in December 1999 and January 2000. Ten different groups recited the prayers turn by turn three times, then twice, then once.

Part 3
Sri Chinmoy offered the following morning prayers during his visit to Brazil and Paraguay in December 1999 and January 2000. Ten different groups recited the prayers turn by turn three times, then twice, then once.

Part 4
Sri Chinmoy offered the following morning prayers during his visit to Ayutthaya, Thailand and Yangon, Myanmar in December 2000.

Part 5
Sri Chinmoy offered the following morning prayers during his visit to Myanmar in December 2000.

Part 6
Sri Chinmoy offered the following morning prayers during his visit to Myanmar in December 2000 and Indonesia in January 2001.

Part 7
Sri Chinmoy offered the following morning prayers during his visit to Bali, Indonesia in January 2001.

Part 8
Sri Chinmoy offered the following prayers during his visit to Hawaii in November-December 2001.

Part 9
Sri Chinmoy offered the following prayers during his visit to Hawaii, Cambodia, Viet Nam and Malaysia from November 2001 to February 2002.

Part 10
Sri Chinmoy offered the following prayers during his visit to Malaysia and Cambodia in December 2001.

Part 11

Sri Chinmoy offered the following prayers during his visit to Cambodia in December 2001 and January 2002.

Part 12
Sri Chinmoy offered the following prayers during his visit to Cambodia and Viet Nam in January 2002.

Part 13
Sri Chinmoy offered the following prayers during his visit to Viet Nam and Brunei Darussalam in January 2002.

Part 14
Sri Chinmoy offered the following prayers during his visit to Malaysia in February 2002.

Part 15
Sri Chinmoy offered the following prayers during his visit to New Zealand in November and December 2002.

Part 16
Sri Chinmoy offered the following prayers during his visit to New Zealand in December 2002.

Part 17
Sri Chinmoy offered the following prayers during his visit to New Zealand in December 2002.

Part 18
Sri Chinmoy offered the following prayers during his visit to Christchurch, New Zealand and Cairns, Australia in December 2002 and January 2003.

Part 19
Sri Chinmoy offered the following prayers during his visit to Australia in January 2003.

Part 20
Sri Chinmoy offered the following prayers during his visit to Australia in January 2003.

Part 21
Sri Chinmoy offered the following prayers during his visit to Australia in January 2003.

Part 22
Sri Chinmoy offered the following prayers during his visit to Singapore and Solo, Indonesia in November 2003.

Part 23
Sri Chinmoy offered the following prayers during his visit to Solo, Indonesia in November and December 2003.

Part 24
Sri Chinmoy offered the following prayers during his visit to Solo, Indonesia in December 2003.

Part 25
Sri Chinmoy offered the following prayers during his visit to Solo and Yogyakarta, Indonesia in December 2003.

Part 26
Sri Chinmoy offered the following prayers during his visit to Yogyakarta, Indonesia in December 2003.

Part 27
Sri Chinmoy offered the following prayers during his visit to Jakarta and Yogyakarta, Indonesia in December 2003.

Part 28
Sri Chinmoy offered the following prayers during his visit to Yogyakarta and Bali, Indonesia in December 2003 and January 2004.

Part 29
Sri Chinmoy offered the following prayers during his visit to Bali, Indonesia in January 2004.

Part 30
Sri Chinmoy offered the following prayers during his visit to Bali, Indonesia in January and February 2004.

Part 31
Sri Chinmoy offered the following prayers during his visit to Sanya, China in November 2004.

Part 32
Sri Chinmoy offered the following prayers during his visit to Sanya, China in November and December 2004.

Part 33
Sri Chinmoy offered the following prayers during his visit to Sanya and Xiamen, China in December 2004.

Part 34

Sri Chinmoy offered the following prayers during his visit to Xiamen, China in December 2004.

Part 35
Sri Chinmoy offered the following prayers during his visit to Qingdao, China in December 2004.

Part 36
Sri Chinmoy offered the following prayers during his visit to Qingdao, China in December 2004.

Part 37
Sri Chinmoy offered the following prayers during his visit to Qingdao and Xian, China in December 2004 and January 2005.

Part 38
Sri Chinmoy offered the following prayers during his visit to Xian and Huangshan, China in January 2005.

Part 39
Sri Chinmoy offered the following prayers during his visit to Huangshan and Nanjing, China in January and February 2005.

Part 40
Sri Chinmoy offered the following prayers during his visit to Pangkor Island, Malaysia in November 2005.

Part 41
Sri Chinmoy offered the following prayers during his visit to Pangkor Island and Kuantan, Malaysia in December 2005.

Part 42
Sri Chinmoy offered the following prayers during his visit to Pangkor Island and Kuantan, Malaysia in December 2005.

Part 43
Sri Chinmoy offered the following prayers during his visit to Kuantan, Malaysia in December 2005.

Part 44
Sri Chinmoy offered the following prayers during his visit to Kuantan, Malaysia in December 2005.

Part 45
Sri Chinmoy offered the following prayers during his visit to Kuantan and Kijal, Malaysia in December 2005 and January 2006.

Part 46
Sri Chinmoy offered the following prayers during his visit to Kijal, Malaysia in January 2006.

Part 47
Sri Chinmoy offered the following prayers during his visit to Kijal, Malaysia in January 2006.

Part 48
Sri Chinmoy offered the following prayers during his visit to Kijal, Malaysia in January 2006.

Part 49
Sri Chinmoy offered the following prayers during his visit to Kijal and Penang, Malaysia in January and February 2006.

Part 50
Sri Chinmoy offered the following prayers during his visit to Penang, Malaysia in February 2006.

Part 51
Sri Chinmoy offered the following prayers during his visit to Penang and Langkawi, Malaysia in February 2006.

Part 52
Sri Chinmoy offered the following prayers during his visit to Langkawi, Malaysia in February 2006.

Part 53
Sri Chinmoy offered the following prayers during his visit to Istanbul and Belek, Turkey in November and December 2006.

Part 54
Sri Chinmoy offered the following prayers during his visit to Belek and Antalya, Turkey in December 2006.

Part 55
Sri Chinmoy offered the following prayers during his visit to Antalya, Turkey in December 2006.

Part 56
Sri Chinmoy offered the following prayers during his visit to Antalya, Turkey and Varna, Bulgaria in December 2006.

Part 57

Sri Chinmoy offered the following prayers during his visit to Varna, Bulgaria in December 2006 and January 2007.

Part 58
Sri Chinmoy offered the following prayers during his visit to Varna, Bulgaria and Bangkok, Thailand in January 2007.

Part 59
Sri Chinmoy offered the following prayers during his visit to Bangkok and Cha-Am, Thailand in January 2007.

Part 60
Sri Chinmoy offered the following prayers during his visit to Cha-Am and Chiang Mai, Thailand in January and February 2007.

Part 61
Sri Chinmoy offered the following prayers during his visit to Chiang Mai, Thailand in February 2007.

MY EARLY MORNING PRAYER JOURNEYS

Part 1
During his trip to China, from November 2004 to February 2005, Sri Chinmoy was inspired to offer a number of prayers very early in the morning, when he came down from his hotel room to go out walking. These 160 prayers are published in two volumes.

Part 2
During his trip to China from November 2004 to February 2005, Sri Chinmoy was inspired to offer a number of prayers very early in the morning, when he came down from his hotel room to go out walking. These 160 prayers are published in two volumes.

BIBLIOGRAPHY

— MY CHRISTMAS-NEW YEAR-VACATION-ASPIRATION-PRAYERS
(61 VOLUMES)

SRI CHINMOY:
— *My Christmas-New Year-Vacation Aspiration-Prayers, part 1*, New York, Agni Press, 2000.
— *My Christmas-New Year-Vacation Aspiration-Prayers, part 2*, New York, Agni Press, 2000.
— *My Christmas-New Year-Vacation Aspiration-Prayers, part 3*, New York, Agni Press, 2000.
— *My Christmas-New Year-Vacation Aspiration-Prayers, part 4*, New York, Agni Press, 2001.
— *My Christmas-New Year-Vacation Aspiration-Prayers, part 5*, New York, Agni Press, 2001.
— *My Christmas-New Year-Vacation Aspiration-Prayers, part 6*, New York, Agni Press, 2001.
— *My Christmas-New Year-Vacation Aspiration-Prayers, part 7*, New York, Agni Press, 2002.
— *My Christmas-New Year-Vacation Aspiration-Prayers, part 8*, New York, Agni Press, 2002.
— *My Christmas-New Year-Vacation Aspiration-Prayers, part 9*, New York, Agni Press, 2002.
— *My Christmas-New Year-Vacation Aspiration-Prayers, part 10*, New York, Agni Press, 2002.
— *My Christmas-New Year-Vacation Aspiration-Prayers, part 11*, New York, Agni Press, 2002.
— *My Christmas-New Year-Vacation Aspiration-Prayers, part 12*, New York, Agni Press, 2002.
— *My Christmas-New Year-Vacation Aspiration-Prayers, part 13*, New York, Agni Press, 2002.
— *My Christmas-New Year-Vacation Aspiration-Prayers, part 14*, New York, Agni Press, 2002.
— *My Christmas-New Year-Vacation Aspiration-Prayers, part 15*, New York, Agni Press, 2003.
— *My Christmas-New Year-Vacation Aspiration-Prayers, part 16*, New York, Agni Press, 2003.
— *My Christmas-New Year-Vacation Aspiration-Prayers, part 17*, New York, Agni Press, 2003.
— *My Christmas-New Year-Vacation Aspiration-Prayers, part 18*, New York, Agni Press, 2003.
— *My Christmas-New Year-Vacation Aspiration-Prayers, part 19*, New York, Agni Press, 2003.
— *My Christmas-New Year-Vacation Aspiration-Prayers, part 20*, New York, Agni Press, 2003.
— *My Christmas-New Year-Vacation Aspiration-Prayers, part 21*, New York, Agni Press, 2003.
— *My Christmas-New Year-Vacation Aspiration-Prayers, part 22*, New York, Agni Press, 2003.
— *My Christmas-New Year-Vacation Aspiration-Prayers, part 23*, New York, Agni Press, 2003.
— *My Christmas-New Year-Vacation Aspiration-Prayers, part 24*, New York, Agni Press, 2003.
— *My Christmas-New Year-Vacation Aspiration-Prayers, part 25*, New York, Agni Press, 2003.
— *My Christmas-New Year-Vacation Aspiration-Prayers, part 26*, New York, Agni Press, 2003.
— *My Christmas-New Year-Vacation Aspiration-Prayers, part 27*, New York, Agni Press, 2003.
— *My Christmas-New Year-Vacation Aspiration-Prayers, part 28*, New York, Agni Press, 2003.
— *My Christmas-New Year-Vacation Aspiration-Prayers, part 29*, New York, Agni Press, 2004.
— *My Christmas-New Year-Vacation Aspiration-Prayers, part 30*, New York, Agni Press, 2004.
— *My Christmas-New Year-Vacation Aspiration-Prayers, part 31*, New York, Agni Press, 2005.
— *My Christmas-New Year-Vacation Aspiration-Prayers, part 32*, New York, Agni Press, 2005.
— *My Christmas-New Year-Vacation Aspiration-Prayers, part 33*, New York, Agni Press, 2005.
— *My Christmas-New Year-Vacation Aspiration-Prayers, part 34*, New York, Agni Press, 2005.
— *My Christmas-New Year-Vacation Aspiration-Prayers, part 35*, New York, Agni Press, 2005.
— *My Christmas-New Year-Vacation Aspiration-Prayers, part 36*, New York, Agni Press, 2005.
— *My Christmas-New Year-Vacation Aspiration-Prayers, part 37*, New York, Agni Press, 2005.
— *My Christmas-New Year-Vacation Aspiration-Prayers, part 38*, New York, Agni Press, 2005.

— *My Christmas-New Year-Vacation Aspiration-Prayers, part 39*, New York, Agni Press, 2005.
— *My Christmas-New Year-Vacation Aspiration-Prayers, part 40*, New York, Agni Press, 2005.
— *My Christmas-New Year-Vacation Aspiration-Prayers, part 41*, New York, Agni Press, 2005.
— *My Christmas-New Year-Vacation Aspiration-Prayers, part 42*, New York, Agni Press, 2006.
— *My Christmas-New Year-Vacation Aspiration-Prayers, part 43*, New York, Agni Press, 2006.
— *My Christmas-New Year-Vacation Aspiration-Prayers, part 44*, New York, Agni Press, 2006.
— *My Christmas-New Year-Vacation Aspiration-Prayers, part 45*, New York, Agni Press, 2006.
— *My Christmas-New Year-Vacation Aspiration-Prayers, part 46*, New York, Agni Press, 2006.
— *My Christmas-New Year-Vacation Aspiration-Prayers, part 47*, New York, Agni Press, 2006.
— *My Christmas-New Year-Vacation Aspiration-Prayers, part 48*, New York, Agni Press, 2006.
— *My Christmas-New Year-Vacation Aspiration-Prayers, part 49*, New York, Agni Press, 2006.
— *My Christmas-New Year-Vacation Aspiration-Prayers, part 50*, New York, Agni Press, 2007.
— *My Christmas-New Year-Vacation Aspiration-Prayers, part 51*, New York, Agni Press, 2007.
— *My Christmas-New Year-Vacation Aspiration-Prayers, part 52*, New York, Agni Press, 2007.
— *My Christmas-New Year-Vacation Aspiration-Prayers, part 53*, New York, Agni Press, 2007.
— *My Christmas-New Year-Vacation Aspiration-Prayers, part 54*, New York, Agni Press, 2007.
— *My Christmas-New Year-Vacation Aspiration-Prayers, part 55*, New York, Agni Press, 2007.
— *My Christmas-New Year-Vacation Aspiration-Prayers, part 56*, New York, Agni Press, 2008.
— *My Christmas-New Year-Vacation Aspiration-Prayers, part 57*, New York, Agni Press, 2008.
— *My Christmas-New Year-Vacation Aspiration-Prayers, part 58*, New York, Agni Press, 2008.
— *My Christmas-New Year-Vacation Aspiration-Prayers, part 59*, New York, Agni Press, 2008.
— *My Christmas-New Year-Vacation Aspiration-Prayers, part 60*, New York, Agni Press, 2008.
— *My Christmas-New Year-Vacation Aspiration-Prayers, part 61*, New York, Agni Press, 2008.

Suggested citation key is APR.

MY EARLY MORNING PRAYER JOURNEYS (2 VOLUMES)

SRI CHINMOY:
— *My Early Morning Prayer-Journeys, part 1*, New York, Agni Press, 2005
— *My Early Morning Prayer-Journeys, part 2*, New York, Agni Press, 2005

Suggested citation key is EMP.

MY EARLY MORNING HEART-CLIMBING PRAYERS

SRI CHINMOY:
— *My Early Morning Heart-Climbing Prayers*, New York, Agni Press, 2006

Suggested citation key is EMH.

POSTFACE

Publishing principles

This edition of *The works of Sri Chinmoy* aims to obey the Author's wish: scrupulous fidelity to his original words, use of typographical style by him selected, specific spelling choices, end placement of any editorial content (i.e. not written by Sri Chinmoy himself), particular treatment of some personal nouns in special cases, etc.

Textual accuracy

The text of this edition has been checked to ensure faithful accuracy to the originals. Although much effort has been put in proofreading and comparing different versions of the text, this print may still present a few lingering errors.

The publisher would be grateful to be apprised of any mistypes, possibly with scan of the original page where the text is different. Please use original books only, specifying the year of publication. Online versions may be as accurate and should not be considered authoritative.

Acknowledgements

Our deepest gratitude to Sri Chinmoy. His living presence can be felt breathing throughout his writings. It is a privilege to be involved with his works, in any form.

TABLE OF CONTENTS

MY CHRISTMAS-NEW YEAR-VACATION ASPIRATION-PRAYERS	1
MY EARLY MORNING PRAYER JOURNEYS	539
MY EARLY MORNING HEART-CLIMBING PRAYERS	559
NOTES TO CURRENT EDITIONS	570
APPENDIX	581
BIBLIOGRAPHY	589
POSTFACE	595
TABLE OF CONTENTS	599

www.ingramcontent.com/pod-product-compliance
Lightning Source LLC
Chambersburg PA
CBHW030110240426
43661CB00031B/1360/J